CW00747159

DANCING FOR HATHOR

Dancing For Hathor
Women in Ancient Egypt

Carolyn Graves-Brown

continuum

Continuum UK, The Tower Building, 11 York Road, London SE1 7NX
Continuum US, 80 Maiden Lane, Suite 704, New York, NY 10038

www.continuumbooks.com

Copyright © Carolyn Graves-Brown 2010

All rights reserved. No part of this publication may be reproduced or transmitted
in any form or by any means, electronic or mechanical, including photocopying,
recording or any information storage or retrieval system, without prior permission
from the publishers.

First published 2010

British Library Cataloguing-in-Publication Data
A catalogue record for this book is available from the British Library.

ISBN 978-1-8472-5054-4

Typeset by Pindar NZ, Auckland, New Zealand
Printed and bound by MPG Books Group Ltd

Contents

Illustrations

Preface

This book is about women in ancient Egypt, and is mainly concerned with the Predynastic and Pharaonic periods, from 5000 BC to 300 BC. The later periods are only briefly included as Egypt was increasingly subject to influence from Greece and Rome. There have been many fine books on women in ancient Egypt but those purporting to be for a general readership often gloss over controversy and those written for scholars can appear dull. The aim of this book is to appeal to the general reader but also to introduce contemporary scholarly research in Egyptology. The book is intended to make people think; it is a book for the educated lay person and the student of Egyptology or women in history, a book which makes an understanding of the past relevant to the present.

The book's title should be explained. For most of this long period of history, and for both rich and poor, Hathor, or goddesses linked to her, influenced how human women were perceived and, in turn, human women would have influenced how this goddess was perceived. For the Egyptians, Hathor was the goddess of female sexuality par excellence, and more temples were built to her than any other Egyptian goddess. She was revered in statues, paintings, feasts and dance. While it was mainly women who danced for her, men at times also did so; the king himself danced for Hathor.

However, we should not assume that all aspects of gods and goddesses were mirrored in the lives of everyday men and women. While ancient Egyptian gods were not the distant all-powerful beings of religions such as Judaism, Islam and Christianity, they were still different from humanity. So, while they might appear human, eating, drinking and making love, and were even being subject to practical jokes, or illnesses, deities were not human. Gods and goddesses, for example, might be portrayed as androgynous, but normal people were not. Kings, however, who were in part gods, could be portrayed as both male and female.

I would like to thank several individuals who in some ways contributed to this book. Firstly, my husband, Paul Graves-Brown, who has been encouraging and supportive, should have some of the credit, though none of the blame, for mistakes herein. Additionally, many thanks to all those women who have believed in me, helped, encouraged and acted as role models, in particular, my mother Carol Brown, but also Rosemary Cramp, Daphne Stanford and most recently, Wendy Goodridge. Finally, I should like to thank Continuum for allowing me to publish this book.

Chronology

It is important to note that Egyptologists dispute the exact dates of the various periods here, but most would generally agree on the following.

Predynastic	5500–3100 BC
Badarian	5500–4000 BC
Naqada I	4000–3500 BC
Naqada II	3500–3200 BC
Naqada III	3200–3100 BC
Early Dynastic	3100–2686 BC
Old Kingdom	2686–2181 BC
First Intermediate Period	2181–2055 BC
Middle Kingdom	2055–1650 BC
Second Intermediate Period	1650–1550 BC
New Kingdom	1550–1069 BC
Third Intermediate Period	1069–747 BC
Late Period	747–332 BC
Ptolemaic Period	332–30 BC
Roman Period	30 BC–AD 395

During the Badarian Period, domestication of cattle, sheep and goats began in Egypt. During Naqada I, cereal farming played a major and important role and increased human settlement is evident. Towards the end of the fourth millennium, plough agriculture was well established. The Naqada III Period, or Dynasty 0, constitutes the formative years of the unification of Egypt and the formation of the state.

Introduction

Ancient Egypt is well known for its exoticism, its otherness. The ancient Egyptians worshipped strange gods with animal heads, built huge monuments and wrapped their dead in yards of bandages. Yet, at the same time, ancient Egypt seems strangely familiar. People went to work, made fun of those in authority, fell hopelessly in love, drank too much, and made fools of themselves. For us, in the twenty-first century, ancient Egyptian art, including depictions of women, is appealingly sensual and 'modern,' but at the same time exotic and distant. It is this combination of the familiar and the fantastic that makes ancient Egypt so compelling.

Even the ancients thought Egypt and its women strange. Herodotus, a Greek writer of the fifth century BC makes this quite clear, claiming the Egyptians had completely reversed normal gender roles. Such emphasis on the exoticism of Egypt, and its women, continues through to the works of Shakespeare and even to modern films such as *The Mummy*. In order to further entice us, sexuality, which is traditionally associated with women, is added to the pot.

We might suspect that the idea of weird, exotic women with lax morals and wanton sexuality was perhaps exaggerated by those wanting to show the superiority of the Greek and Roman, or our own, worlds, or just to tell a good story. However, this book will show that in many ways, ancient Egyptian women really were 'strange' when compared with us. This is hardly surprising as the period under discussion began over 3,000 years before the birth of Christ. One might expect to see a rather unfamiliar society with unusual attitudes to women. The bizarre picture presented here shows the absolute impossibility of ever fully understanding the past. Quite apart from the problems of lack of evidence or the myriad of ways one set of evidence may be understood, how can we empathize with totally alien beliefs?

In most societies, women are subservient to men. Generally, women have fewer rights and their work is confined to the home. When they work outside the home, they are not usually rewarded as well as men. It has sometimes been claimed that in ancient Egypt, women's work always centred round the home, hence the pale skin of Egyptian women depicted in painting. However, a Fifth Dynasty tomb scene from Saqqara shows a woman steering a cargo ship while ordering a man to get her food, but not to obstruct her view. Not only is this women strikingly bossy – some might claim 'unfeminine' in her demands – she is in charge of a vessel and clearly not confined to the home. In this same period, Egyptian women are shown engaged in marketplace trade with men. Women weavers are rewarded with necklaces in the same way that men were given rewards by the king, and they also received bread, beer, oil and wheat, just like the male tomb workers. At least in the Old Kingdom, women conceivably had a certain amount of independence and status, though of course we do not know if they found it difficult to juggle demands of work inside and outside the home.

In later Egyptian history, women still seem remarkably liberated in many ways. We have a papyrus written by a woman weaver to the king. Despite the fact that he is the most important person in the land, a god on earth, this woman is not cowed, but audaciously points out that he is lucky to have her in his employment. In much later periods, the Divine Adoratrice, a female priestly postholder, held such wealth and status that she was second only to the king.

In the New Kingdom, Egyptian love poems describe the woman as the more active partner, seeking out and ensnaring male lovers. Furthermore, while it is usually assumed that, historically, most prostitutes were women, the earliest Egyptian tales where prostitution is mentioned describe women paying for sex. In one story, the wife of the high priest sends a box of clothing to a man in the town to get his attention. In another, a wife offers to make her brother-in-law fine clothing if he will sleep with her. In this period, textiles were a form of currency. All this might suggest that ancient Egyptian women were early feminists.

Attitudes to women's procreation may also seem bizarre. In most societies, women are at the centre of the procreative process. Some would claim that this ability to create is the essence of female power. On the negative side, in such societies, the woman is usually blamed if a couple cannot produce children. However, in ancient Egypt, it was men who were considered the creators. In New Kingdom Deir el-Medina, a man is criticized because he cannot make his wife pregnant 'like other men'. The woman was important in creation, but only as the arouser of the male and as a vessel for his child. This idea of the male creator extended to the world of the gods. There was no concept of mother earth, but rather the earth was personified as the male god, Geb.

The importance of the male as the centre-point for rebirth meant that for most of Egyptian history the deceased was identified with the reborn male god Osiris. Mythically, Osiris had to be revived from death by the sexual allure of his sister/wife, Isis. This belief led to depictions of the goddess Isis in the form of a bird hovering over the genital area of the deceased in order to sexually stimulate his phallus to life. As the deceased, whether male or female, is associated with the male god Osiris, the motif of Isis bird hovering over the genital area was even used if the deceased was female.

Other attitudes toward women may appear unusual. In many societies, women are not allowed the same freedom to drink alcohol as are men. Heavy drinking is considered especially immoral for women and certainly unfeminine. Often it is felt that since women are in charge of children, they need to be especially moral. While drinking was often discouraged in ancient Egypt, at times it appears to have been celebrated by both sexes. An ancient Egyptian tomb painting shows an elite woman vomiting through overindulgence in alcohol. A woman at a drinking party asks for 18 cups of wine because her throat is as dry as straw. The gentle goddess Hathor turns into a blood-lusting lioness, but is tricked into drinking huge quantities of beer which have been dyed red to look like blood. As a result, she returns to her peaceful and beautiful state. The return of the pacified goddess was celebrated by Egyptian men and women with a festival of drunkenness.

The opening lines of L. P. Hartley's *The Go Between*, 'The past is a foreign country', contain a metaphor often quoted to emphasize the specificity, contingency and particularity of the past, and the fact that any attempt to understand it is thus an illusion. Furthermore, this strangeness (to our eyes) of the lives of ancient Egyptian women also disabuses the notion of the prototypical sisterhood claimed by some branches of feminism. One might also add that the problems of lack of evidence and the interpretation of ancient material in modern terms reinforce the futility of trying to understand past events.

But is the aim of understanding the past really so hopeless? One might argue that at the same time, all humans do share commonality, that there is some universal human experience, that we all live in the same world and that we are, more or less, all biologically the same.

Thus, certain aspects of ancient Egyptian women seem remarkably similar to those of today's women. That we can appreciate this similarity is made possible by the incredible amount of surviving evidence. We can even witness poignantly personal events, both of ecstatic celebration and terrible tragedy. The birth of a girl child was celebrated at 'the place of hard drinking' and we can imagine her parents' joy. Concerning tragedy, it is sometimes claimed that high infant mortality meant that mothers dared not become attached to their children and therefore, personhood was not ascribed until an individual had passed childhood. However, the evidence of a severely disabled child from Deir el-Medina – a young boy who could not have survived had he not received considerable help in his short life – shows that children were cared for. Mothers loved their children dearly. After death, the child was lovingly buried with bread, dom-fruit and jewellery, no doubt by his tearful carers.

Such incidents would have engendered high emotion; they are occurrences with which we can all sympathize and make us feel as though we can almost touch the past.

When we look beyond the individual at the broader picture, it sometimes seems that in over 4,000 years, the lives of most women are remarkably unchanged. Although we think of Egypt as being incredibly developed, it was a pre-modern country and sanitation, nutrition and health care were not as they are today. As was the case in the early twentieth century West, for most ancient Egyptian women, life was short and infant mortality high. A 40-year-old woman would have been considered old. For most individuals, lives would have involved the physically drudgery of carrying children and water, and hours spent grinding corn would have taken its toll on health. This tedious and labour-intensive activity remains the unenviable lot of millions of women today.

Women generally did not have the same rights or wealth as men. Ancient Egypt was a patriarchal society. Upper-class women rarely had their own tomb chapels or funerary stelae, but were instead interred in those of their male relatives. Texts from New Kingdom Deir el-Medina suggest that while both men and women could initiate divorce, it was largely men who did so. Where marriages broke down, women were socially and economically excluded, resulting in single mothers struggling to bring up families. This difference in status between men and women is something which many would recognize today. Today there are few, if any, instances of matriarchal societies.

Not only do women, at least from the Middle Kingdom, appear to have fewer grave-goods, but also, to some extent, seem to be the chattels of men. A man committing adultery wrongs the husband of his paramour, not his own wife. Wife beating does not seem to have been considered shocking, though it could be brought before the courts. Unfortunately wife beating is still considered acceptable in many societies today.

Most women would have worked on the land and/or within the household. Men then, as now, dominated the administrative hierarchy. Where there were female supreme heads of state, and there were only around six in 3,000 years of Egyptian history, these women made use of male symbols of kingship and may be better regarded as female kings, rather than queens.

However, not all women were confined to the home. Wealthy women could be spared continual nursing, sagging breasts and childcare by the wet nurse and maids, just as today, wealthier career women have nannies. Childcare then, as now, could be off loaded onto other, less wealthy, women. This of course suggests that then, as now, childcare was not rewarded quite so well as other forms of labour, though again, caring for the offspring of the wealthy might be one of the few means of enhancing status for more lowly born women.

While women worked just as hard as men, work in the home, or women's work then, as now, does not appear to have been so highly regarded as men's work. Cross culturally, work in the home is associated with less prestige than that outside the home; it is also associated with women. The pale skin colour of ancient Egyptian women suggests that ideally they worked indoors, protected from the sun. This artistic convention is used in many societies to differentiate male and female. It is also true that then, as now, women's work, although largely domestic or related to the domestic, may well have greatly added to the family income. Women's 'kitchen gardens' could earn enough to pay for servants and their weaving could purchase land. They also, of course, were vital in the upbringing of children and thus in the social conditioning of the populace.

As a curator of Egyptian antiquities, I have often heard male visitors to our galleries explaining excitedly to their wives and girlfriends that in ancient Egypt women wore very little. This is a common view of ancient Egypt, largely a result of the sensuous tomb paintings of Egyptian women displaying their charms, and enhanced by film and television. In many ancient reliefs, women are shown standing with their husbands; the women are holding a lotus, (a symbol of love), wearing a heavy wig (an erotic symbol) and are associated with animals representing sexuality such as the monkey, the duck and the goose. They are shown as perfumed, eternally young and beautiful, and wearing tight, see-through outfits. The Westcar Papyrus describes diaphanous net dresses worn by young women to amuse the king. This emphasis on female sexuality in Egyptian representation may not have been an accurate reproduction of most ancient Egyptian women, but the emphasis on female, as opposed to male, sexuality is again strangely familiar.

At the same time, women's sexuality was both celebrated and feared. The dichotomy between the femme fatale and the faithful wife and mother is modern. The traditional Mills & Boon heroine is gentle, passive and good. James Bond's female adversaries are dangerous and active, using their sexual wiles to entrap the male. This duality seems to have extended as far back as ancient Egypt. The ideal woman does not actively stride forward, but stands passively by her partner's side. However, there are stories of women who use their feminine wiles to entrap men. Women were often blamed for the sexual weakness of men. A lone woman is a threatening siren to a good man. The dual nature of womanhood is also manifest in the portrayal of female goddesses. On the one hand, there are beautiful nurturing goddesses such as Hathor and Bastet, and on the other, fierce blood-lusting goddesses such as Mut and Sekhmet. Women's passion is shown to move from one extreme to another.

Thus, a study of women in ancient Egypt seems to show that the particular and the universal are possible at the same time. While, generally, ancient women are much the same as modern women, when we look at the specifics, there are differences. The study of the past at once shows striking similarities and striking dissimilarities.

However, the purpose of this book is to encourage debate, and it is appropriate to end this introduction with some questions. Are we deluding ourselves that the ancient Egyptians were in any way similar to us? Do we not impose ourselves on the past, familiarizing that which is essentially exotic? The famous Berlin bust of Nefertiti conforms to modern stereotypical ideas of feminine beauty, and in popular works, Nefertiti is said to be the most beautiful woman the world has ever seen. At the same time, she is strangely distant; her enigmatic smile hides the secrets of 3,000 years. She has been considered the archetypal black woman, the stereotypical Nazi Aryan and the role model of modern Egyptian womanhood. Can we ever really understand her?

1

Rich women, poor women

> *The citizeness Taaper was brought. She was examined by beating with the stick. They said to her, Come tell us the story about this piece of copper which you said was in the possession of the field labourer Peikharu . . . She said . . . Now I happened to be sitting hungry under the sycamores and the men chanced to be trading copper as we were sitting hungry . . .*

> *There was brought the citizeness Shedehnakht the wife of the field labourer Peikharu who was a maid servant . . . She was examined by beating with a stick; her feet and hands were twisted. She was given the oath by the Ruler on pain of mutilation not to speak falsehood . . . They said to her, When you were a maid-servant with the wab-priest and thief Tetisheri it was you who opened for those who went in . . . tell me of men whom you saw . . . She said I did not see it. If I had seen it I would tell you. She was examined again by beating with the stick. She was given the oath by the Ruler not to speak falsehood. She said, I saw no one at all. If I had seen I would tell you.[1]*

These two extracts from a 3,000-year-old court document now in the British Museum, poignantly describe the questioning of several people, including two women, concerning the theft of a copper carrying pole from the tomb of a chief priest of Amun worth the equivalent of about eight months' wages for a workman.[2] These women are obviously not of the elite as one of them describes herself as 'sitting hungry'. Both are subject to torture to extract confessions. The paltry amount of metal about which they are questioned contrasts with the great wealth of goods placed in royal tombs. The gold coffin of Tutankhamun, which alone weighed c. 100 kg, would have been worth 3,000 years' wages for a labourer.[3]

These accounts remind us that life for the majority of Egyptians – most of whom were field labourers and wives of labourers – was not one of ease, and contrasted with the vast wealth of royalty. This book is about rich and poor – the wives of field labourers and the wives of kings. I begin by considering whether their lives were so vastly different from one another.

In many societies, including our own, the majority of wealth is in the hands of only a very few people. In ancient Egypt, the king was the most important person and around him, the royal family and courtiers were the elite. Below these people were scribes, the men of the bureaucratic machinery of state, and skilled artisans. Next came the largest group, which consisted mainly of agricultural workers, peasant farmers, herdsmen, fishermen and labourers. Finally, there would be the poorest of poor who were destitute, such as beggars. It is a popular, and entirely erroneous myth, that the ancient Egyptians employed vast teams of slaves. In fact, there was no specific term for the slave in ancient Egypt, though the terms *ḥm* (hem) or *b3k* (bak) are sometimes translated as 'slave'. Hem is used of servants dependent upon a household; bak is similarly used, but implies a strong sense of loyalty to the lord (often the god or king). While certainly some of these people might have had little freedom, only very few of them could be bought and sold, and it is usually agreed that compared to other societies in the ancient world, the Egyptians had very few slaves.

There was a certain amount of social mobility, although a peasant farmer would not have been expected to become a scribe. In addition to the social inertia caused by lack of mixing among the classes, the lower social orders could never aspire to be members of the bureaucracy because this depended on the ability to read and write. Estimates for the percentage of people who could read and write in ancient Egypt generally vary between 1 and 4 per cent.

Of course, women were not a homogeneous group, but whether rich or poor, all women were certainly disadvantaged in comparison to men of the same social class. Women had fewer life chances and, for all classes, their lives were overshadowed by the dangers of giving birth. Additionally, it seems to have been acceptable to physically punish disadvantaged adults. Rich women may not have been as subject to beatings from social 'betters', but they still may have endured such from higher status relatives, and in turn beaten their social inferiors. Generally, women were seen as more passionate than men and whether as dangerous femmes fatales, or nurturing housewives and mothers, their role was to encourage and support the male. This does not mean that all ancient Egyptian women had unhappy lives; the role of women may have lacked the status and advantages of men, but it does not follow that ancient Egyptian women felt oppressed. Exclusion from active and aggressive professions, for example, meant they were not coerced into the army. Ancient Egyptian women do not appear to have been unable to ask for what they wanted and, as is the case today, the role of wife and mother was exactly what many ancient Egyptian women desired.

While all social classes of women in ancient Egypt shared some things in common, there were differences between the rich and poor. The huge difference in social status in ancient Egypt is often underplayed, partly due to intrinsic bias in the evidence and partly due to romanticism; representations of women tend to concentrate on the wives of the great and the good, and this elite lived differently from the poor.

It is difficult to judge the extent of poverty in ancient Egypt, but we can say that compared to the twentieth century in the developed world, the lives of most ancient Egyptians were short and marked by grinding poverty and drudgery. Women who survived childhood would be lucky to live beyond forty. Work was hard and monotonous; bosses ill-treated workers and there was little recourse to courts and justice. Children grew up quickly and were sent out to work at an early age to support the family. Egyptian women in such households had neither the luxury of leisure, nor the time to beautify themselves. Instead, they would spend hours each day in the back-breaking tasks of grinding corn to make flour, weaving and looking after children. Some would have helped in the fields. These women wore clothes that would have been darned and redarned and they would have had few possessions.

Lower-class women, like other less advantaged groups, would have been abused by their superiors. The *Tale of the Eloquent Peasant* explains the difficulty experienced by the non-elite in gaining justice. While the title suggests the hero of the story is of the lowest social class, he is actually a merchant or pedlar and yet is subject to abuse by those of higher status. Women seem not to have used the courts as much as men (see Chapter 3), and justice would have been doubly difficult for poorer woman. Poorer women would have been more dependent upon male relatives than richer women, and thus widowhood, especially without family support, would have caused great hardship. The beautifully painted wooden coffins we so commonly see in museums were simply unaffordable for the average Egyptian.

Elite women, such as the wives of courtiers, had very different lives. However, while more of this group might have been expected to live to old age, this rarely in fact occurred. Many of these women would have died in childbirth and, like their poorer sisters, would have been expected to produce large families. Wet nurses would have taken charge of children, and later, tutors would have freed such women from constant childminding. They would have had maidservants to assist them and, thanks to a better education, might well have been able to read and write. Thus, they could easily run large households, keeping accounts of goods and chattels. Many would have been priestesses, working one month in four in the temple. At banquets, such women would have been clad in fine linen, perfumed and adorned with colourful collars of semi-precious stones. If widowed, elite women would have been able to keep their own property, plus one third of that acquired while married; they would not have been destitute. In death, elite women would have been interred in the tombs of their male relatives.

Sex and gender are often confused. Put simply, sex consists of the biological and psychological differences that define men and women, whereas gender refers to the socially constructed roles and activities considered acceptable for both men and women. Thus, women are sexually different from men in that they can give birth, while modern female gender differs from that of men in that women are still likely to do more housework than men. As gender is socially constructed and varies from society to society, other aspects of society, such as class, may influence it. Some scholars have even suggested that class differentiation gives rise to gender, that is, the division of people into rich and poor, or powerful and less powerful, has forced men and women into different roles.

There is some evidence from ancient Egypt that differences in the roles of men and women are, indeed, more apparent among the rich than the poor. A study of artefacts from Deir el-Medina tombs suggests that middle and upper-class men were buried with more jewellery and other possessions than their wives, whereas, for the lower classes, there is very little differentiation in grave goods between the sexes.[4] However, this may simply indicate that archaeology cannot show gender differences among the poor since they had very few objects anyway; it could well be that the behaviour and treatment of poor men and women was very different, but not in ways which would show up in their tombs.

Studies have shown that higher status women in ancient Egypt would have found themselves better off in terms of access to good food and luxury goods, but at the same time their personal freedoms would have been more restricted than that of their less wealthy sisters. Poor women would have needed to work in the fields to feed their families and this would have been seen as an unladylike activity by wealthier women. However, such outdoor toil possibly allowed for a freer way of life which may have been the envy of wealthy women restricted to more feminine, indoor activities.

One argument for viewing class, rather than gender, as a dividing principal in ancient Egypt is that richer women were freed from childcare and housework. This should have meant that in ancient Egypt wealth reduced gender differentiation. Needless to say, by hiring maidservants and wet nurses, richer women simply pushed the burden of domestic work onto poorer women.

In 1884, Friedrich Engels (in *The Origin of the Family, Private Property and the State*) suggested that the status of women declined with the emergence of economic classes. Engels saw private property as disadvantaging women. Men would want to pass property on to sons, hence the need to control the virginity and fidelity of women. In ancient Egypt, evidence that class difference creates gender might be found in the transition from Predynastic Period sexual equality to inequality within the hierarchical Dynastic society. This is discussed in the next chapter. The situation is complex, as we cannot say which factors in the growth of the state may have led to loss of female power. Some have seen kinship, rather than economics, as important, while others have looked to the rise of militarism.

2

Changing worlds

The Cleopatra of legend (Cleopatra VII) was not buried in a massive stone pyramid. Such monuments were built over 2,000 years before she was born and were probably almost as mysterious to her as they are to us. Studies of Egypt often ignore chronological variation and consider the lives of women from the age of the great pyramids to be the same as those of women in the age of Cleopatra.[1] This would be like describing contemporary British women through evidence from the time of the rebel queen Boudicca. The perception of Egypt's great achievements, and their seeming timelessness, is partly due to the monumentality of its material culture, which suggests an unchanging never-never land, focusing our minds on kings and great men.

Women's fortunes waxed and waned from the Predynastic Period to the Middle Kingdom. The Predynastic Period is sometimes represented as a golden age for women, or a time when women ruled the land. From this period until the Middle Kingdom, the status of women appears to have declined, although as we shall see, the evidence is open to question.

THE GOLDEN AGE

In times of disillusionment, people may seek a golden age in either the past or the future. Some feminists have situated such an age in the prehistoric past, a period in which they believe women were at least equal in status with men. Perhaps the most well-known proponent of this golden age has been Marija Gimbutas, a respected but controversial scholar who claimed that the period up to the Late Neolithic was the age of the Mother Goddess, a peaceful and egalitarian era compared to later aggressive, hierarchical and patriarchal times. The idea of a golden age is attractive but did it ever exist, and if it did, what caused its demise? As usual, reality is more mundanely complex than romantic vision.

THE GREAT MOTHER GODDESS

Marija Gimbutas (1921–1994), a Lithuanian scholar who later became professor of archaeology at the University of California, saw the period up to the
late Neolithic as one in which women had particular power and status, largely
through the religion of the Mother Goddess. Gimbutas was mainly interested
in the European Old World, although her vision of the Mother Goddess and
corresponding pre-Bronze Age golden age has been applied to ancient Egyptian
culture. Sadly for romantics, her attractive ideas are now rarely taken seriously in
academia. Gimbutas claimed, for example, that certain figurines are evidence of
the Mother Goddess, even though they are often separated in time by thousands
of years, and geographically by thousands of miles. It is now recognized that some
of these figurines may not be goddesses at all, but rather toys, self-representations,
or depictions of other categories of non-divine women. It has also been argued
that some of these figurines may not even be women.[2] However, while one may
dismiss many of Gimbutas' ideas as speculative, more recent scholars still support
the notion of a Mother Goddess in Predynastic Egypt. Others believe that before
the rise of the state, women in ancient Egypt had more status.

It is undeniable that in Dynastic Egypt, Hathor and later Isis were paramount
female goddesses. While not usurping the role of male gods, Hathor and Isis were
essential to kingship, and thus to the survival of the state in Egypt. However, we
know little of the importance and function of Predynastic and earlier goddesses.
In the 2,000 years of Predynastic Egyptian history, it seems likely that some deities
were female.

It is sometimes claimed that the fact that only women can give birth must
have given rise to the idea of a female goddess.[3] However, the knowledge that the
male is also vital for life is not unique to modern societies, and indeed, for the
Pharaonic Egyptians it was the male who was considered crucial to life. Besides
this, patriarchal societies with a male godhead can exist in societies where the
woman is regarded as more important for reproduction.

One of the early proponents of the Egyptian fertility goddess was a pioneering
Egyptologist of the twentieth century, Elise Baumgartel,[4] who cited the evidence
of the female form of some pottery vessels and so-called 'cow amulets'. More
recently, the respected Egyptologist, Fekri Hassan,[5] argued for the importance
of a Mother Goddess, usually taking cow form, in Predynastic Egypt, extending
the idea of a mothering cow goddess back to 7000 BC. Writing in 1992, Hassan
suggested that this goddess was the paramount deity, although by 1998 he admits
that she was not to the exclusion of male gods. He sees the location and economy
of Egypt as being critical to the importance of the female cow goddess – the

life-giving importance of the woman, milk and water in an increasingly desert environment. The idea of a Predynastic cow goddess is also supported by other Egyptologists,[6] although this goddess is not seen as a paramount deity.

It is certainly true that many pastoral cultures revere the cow, and see her as a nurturing entity, or perfect mother. However, this does not mean that all pastoralists inevitably adopt a cow goddess. Evidence for a paramount cow goddess in Predynastic Egypt appears based upon three related and contestable assumptions: that beliefs surrounding Hathor, or other cow goddesses of the Dynastic Period, can be extended backward into the Predynastic Period; that depictions of cattle are to be identified as cow goddesses; and that women are associated with cattle.

There is clear evidence of the symbolic importance of cattle in Predynastic Egypt, but little evidence of the particular importance of the cow, as opposed to the bull.[7] The most cited 'evidence' for a Predynastic cow goddess is that of the Naqada II to First Dynasty depictions of a bovine head shown facing forward in conjunction with five stars, one on each ear and horn, and one on top of the head. This head is similar to a later, little-known deity, Bat, a bovine with curled horns and human-shaped eyes and mouth; it is also sometimes said to be like Hathor.

Bat[8] represented the seventh nome (Egypt was divided into territories called 'nomes' and the authority of the nome deity was usually restricted to this territory). She is shown, for example, in one of a series of triads depicting King Menkaure of the Fourth Dynasty accompanied by Hathor and one male or female nome deity.[9] Thus, as far as we can tell, she was never a major deity. Hathor, as we shall see, was a major goddess who sometimes took cow form.

Three particular depictions of a Predynastic bovine head with stars are commonly cited as evidence of a sky goddess, but other images of bovine heads without stars are also claimed to be cow goddesses. The most famous depiction with stars is a Naqada II oversize palette from Gerza. A palette is a flat piece of stone used for grinding minerals to make make-up. Its large size and decoration suggest that it was a ceremonial object. Another bovine occurs on a First Dynasty black and white porphyry bowl from Hierakonpolis reconstructed from fragments held by the Ashmolean and Petrie Museums.[10] The third is on a seal impression of the Naqada II Period from a burial at Abydos.[11] In all three cases, the bovine is not identical to the later Bat (in particular, the horns of the later Bat appear to end in spirals) and the head is certainly unlike that of Hathor.

The cow depicted in the Gerza palette, in particular, has been cited by scholars as evidence for a celestial cow goddess as her head is surrounded by 'stars'.[12] Some even go so far as to identify the stars as Orion. Admittedly, the 'stars' may be a device to set apart these depictions from those of earthly bovines, and might indicate a bovine sky goddess. The 'stars' on either side of the face of the bovine could alternatively be 'rosettes', which some have seen as depicting kingship,[13] though the symbols between the horns look more starlike than rosette-like. However, stars do not prove that this is Hathor or Bat. The *Pyramid Texts* describe a celestial goddess as 'the Great Wild Cow who dwells in Nekheb'[14] and as 'She who bears a thousand *bas*'[15] (the *ba* here may be simplistically equated with the soul). The *Pyramid Texts* are a collection of religious texts which were carved on the walls and sarcophagi of the pyramids at Saqqara during the fifth and sixth Dynasties of the Old Kingdom. Unlike the *Book of the Dead* into which parts of the *Pyramid Texts* later evolved, these spells were reserved for the king. Moreover, the *Pyramid Texts* also described the deceased king as a 'Bull of the Sky'.[16] The Gerza palette cow could just as easily be a bull. Thus, we seem to have two main contenders for the starry bovine, either the king in the sky, or a celestial goddess, and it is difficult to say which is correct.

Other items that are sometimes claimed to represent the cow goddesses are not associated with stars. Particularly well known is the Narmer palette, a Naqada III or Early Dynastic ceremonial item, which was found at Hierakonpolis over a century ago. Like the Gerza Palette, this too is an oversized ceremonial item. The Narmer palette has depictions of bovines on the top row of decoration, two on each side, which have been interpreted as Bat or Hathor. Again, these bovines are shown face on, and here, as on the Hierakonpolis bowl, the features of eyes, nose and mouth look human. Elsewhere on the Narmer palette, bulls represent the victorious power of the king. It is difficult to understand why examples such as those depicted on the Narmer Palette should be assumed to be cows, rather than bulls. Egyptologists do not always present such images as female. One such example is the frontal view bovine head, with straight horns, upon a serekh or shrine excavated from a Tarkhan grave (dating to the time of Narmer) which has been considered a bull.[17]

A further problem with assuming that the Predynastic bovine is related to Bat or Hathor is that we cannot simply assume that the same divinities continued from the Predynastic Period into the Dynastic Period. Even though it is usually claimed that religions are slow to change, it is dangerous to extend the importance of known deities far back into little-known periods; the state emerged in Egypt during the Predynastic Period, a time when religious change may have been momentous. The earliest clear indication of Bat comes from *Pyramid Text 1096*, where the king is identified as 'Bat with her two faces'. Although written down in the Old Kingdom, the *Pyramid Texts* were composed much earlier. However, whether this was as early as the Gerza and Narmer Palettes, is debatable. Other indications of Bat are from later periods and include a Sixth Dynasty stela depicting a woman said to be an overseer of the *ḥnr*[18] (khener, meaning musical troupe) of Bat. The first clear attestation of Hathor is in the reign of Khafre of the Fourth Dynasty.[19]

We cannot say that there is clear evidence of a Predynastic cow goddess, but assuming such a deity existed, is there evidence for her link with human women? The apparent connection between cow goddesses and human women is sometimes cited to further the idea of a Golden Age for women in the Predynastic Period. Evidence for the link between women, cattle and goddesses is sometimes said to lie in depictions of women with arms curved enigmatically upward. These depictions occur in different forms, on pottery and as figurines, which some Egyptologists have interpreted as goddesses with arms raised in imitation of cow horns. Several of these figurines with curved arms are known from two Naqada I Period tombs at Ma'amerieh,[20] but their purpose is unclear. They are found in graves, but were they intended to serve the deceased in the afterlife, or facilitate an afterlife? They may be depictions of goddesses, but equally they could be fertility figurines, or depictions of the deceased or other women. Fekri Hassan,[21] following the lead of Elise Baumgartel,[22] sees a connection between the curved arms of these figurines and cow horns. The present-day Sudanese Dinka (Nilotes) women have a dance termed the 'cow dance', which they perform with their arms upraised in a similar posture.[23] However, the Dinka are far removed in time from the period under discussion, and there are several other problems with the assumption that the figurines are dancing in imitation of the cow. One of these problems is that the figurines are known mainly from two tombs and generally, female figurines without arms are more common than those with arms,[24] suggesting no general correlation between women and pottery figurines with upraised arms. Another problem is that the fact that the arm positions are similar to a dance known from the Fifth Dynasty[25] does not mean that the Predynastic representations of raised arms are also a dance. There are major differences between the Dynastic and Predynastic images. The Dynastic scenes, for example, show dancers in groups, while the Predynastic scenes show single individuals with raised arms; the arm position could alternatively represent birds flying, or women dancing (possibly imitating cows or birds), praying, or perhaps simply exuberance. Indeed, the beak-like faces of these figures suggest more affinity with birds than cows.

Women with such raised hands are also shown in two dimensions on a type of pottery called 'Decorated Ware' (D-ware) which is common in the Naqada II Period. The figures on the pottery are often shown in association with boats, and figures with raised hands are recognized as females by their wide hips. Ithyphallic males accompany them and have been seen in some quarters as precursors to the Dynastic god, the ithyphallic Min. Alternatively, these could simply be earthly men. The women are often shown larger than the men, perhaps indicating their superior, or god-like, status. Again, like the pottery figures, the women with upraised arms may not necessarily be mirroring cows' horns, but by their size, they do seem to at least show important female figures.

The situation gets more complicated if we consider the rarer white, cross-lined ware (C-ware) pots of Naqada I. On first impression, these vessels show only male figures with raised arms.[26] There is, however, some ambiguity of gender here; three vessels appear to show taller human forms among smaller ones. The taller ones have raised arms and protuberances from the tops of their heads. In two cases, these larger figures have elongated protuberances with swollen ends extending from their waists, while the hips are not enlarged. The assumption might be that these protuberances are phalli. The third figure does not have any semblance of a phallus, but is placed among a group carrying maces. Thus, we might interpret the elongated objects with swollen ends appearing from the waist area as maces. Hence, the figures could be women carrying maces, though there is debatable evidence that it was mainly men who were associated with maces.[27]

There is a fourth source of figures with upraised arms, but again this source does not give any definitive answer. The rock art of the Eastern Desert includes several sites depicting figures with arms positioned in this manner.[28] Like the D-ware pottery representations, rock art figures are found in association with boats, but the rock art examples are notoriously difficult to date and the gender of the figures is unclear.[29] Not all the figures with upraised arms exhibit the enlarged hips usually associated with women.[30] Occasionally, figures with raised arms are depicted with apparent phalli which are clearly not maces.[31]

To sum up, the idea of a Prehistoric, nurturing cow goddess, while plausible, needs further study, as indeed does Predynastic religion more generally. As is frequently said of prehistoric archaeology, 'absence of evidence is not evidence of absence'; while a paramount mother goddess seems unlikely, it also seems unlikely that there were not at least some female goddesses, though identifying them is not easy. We have more evidence for Neith, a primeval goddess often shown with a bow and arrow, than for any other goddesses. She is discussed more fully in Chapter 8.

THE STATUS AND ROLE OF PREDYNASTIC WOMEN

Although we cannot prove the existence of a Predynastic mother goddess, this does not demolish the notion of women's high status in this period. Many scholars have postulated that pre-state Egypt was an age when the sexes were more equal compared to later periods. The large women of D-ware vessels have already been discussed, and there is other tantalizing evidence that Predynastic women had higher status.

Initially, it should be conceded, on the basis of mortuary evidence, that while men and women had different roles in Predynastic Egypt, there is little evidence for a significant difference in status.[32] However, use of mortuary evidence is problematic, involving the assumption that how a person is buried relates to his or her role in life. This might not be the case since in death, social roles may be inverted and, moreover, mortuary evidence reflects the ideal rather than the actual. There are also problems with the quality of data; most burials were excavated in the early twentieth century, when sexing of human remains was relatively inaccurate. Additionally, excavations were not always recorded to 'modern' standards and graves were often found to have been plundered. In studies of Predynastic data, 2,000 years of evidence is often conflated so that any chronological variation in status or role of women remains hidden. Nevertheless, the studies of mortuary evidence which have been carried out suggest that generally in Predynastic Egypt, men and women were relatively equal.

The richest Badarian grave at Mahasna contained a woman's skeleton.[33] She wore several ivory bracelets, and necklaces of carnelian and green glazed steatite beads. Nearby were two tusks, one hollow and one solid, which were interpreted as ritual objects representing the male and female. The grave also contained a pottery bowl decorated with depictions of hippopotami and an ivory statue of an ithyphallic male. However, was it only in exceptional circumstances that women achieved high status, or were they generally equal with men?

A study of Predynastic–Early Dynastic graves at Tarkhan showed that women's graves contained more artefacts and more types of artefact than those of men, but men's graves were larger and more variable.[34] Slate palettes and beads were more common in women's graves. At Predynastic Naga-ed-Deir Cemetery N7000, excavated in 1902–1903, a recent study showed no differences in sizes or shapes of graves between the sexes.[35] This cemetery dates largely from Naqada I-II, with a few possible Naqada III graves. Clusters of artefacts occurring together were studied and assumed to indicate social roles. Results showed women had a greater variety of clusters, and thus a greater variety of social roles, than men. However, we need not assume that this relates to status. An early study of 635 Naqada I-II graves from Naga-ed-Deir showed that fishtailed knives and maceheads were associated with male graves, and hairpins, blue beads, tusks, tusk amulets and palettes were most common in female graves.[36] However, as a significant number of unsexed graves were also associated with palettes, and only two maceheads were actually found, these correlations with gender may not be real. In size of tomb and diversity of grave goods, there was no real difference between men and women.

In a study of 426 graves from five cemeteries of Predynastic Egypt – once again from early excavations – it was apparent that while male graves appeared hierarchical, female graves were more homogeneous.[37] However, there was no significant gender difference between size of tomb and number of grave goods. Women were buried with more toiletries, amulets, ornaments, red and rough pottery, high-value items and possibly cattle in the form of figurines. They also seemed to have been associated with the colour green. Men had more projectile points, stone artefacts and skins. One may wonder if projectile points were associated with warfare, hunting, or both (on rock art and grinding palettes, men seem to be associated with hunting).

Using not only evidence from graves, but also rock art and other representations, some scholars identified a connection between women and water, and women and birds, with the bird representing the soul. Pottery figurines of women, which had not only raised arms but also bird beaks, have been discussed above. Additionally, palettes used for grinding eye paint[38] often have bird-like beaks, or occasionally cow heads. It is suggested that the ostrich, in particular, was associated with the female, a connection which continued in the equation of the female goddess Maat with the ostrich feather. Ostrich eggshells were frequently used in Predynastic times and ostriches appear on pottery.

There has been speculation that women were connected with vegetation in the Predynastic Period[39] as some figurines seem to depict females decorated with symbols which could be interpreted as vegetation.[40] This may link female goddesses with the earth,[41] and *Pyramid Text* references to Isis and Nephthys as the two banks of the River Nile may be a throwback to this earlier belief. However, there is no proof that the figurines are goddesses. It would be interesting if women were associated with the earth in the Predynastic Period, as this appears to contradict a later association of goddesses with the sky. It has been suggested[42] that the Dynastic Period association of men with the earth and women with the sky arose because the water supply in Egypt derived from the annual inundation, rather than rainfall. However, in the Predynastic Period, there were much higher levels of rainfall.

Thus, there is evidence of a difference in the roles of men and women in Predynastic Egypt and some evidence supporting equality of the sexes, though this is not to suggest a Predynastic matriarchy or matrilineal descent. The general equality in the Predynastic Period contrasts with later times; by Naqada III, male graves 'began to outpace' female graves.[43] As time progresses, there is increasing evidence of male dominance, though as we shall see, not all women of later periods were lacking in status. The question is, 'Does the decline in women's status lie in the increased power of the state, or is it due to some other factor, such as the growth of agriculture?' This question is not easy to answer. The later Predynastic Period coincides with the decline in the status of women, the secondary products revolution (the exploitation of animals for milk, blood, traction and wool, rather than simply for food is discussed below), and the growth of the state. Both the secondary products revolution and the growth of the state have been blamed for loss of women's power.

INEQUALITY AND THE RISE OF THE STATE

The loss of equality with the rise of the state is not confined to Egypt, and several gender theorists have considered the problem of why women seem to lose power at this time.[44] Some see this loss of power as inevitable in a state-level society, but arguably gender equality can continue to exist so long as elites are organized through kinship.[45]

Fekri Hassan[46] specifically considers the relationship between gender inequality and state formation in Egypt. He interestingly suggests that while the female goddess was used to legitimize male rule and formation of the nation state, women lost power partly because it was transferred from the female domain of kinship and the home to the male domain of the state. The idea of the female goddess aside, support for this argument demands proof that women were confined to the family and the home. The claim that it is natural for women to work in the home due to the restrictions of child rearing is debatable. Furthermore, while it is clear that the early Egyptian state did indeed rely to some extent on kinship, this is an area which is not clearly understood. The continuing importance of kinship perhaps explains the importance of the king's mother (discussed below), and the family ties in Hathorian priesthood (see below). Hassan[47] also emphasizes the part played by warfare, an area from which women were largely excluded, in the construction of the state. Not only was warfare seen as prestigious, but women were possibly given as rewards to the victors.

Finally, it is sometimes stated that gender is produced by economic class; certainly, the growth of class and gender division in Egypt coincides with state formation. One expert has shown[48] that in the Naqada III Period, control was increasingly in the hands of a small elite and this continued until the Early Dynastic Period. The mechanisms by which class disadvantages women are, however, debatable.

WOMEN'S STATUS AND THE GROWTH OF AGRICULTURE

Cereal production became increasingly important in Egypt between 4000–3500 BC,[49] roughly coinciding with the beginning of a decline in women's status. Those studying the Old World often claim that the farming revolution resulted in the loss of women's status.[50] It is argued that in the Early Neolithic Period, women would have played a vital part in horticulture, sowing, weeding and harvesting. The later Neolithic Period saw a change in subsistence with the development of farming innovations. This, it is claimed, led to men playing the dominant role in handling large livestock, while women were relegated to the less prestigious domestic sphere and were particularly occupied in spinning and weaving wool. Why domestic work should be considered inferior is not usually explored.

Can this model be applied to Egypt? The so-called 'secondary products' revolution (the harvesting of milk, wool and other goods) would have taken place during the Fourth Millennium BC,[51] and the problem is that we do not have finely detailed chronological frameworks for women's status. Moreover, cross culturally this model assumes women would have been primary producers in the Early Neolithic Period, an assumption for which there is no evidence.[52] It also assumes that only men would have handled livestock in the Late Neolithic Period, again something for which there is no evidence. Finally, in Egypt, linen, not wool, was the main textile produced and this dates back to the Badarian Period,[53] thereby pre-dating the Egyptian secondary products revolution.

WOMEN'S STATUS FROM THE OLD KINGDOM TO THE MIDDLE KINGDOM

There does appear to be evidence for the decline of the status of women from the Old to the Middle Kingdom. In the Old Kingdom, there is evidence that royal women, especially the queen mothers, were particularly important. By the Middle Kingdom, this was no longer the case. Secondly, women seem generally to have had fewer administrative titles in the Middle Kingdom than in the Old Kingdom.[54] Thirdly, in temple hierarchy, women appear less important[55] and the decline of the priestess of Hathor is particularly noticeable during the Middle Kingdom. Finally, it has also been suggested that in the Old Kingdom women were particularly well rewarded as weavers and perhaps were even important in trade.

This change may well have been a part of the general social upheaval of the First Intermediate Period. This period is generally thought to have been one of weak kings and a growth of the middle classes. Inscriptions describe civil war and the possibility that women actually gained in status in this period is discussed below. However, other theories could be posited. The Middle Kingdom decline in women's status might be seen as related to the decline of kings. If, as has been suggested,[56] the kings of the Old Kingdom were all part of a single extended kin-group, the changing roles of women, and indeed other social changes, might all be ascribed to the decline of this group. Indeed, the areas I now describe are largely those of elite women who would most likely have been affected by change in a ruling group. We need not assume that this was also part of a general change in the status and roles of all women. For this, we would need to look more extensively at evidence encompassing the non-elite.

QUEENS OF THE OLD KINGDOM

In 1910, the American archaeologist George Reisner unearthed an enigmatic, stone statue from the Valley Temple of King Menkaure. The statue, now in the Museum of Fine Art at Boston, showed two figures standing side by side – a woman embracing a king. The male figure was clearly Menkaure of the Fourth Dynasty as comparable named statues of him were known, but the woman was more of a mystery. She was obviously of high-status and some have even suggested she was a goddess. She is not only shown as being as tall as the king but, like him, strides forward with her left foot. Statues of Egyptian women of the period would generally show wives as shorter than their husbands, and with their feet passively together. So who was this high-status individual? The statue was tantalizingly uninscribed, but Reisner assumed the woman to be the principal wife of the king. However, the status, particularly of queen mothers of reigning kings, appears particularly high in the Old Kingdom and we may wonder if this was, in fact, his mother rather than his wife (against this theory, in private sculpture when a man and woman are modelled together, the woman is usually indicated by text as the man's wife and private sculpture tended to copy royal sculpture). The mother of the reigning king was always important in ancient Egypt, partly because of her influence upon the head of state, but also because of her religious role. It is also clear that for much of Egyptian history, the mother, whether royal or non-royal, was held in high regard. However, in the Old Kingdom, the role of the elite mother is particularly pronounced. During this period, the mother of the royal heir, not his wife, was his official consort.[57]

A number of queens of the Old Kingdom appear to have been accorded particularly high status. Old Kingdom queen mothers were listed on the Palermo

Stone, a large fragment of a stela that records the names of the kings of Egypt and which is known as the Royal Annals of the Old Kingdom. The first known royal mother, Merneith, had a tomb of similar size to other First Dynasty rulers. Two queens, both called Khentkawes, appear to have been regents[58] and had pyramid complexes of their own. Pepi II, who ascended to the throne at the age of five, is shown in a smaller scale than his mother, and is seated on her lap.

The importance of the queen mother in the Old Kingdom may have been in part due to the importance of kinship at this date. It may also have been due to the general prominence of the mother during the Old Kingdom; while women are generally shown as having secondary status to men in ancient Egypt, in tombs of the Old Kingdom, some prominence is given to them.[59] This may also be due to inheritance of wealth which, in some cases, was passed on from the mother. A First Intermediate Period inscription declares: 'I acquired the house of my father, Iti; it was my mother, Ibeb, who did it for me'.[60] But lest we get carried away with the high status of Old Kingdom mothers, outside the tomb, the father is also usually mentioned.

However, none of this explains the decline of the queen mother's importance. Perhaps, during unstable times, kings died young and the young were more easily influenced by their mothers. A long period of stability allowed for kings to develop into adults, and possibly lessened the power of the queen mother.[61] During the Middle Kingdom, the king's mother was given a tomb, often near her son's pyramid, and often larger than that of the principal queen. In fact, until the New Kingdom, the royal mother remained more important than the spouse.[62] However, in general, the status of royal women significantly declined during the Middle Kingdom and queens were no longer depicted alongside kings in statues and reliefs.[63]

In contrast to the declining importance of the royal mother, there is some evidence of the importance of elite, non-royal mothers continuing into the Middle Kingdom. On Middle Kingdom stelae, there is a strong maternal bias,[64] though this varies throughout the period.[65] In the Twelfth Dynasty, the mother is even more important than the wife, although in the Eleventh Dynasty it is the wife who is more important. A study of 600 Middle Kingdom documents show that 48 per cent name both parents, 46 per cent name the mother only and 5 per cent the father only.[66]

ADMINISTRATIVE TITLES

Administrative roles taken by women are more thoroughly explored in Chapter 5. In all periods, women's important administrative titles tended to be held by royal women, or those who served royal women. In the Old Kingdom, women held particularly powerful political offices.[67] We even know of a woman vizier, an official of the highest rank in ancient Egypt, second only to the king himself, and a possible overseer of women physicians. It is possible that the evidence is biased; in the Old Kingdom, most records come from courtiers buried near Memphis, while Middle Kingdom evidence largely consists of stelae listing female servants. Additionally, it should be pointed out that far more tomb inscriptions are known for the Old Kingdom than later periods. Tomb inscriptions would be more likely to document royal women.

PRIESTESSES OF HATHOR

In the Old Kingdom to the First Intermediate Period, women held high-status roles with the title *ḥmt nṯr* (meaning 'servant of the gods' or more loosely, 'priestess'), but this role seems to have declined during the Middle Kingdom. This general decline of female priests has been seen as a product of the nature of ancient Egyptian priesthood which was more suited to men than women. It is also possible that this decline may have been caused by a more general weakening of women's power within the higher rungs of Egyptian society. The decline of the role of priestesses of Hathor, in particular, has received much attention. Some have seen this decline as part of royal policy.

From the Old Kingdom until the Middle Kingdom, large numbers of elite women were servants of the gods,[68] or priestesses. The title was not inherited but its allocation, whether given according to aptitude, or purchased, is unclear. It seems most likely that it depended on knowing the 'right' people, as is the case throughout history.

The first known Priestess of Hathor was Neferhetepes, daughter of King Radjedef,[69] though in the Old Kingdom, over 400 women seem to have held the title. In the Fourth Dynasty, royal women often took the title,[70] but these were princesses, not wives or mothers of kings, and thus not mythically important to kingship. The fact that the title *rḫt nswt* (Royal Acquaintance) is often linked with the title 'Priestess of Hathor' suggests that Hathorian priestesses were part of the court circle. A few women who were priestesses also held what appears to be the higher title *ḥkrt nswt* ('King's Ornament'[71]).

In some cases, *ḥmt nṯr ḥt-ḥr* (Priestesses of Hathor) had their own tombs (one example is Hetep[72]), although this fact does not mean that they gained their wealth solely through their profession. While at least some were paid a stipend, this need not have been a large amount. Priestesses of Hathor in the Old Kingdom and First Intermediate Period came from several levels of Egyptian society, but were nevertheless always drawn from the elite.[73] This was not a means by which women from poverty-stricken families could improve their lot.

While Priestesses of Hathor did not inherit hereditary titles, their families were often involved in the cult.[74] However, the fact that not all in-laws of the Priestesses were titled suggests that in the Old Kingdom the social status of women was not defined by relation to their husbands or fathers.

It is clear that the role of Priestess of Hathor was not simply an honorary one, certainly in the Middle Kingdom,[75] but this role is not entirely understood. Given Hathor's strong links with music and dance, we may assume that all priestesses of the goddess would have played musical instruments and danced, but it seems, with few exceptions, Hathor's Priestesses did not play instruments.[76] While there are Old Kingdom depictions of women dancing, shaking sistra and offering *menit*-necklaces for Hathor, such as in the tomb of Senebei at Meir,[77] these are rarely specifically identified as 'priestesses'.

Examination of the role of priestesses of other deities in the pantheon gives further clues. There were general differences between the roles of male and female priests, whatever god or goddess was being served. Only male priests performed the purification rituals and rites associated with the god's morning toilet.[78] Instances of women offering and censing for deities are not extant in this period. However, female administrators are known in the Old Kingdom, and it seems likely that women also took administrative duties in serving the deities, although perhaps not always of the same rank as the men. In the Old Kingdom, most priests of Hathor were female, but it was men who were overseers of these priests. Women were sometimes overseers of dancers and singers, while professional musicians are nearly always men.[79] Additionally, there are no female lector priests – the priests who spoke the ritual texts in funerary and temple rites – and it has been suggested that women funerary priests held their titles in name only.

The roles of men and women did however overlap; women serving at the temple of Min at Akhmim in the Old Kingdom, like the men, kept watch through day and night.[80] A Fifth Dynasty papyrus from Abusir[81] shows that priestesses received the same payment as men, and were therefore not considered of lesser status.

We gather some clues about the different priestly roles of men and women through a study of *iri ḥt* (iri khet, meaning 'doing things'). Carolyn Routledge[82] has studied the term and shown that it is used of elite males carrying out cultic duties. It refers to the maintenance of cosmic order and is never applied to women. While women could certainly perform certain cultic duties, Routledge explains that in such roles they are described as *iri irw* (iri iru, meaning 'performing performances') and were excluded from others which involved *iri ḥt*. The latter phrase is used of lector priests, a role which women never fulfil. There is little evidence that acts listed as *iri ḥt*, such as giving of offerings to deities, or libating and censing in temples are practised by women priests. However, it should also be noted that this avoidance of labelling women as those practising *iri ḥt* probably reflects an ideal rather than a reality. The question, of course, remains as to why it was only men who were involved in maintaining cosmic order.

The title, Priestess of Hathor, seems to have been very common for elite women in the Old Kingdom, but by the end of the Middle Kingdom, it had all but disappeared.[83] Instead, men took on this role. By the end of the Old Kingdom, Priestesses of Hathor held such authority that King Mentuhotep Nebhepetre married at least one of them to legitimize his claim to the throne. However, not long after, priestesses of this goddess disappear from the record, perhaps because kings used their own wives and children in this role to the exclusion of others.[84] So, only royal women remained Priestesses of Hathor and the role was increasingly associated with kingship and state fertility. By the New Kingdom, royal figures such as Meritamun, daughter of Rameses II, occasionally held the title, but by then it was only given to demonstrate legitimacy.[85]

The decline in the role of Priestess of Hathor seems to have been linked to a decline of priestesses more generally. Was this general decline a 'natural' usurpation of power on the part of men? There are several possible explanations. One is the possibility that priests had to be pure or *wab*, and women may have been considered impure because of menstruation and childbirth. Certainly, following childbirth women underwent a 14-day period of purification and there is some evidence for purification rites at menstruation. But if we believe that the decline of women priests was due to women's impurity, there remains the question of why women were not considered impure in the Old Kingdom.

The *wab*-priests, or 'Purifiers' were usually men; these were lay priests who assisted the *ḥmt nṯr* in rotas, of one month in every four. However, we know that in at least one instance in the Old Kingdom, at Tehneh, a Hathorian priestess performed *wab* for the goddess.[86] Female *wab*-priests are also known from two Middle Kingdom stelae; one was a *wab*-priest of Khons and another of Wepwawet.[87] As is shown from a Fifth Dynasty papyrus from Abusir,[88] *wab*-priestesses received the same payment as men.[89] It may be assumed that, like men, they served in phyles (work crews);[90] evidence from a Twelfth Dynasty papyrus (the Kahun Papyrus discovered by Flinders Petrie in 1889; its many fragments are kept at University College, London) records that Irer, a Mistress of the House, needs to take one month of leave from the weaving workshop to fulfil temple duty as a *wab*-priestess. However, an alternative translation gives a different interpretation,[91] stating that the woman went to the temple on day 20 for purification.

Perhaps the decrease in women priests was due to the increasing extent to which the priesthood had become part of state bureaucracy. The growing professionalism and specialization of the priesthood may have been to blame.[92] In earlier periods, priestly functions were carried out on a part-time basis, thus purity was only required part-time and women didn't need to be excluded. Indeed, one might explain the general decline in the power of women from the Old Kingdom as a rise in state bureaucracy which placed increasing value on the male role of scribe.

However, women retained an important role in religion, particularly as providers of music. And they were not always to remain secondary to men; during the Late Period, the roles of God's Wife of Amun and Divine Adoratrice are almost on a par with the king himself. These exceptional women are discussed later in this book.

WOMEN TEXTILE WORKERS

Textile production was the second most important industry in Egypt after agriculture. Textiles were essential to clothe the living and the dead, and also to make furnishings, sails for boats, awnings, bags and innumerable other items. Wages were paid in food, but also in metalwork and textiles. For much of Egyptian history, women were at the heart of this industry, and during the Old Kingdom their rewards for such work seem to have been particularly marked.

From the Old Kingdom on, weaving was carried out by women. This is usually seen as a domestic industry, although there is evidence for specialized workshops.[93] Some scholars believe that the term *pr-iriwt*, often translated as 'houses of women' (that is, harems), should rather be construed as 'weaving workshops', while others argue that there is little evidence for domestic weaving in the Old Kingdom (there have been few extensive modern excavations of Old Kingdom settlements that might test this claim). It is likely that weaving was carried out in workshops attached to elite households, thus these places were both extensions of the domestic environment as well as outside the home itself.

In the Old Kingdom, women not only manufactured cloth, but oversaw its production; several women are recorded as overseers in 'the house of weavers' (presumably a workshop) at this period, though men also held the same title.[94]

The hieroglyph for weaver, which represents a sceptre, designates the weaver as 'one who is adorned' or 'rewarded' and suggests the high status of weavers in the Old Kingdom.[95] Women are shown being given costly ornaments for their services, something which does not appear in later representations. It has been claimed[96] that the depictions of women weavers receiving necklaces were a public recognition of their worth, and furthermore[97] that the payment of weavers can be equated to payment given to Old Kingdom tomb workers. Women engaged in such activities would have had a certain amount of financial independence and thus would have been more able to build their own tombs.

By the Middle Kingdom, texts show that weaving was still primarily the job of women, though there is not the evidence for their being given such substantial rewards as earlier. A papyrus from Kahun suggests that several servant women were employed together as weavers[98] and another document shows that of 29 servants within a particular household, 20 were employed in weaving.[99] At other times, production seems to be within the family.[100] Tomb paintings suggest that although women were largely involved in spinning and weaving, men generally took charge as overseers.

WOMEN IN TRADE

In Old Kingdom tomb scenes women were not only shown engaged in the cloth trade, but are often represented as both buyers and sellers of goods more generally, although they are still outnumbered by men. These women appear to have worked near harbours selling bread, beer, fish and vegetables, as well as manufactured goods such as cloth and sandals.[101] The most important market-place scene is perhaps the Fifth Dynasty scene from the tomb of the two 'brothers', Niankhkhnum and Khnumhotep, at Saqqara.[102] Both women and men seem to be engaged in buying and selling at the port. The tomb of Feteka shows a similar scene, but here only men are shown trading, with women as customers.[103] There are rare depictions of women engaged in trade from ships. 'Give bread (with) thy arm' and 'Don't obstruct my face while I am putting to shore' commands a woman steering a cargo ship, which, in other words, means 'Get me food and keep out of my way as I'm doing something important'.[104] This is depicted in a scene from a Fifth Dynasty chapel at Saqqara.

There is also some evidence of women in the marketplace in the New Kingdom[105] and it is possible that the extensive number of Old Kingdom scenes is more a product of the wealth of scenes mirroring everyday life in tombs of this date. Again, the type of goods women sell in the marketplace could be seen as an extension of domestic production.[106]

DID WOMEN'S STATUS DECLINE FROM THE OLD TO THE MIDDLE KINGDOMS?

While it seems that in grave goods, religious practice and trade, women of the Old Kingdom enjoyed more parity in status with men than in the Middle Kingdom, we must be aware that there are problems with the evidence. Old Kingdom and Middle Kingdom evidence differs significantly; while Old Kingdom material may be biased because it focuses on women of the royal court, the Middle Kingdom may give more evidence on women outside the court. Thus, we may simply be seeing a weight of evidence for the high status of elite Old Kingdom women compared to their lower-class sisters. Additionally, we must not assume that, even in the Old Kingdom, women held the same status as men. In Egyptian art, status was often depicted by size and Old Kingdom royal princesses are shown dwarfed by their husbands.

It has been suggested that the status of the Priestesses of Hathor may have declined due to the changing fortunes of kingship but other theories may be posited. It could be that the decline in women's status was a deliberate policy or a side effect of increasing male bureaucracy. Another possibility can be suggested from tantalizing evidence from First Intermediate Period stelae.

The pattern in decline in women's status from the Old to the Middle Kingdom is not a simple linear pattern, nor evident in all areas of material culture. During the First Intermediate Period, for example, there are several stelae which show women standing in front of men. For the rest of Egyptian history, the men always come first, in the position of superiority. During this time of civil war, women had more power at home, built their own tombs, and so on. We might hypothesize that while the men were off fighting and being killed, it was the women who assumed positions of leadership and responsibility at home.

Unfortunately, the First Intermediate Period is an era which is difficult to understand, for while the kings of the Seventh and Eighth Dynasties ruled from Memphis, they controlled very little of the country. During the Ninth and Tenth Dynasties, a series of rulers originating from Herakleopolis Magna controlled the north of Egypt. Around the same time, rulers of the Eleventh Dynasty, from Thebes, in the south, began to assert power. Provincial art flourished and funerary inscriptions of regional governors show their allegiance to either

Herakleopolitan or Theban rulers. Eventually, the Theban King Mentuhotep II (2055–2004 BC) succeeded in controlling the entire country.

One might draw a parallel with the situation during and after World War II. During the war years, women had taken on many of men's roles. After the war, division of labour became more enforced as men took back their jobs. The evidence for a shortage of men in the First Intermediate Period is unproven, although one scholar[107] attests evidence of polygamy in the Herakleopolitan Period, in contrast to earlier periods. This perhaps bears witness to a shortage of men. We cannot assume an increase in women's status from stelae alone, though there are other tantalizing pieces of evidence including a First Intermediate Period false door from a woman's tomb at Busaris in the Delta.[108] Most false doors of men contrast the corpulent appearance of age with the slender youth. Women, by contrast, are shown as eternally youthful. Yet this First Intermediate Period door shows the woman as a naked girl with pigtails and as a thin old woman with sagging breasts. This is the tomb of a woman who is unafraid to flout traditional rules.

LATER PERIODS

Later periods of Egyptian history show further changes in women's status. The Late Middle Kingdom to Early New Kingdom sees resurgence in the apparent status of women. Statuettes of non-royal women of the late Seventeenth Dynasty show women as more active, with the left foot advanced for the first time, and with one arm bent across the chest, either fisted or holding a flower.[109] In the Eighteenth Dynasty, the reign of Thutmose III shows women as more prominent in tomb chapels, making offerings to the deceased and dedicating monuments. This period seems to coincide with an increase in the importance of royal women.[110] There is a small variation in coffin prices between men and women in Rameside Deir el-Medina.[111] Then, in the late Twentieth to early Twenty-second Dynasty, perhaps with Libyan influence, funerary monuments of women appear free of male kin, and one woman, Neskhons, is even charged with governing Kush.

One Egyptologist, in discussing Third Intermediate Period coffins, notes that, 'In statues they [the priestesses] were apparently as prestigious as men, as is obvious from the quality of their coffins. Although qualitatively the corpus can be divided into three main groups – bad, mediocre and (very) good – their distribution shows no significant difference. In other words, women were able to spend as much 'economic resources' or 'money' on their tomb equipment as were men'.[112] The same seems to hold true for papyri as well. We must understand, however, that women did not usually have such high status as men.

One might state that even in today's western world, with its apparent emphasis on equality and understanding of social problems, men are still much more likely to reach positions of status than women. Today, we argue over the reasons for this state of affairs – the most common perception is that women are hampered by their traditional role as homemakers and childrearers and bearers. Indeed, it has been argued that there has never been any matriarchal society and that men have always run the show throughout history. This chapter cannot conclusively answer the question of why women lost status, but the fact that they once held power suggests that it was not exclusively biological factors which were to blame.

3

Reversing the ordinary practices of mankind

*'The Egyptians in their manners and customs, seem to have reversed the
ordinary practices of mankind. For instance, women attend market and
are employed in trade, while men stay at home and do
the weaving'.*

(HERODOTUS BOOK II)

Herodotus (c.490–425 BC), who was more familiar with the restricted lives of
Greek women, was clearly shocked. It may well have been the case that Egyptian
women of this date were among the most independent of the ancient world, but
it seems unlikely that the Egyptians really did reverse 'the ordinary practices of
mankind', contrary to Herodotus' excited claim.

Women in ancient Egypt had many rights, particularly when compared to
other societies of the time – they were able to own property, to divorce and to
take men to court. However, a closer examination reveals inequality. Upper-class
women rarely had their own tomb chapels or funerary stelae, but were instead
interred in tombs of their male relatives and were buried with far fewer possessions than men. Texts suggest that while both men and women could initiate
divorce, it was almost exclusively men who actually did so. Where marriages broke
down, women could be socially and economically excluded, with single mothers
struggling to bring up families. We cannot assume that this was the case for all
times and places in ancient Egypt, but there is evidence to support the notion
that, for much of Egyptian society, women were not equal in status to their men.

It is always difficult to judge how other societies perceive status and the relative importance of one individual in relation to another. The fact that women
in ancient Egypt rarely had administrative roles may not necessarily mean they
were of low status – it could simply be that their status lay in the home. Women
may have had high status in one area, perhaps as musicians, and low status in
other areas. The exclusion of women from certain professions – the army was
one – might mean that women lived longer. The idealized representations of
Egyptian art might show a cosy life for Egyptian women, while the archaeological

record shows a very different reality. Finally, what may be a mark of high status for one sex may be a mark of low status for another: a sexually aggressive male may be attributed a high status, while a woman displaying such behaviour would be considered a low status whore. It is not possible to unravel all of the complexities of Egyptian social status. Rather, this chapter considers what we might consider prestigious, and compares the role of women in these areas with those of men. I consider: women, the law and property; attitudes to adultery and divorce; women's access to wealth; and the overriding trend among ancient Egyptian men to imagine women as either passive and perfect wives or dangerous and active femmes fatale.

Women, although valued, had a status almost equivalent to that of children, as one may observe in the way children and women were similarly depicted. Both take a secondary role in tomb paintings and are shown as smaller than fathers and husbands (even where the child was an adult). At times in the Old Kingdom, adult princesses are shown as particularly miniscule, not even reaching to the knees of their husbands.[1] In the New Kingdom, young boys are sometimes depicted wearing the earrings and below-the-elbow bracelets worn by women.[2] Adult men did not wear these. One might almost see this in a parallel to certain child rearing practices today, where very young boys are allowed to play with dolls, but these are deemed inappropriate once the child becomes older, when he must take on more masculine roles.

THE DANGEROUS TEMPTRESS AND THE PASSIVE WIFE

The passive woman is a frequent sexual stereotype. In our own society, the adventure hero of the cinema often has a beautiful, passive woman at his side – the heroine playing second fiddle to the central male character. But was this the case in ancient Egypt? The short answer is 'yes'. While men were involved in adventures, women stayed at home. Women who did not conform to the passive norm were considered dangerous, with the power to subvert the dominant and sexually active male.

Much Egyptian literature presents the stereotypical passive woman, the good wife, or the active but dangerous temptress.[3] Literature was written largely by men for men, so we may assume that these were male views of women, although in the case of stories, it is likely that they were publicly performed for both men and women. There are always exceptions: in love poetry women are shown as actively ensnaring the male, but this does not seem to be regarded as subversive or dangerous.

In texts, the quiet, obedient wife is praised. An Old Kingdom husband praises his wife in a tomb chapel inscription: 'she did not utter a statement that repelled my heart; she did not transgress while she was young in life'. Another wife is credited as 'one who speaks pleasantly and sweetens love in the presence of her husband'.[4] The Middle Kingdom *Instructions of Ptahhotep* advise: 'love your wife with proper ardor, Fill her belly, clothe her back . . . .'[5] But they also say, 'Remove her from power, suppress her! . . . Restraining her is how to make her remain in your house; a female who is under her own control is rainwater'.

The Middle Kingdom *Tale of the Herdsman*[6] recounts the story of a dangerous temptress: a herdsman sees a woman, possibly a goddess, in the marshes, she unclothes herself and the herdsman is terrified by what he witnesses. Unfortunately, this story survives only in fragments, but what we can piece together invokes the archetypal story of the watery siren, both erotic woman and terrifying monster. A parallel has been drawn in this tale with the story of the Mut goddess who resided in the marshy borders of Egypt and Libya.

In the Middle Kingdom *Instructions of Ptahhotep*, the dual nature of women is described:

> One is made a fool by limbs of fayence
> And then she turns into carnelian.

Here the woman is described as both 'faience' and 'carnelian'. The positive and beautiful blue of faience turns into the aggressive and fiery red of carnelian.[7] The *Tale of the Herdsman* may suggest, in the unclothed nature of the woman, that it is women's sexuality that was feared. However, in the Middle Kingdom there are some positive associations of women, such as the princesses in the *Tale of Sinuhe*, reviving the hero through the shaking of sistra.[8]

The danger afforded by women continues in New Kingdom literature. In the *Instructions of Ani*, a man is warned of women traveling alone:

> A deep water whose course is unknown,
> Such is a woman away from her husband.
> 'I am pretty,' she tells you daily,
> When she has no witnesses;
> She is ready to ensnare you,
> A great deadly crime when it is heard.[9]

In the *Tale of Two Brothers*, Anubis' wife attempts to seduce her husband's younger brother, Bata, and Bata's young wife betrays her husband.[10] In *Truth and Falsehood*, a woman rescues Truth, but then treats him badly after sleeping with him.[11] While men may also be shown in an unfavourable light, in Egyptian tales it is usually suggested that women accomplish sinister deeds through their sexuality.

The dual and dangerous nature of the woman continues into the Late and Graeco-Roman Periods. In the Late Period, the *Instructions of Ankhsheshonq* remark:

> When a man smells myrrh his wife is a cat before him
> When a man is suffering his wife is a lioness before him[12]

In the Graeco-Roman, *The First Tale of Setne Khaemwes*, a character called Tabubu seductively dressed in transparent linen, ensnares the hero and then mysteriously vanishes.[13]

Women are rarely shown actively engaged in any vigorous activity in tomb art, and they appear as passive partners to the male. This is even the case in the Old Kingdom, where it could be argued that women had more status than in later periods. Men are shown striding forward, while women stand with their legs closer together. The man always sits on the right (superior) side and the woman on the left (inferior) side.[14] By tradition, women may cling to, or adore their active husbands, but in a study of 42 New Kingdom couples, only 2 show reciprocal gestures of affection. Men are central, while women show them deference.[15]

Women are also shown as passive in Old Kingdom fowling scenes and in one case a woman urges the male to get a bird for her.[16] Usually, women stand by their husbands, who are actively hunting the birds. Two unusual instances of women depicted alone in fowling scenes have been noted, but the woman's role is ambiguous in both instances as she is described as 'viewing' rather than 'performing' the activity.[17] The lack of active female roles in art may be because Egyptian tomb imagery used women largely as sexualized images, placed in supporting roles to men.

The apparently restrictive nature of women's clothes, as shown on tomb paintings, may have been because they were expected to be less active than men. However, it could equally be true that these clothes were not tight and restrictive, but merely appear so in ancient Egyptian art because the typical wrap dress would have been shown two dimensionally.[18] Certainly, actual Egyptian women's clothing found in tombs is not restrictive, but rather sack-like.

To a certain extent, the passive/aggressive duality and positive associations of passivity extend to deities. In Chapter 8, it will be shown that there are aggressive goddesses, such as the creative and active Eye of Re. While such goddesses are not necessarily seen in a negative light, the story of the dangerous lioness goddess, Sekhmet, sent out on a killing spree by Re shows this goddess must be controlled and changed into the passive and beautiful Hathor if humankind is not to be annihilated. The connection between deities and mortal women is described in Papyrus Insinger: 'the work of Mut and Hathor is what acts among women. It is in women that the good demon and the bad demon are active on earth'.[19]

In contrast, Chapter 6 will show that male gods who act in a passive manner are mocked – in the *Contendings of Horus and Seth*, Horus is spat on for being the passive partner. The ithyphallic male is a symbol of power. Some Egyptologists[20] suggest that the passive depiction of females is a necessary contrast to the active male role in maintaining cosmic order (maat). As we have seen, only men are said to carry out the act of *iri ḥt* (iri khet, meaning 'doing things') which may be interpreted as meaning carrying out acts which maintain maat. Kings are given the title *nb irt-ḥt* (neb irt-khet, meaning 'Lord of Doing Things') and the feminine version is only ever used of two queens. Examples of aggressive female queens cannot support of an argument countering the idea of the disapproval of female aggression since, as explained in the chapter on harems, female kings had to show themselves as in some ways masculine.

While we have, in the maintenance of cosmic order, a specific reason why the passive woman is the ideal in ancient Egypt, the problem is how this situation came about. Is not the idea that only males can keep cosmic order another symptom of the ideal of the passive woman, rather than its cause? In many societies woman are divided into those who are the good and passive wives, and those who are the active and dangerous temptresses. Women may not lead, they may not actively create, but rather they must remain the passive supporters of men. When they do not conform, women are considered dangerous and immoral and must be controlled.[21] Such a situation, feminists may claim, is common to patriarchal societies, where women's status is lower than that of men. In many mammals, males must necessarily be active and aggressive in order to maintain their status and this unfortunately seems true of humans.

WOMEN, WEAPONS AND WARFARE

'Had a woman ever marshaled troops?'[22]

This quotation, which comes from the Middle Kingdom *Instruction of Amenemhat I*, makes it clear that the ancient Egyptians considered it unlikely for women to be in charge of troops; throughout Egyptian history non-royal women are non-combatant. Goddesses, however, were very different, possibly relating to their androgynous nature or perhaps a result of their apartness from human society. Queens, who took on the role of goddesses, that is, women who were the 'King's Principal Wife' or the 'King's Mother', might claim certain aspects of the warring goddess. Queens who took the role of kings, as sole ruler, naturally took over this masculine aggressive role as upholders of maat.

From the Predynastic Period onward, non-royal women, unlike men, were not buried with projectile points, and throughout Egyptian history, there are depictions of men carrying arms, but very few of women. Women are rarely shown carrying any sort of dangerous object which could be used as a weapon. In tomb paintings men are shown holding sickles, or are shown as butchers with knives, cutting joints of meat or butchering cattle. Women did not take these roles and did not prepare meat. When shown carrying out agricultural work, they do not carry sickles. Unlike boys, girls are not shown wrestling, and in every case, all depictions of soldiers are men.

The exceptions to the rule regarding women using weapons appear in the Old Kingdom and these are largely depictions of foreign women. A Sixth Dynasty representation of a besieged town, in the tomb of Inti at Deshasha,[23] shows a woman defender stabbing a bowman with a dagger. Several of the male defenders seem to have beards, thus revealing that they are foreign. The foreign nature of the women is reinforced by a parallel scene from the Saqqara tomb of Kaemhesit[24] which shows women in a siege situation, but none of them appear to be taking an active stance. In this scene the women are clearly foreign, wearing non-Egyptian clothing. Finally, there is the case of the Sixth Dynasty female guard called Merinebti-ankhteti of the pyramid cult of Teti,[25] although here there is no evidence to suggest that she was foreign. Such guards were not mere doorkeepers, as the lady was given a tomb of her own.

Exceptions to the non-aggressive woman also occur later, but only in the royal family. The 'King's Principal Wife' and the 'King's Mother' are shown mirroring aggressive goddesses. This aspect is discussed in more detail in Chapter 7. However, such women, as far as we know, were rarely credited with being engaged in warfare, though there appear notable exceptions at the end of the Seventeenth Dynasty and beginning of the Eighteenth. Nefertiti is shown smiting the female enemies of Egypt, a pose usually reserved for the king. Although it has been surmised that she may have ruled at the end of the Amarna period as a king, this particular scene does not prove that the queen was engaged in warfare. Smiting scenes are more a demonstration of power and destruction of enemies, a ritual, than of engagement in warfare.

There is also the case of the mysterious lady Ahhotep (here called Ahhotep II to distinguish her from Ahhotep I, the mother of Ahmose I). This lady, a possible warrior queen, remains something of a mystery; her tomb was discovered in 1859 at Dra Abu el-Naga, Thebes and her coffin bears the title 'King's Wife'. Many of the objects found in the tomb bear the name of the kings Ahmose (1550–1525 BC) and Kamose (1555–1550 BC), so it is sometimes believed that these were her sons. However, her coffin does not have the title 'Mother of the King', so she had no son who became king by the time of her death. Her tomb has been dated to the reign of Ahmose, but prior to Year 22 of his reign.[26] It has also been suggested that she was the wife of Kamose.

Ahhotep II was buried with a dagger and battle axe, as well as three golden fly pendants. Such pendants were given as awards for military valour, because good warriors were like flies – persistent, impossible to ward off and numerous. Although the dagger and battle axe found in the tomb are usually associated with her, they do not actually bear her name and since the Dra Abu el-Naga tomb was not her original burial place, it is possible that the objects belong to another person altogether. The axehead shows Ahmose smiting his enemies. However, the golden fly jewellery was closely associated with the queen, as the pendants were found inside her coffin.

Another Ahhotep, Ahhotep I, is also credited with aggression. She was the mother of Ahmose, honoured in a stela at Karnak as 'one who pulled Egypt together, having cared for its army, having guarded it, having brought back those who fled, gathering up its deserters, having quieted the South, subduing those who defy her'.[27]

Naturally, queens ruling in their own right were endorsed as real kings partly through use of the warrior image since the king is shown as engaged in warfare in order to maintain cosmic order. Thus, the king's title 'Lord of Doing Things', occurs on many items of warfare in Tutankhamun's tomb.[28] The feminine version of the title is used by only two women, both of whom ruled as kings, Sobekneferu and Hatshepsut.[29] As will be shown, Hatshepsut took part in at least two military campaigns, but whether or not she led from the front, as kings claim to have done, is unknown.

DOMESTIC VIOLENCE

Violence in ancient Egypt was not considered as abhorrent as it is today. Schoolboys were routinely beaten by school teachers, servants by the Mistress of the House, workers by overseers, and peasants by tax collectors. The acceptance that those in authority could physically chastise those with less power naturally extended to the relationship between husband and wife. While it is clear that there were many loving relationships, domestic violence was not uncommon.

Joyce Filer,[30] discussing head injuries in male and female skeletons, concludes that given the unlikelihood of women being engaged in warfare, head injuries to women were most likely the results of domestic violence. Brenda Baker[31] on examining the 4,000-year-old skeleton of a woman buried in a simple wooden coffin among other commoners at Abydos, found that the skeleton showed multiple signs of violence. She seemingly died between 30 and 35 years of age from a stab wound through the back, but she also had injuries which had healed. These injuries could be interpreted as evidence of long-term abuse: three ribs and a bone in her left hand had been broken, and she had suffered from an infection in her fractured right wrist, probably from breaking a fall.[32] We do not know in these cases whether the women were abused servants, or victims of domestic violence by husbands. However, they poignantly raise the question of whether or not wife beating was unofficially sanctioned in ancient Egypt, as it still is in some societies today.

Adultery was considered a crime of property against another man which suggests that women were, at some level, considered the property of their husbands. The practice of the prospective husband paying a bride-price to secure a wife can only have exacerbated this viewpoint. It is no wonder then that there are several textual sources for the beating of women by husbands.[33]

There are also, however, instances of wife beating being brought before the court. The fragmentary Ostracon Nash 5 (an ostracon is a fragment of pottery or stone) may be translated:

> My husband [...]. Then he made a beating, he made a beating [again] and I caused the [...] to fetch his mother. He was found guilty and was caused [...]." And I said to him: "If you are [...] in the presence of the court." And he swore (an Oath of the Lord) saying: "As Amon endures, as (the Ruler) endures [...]".[34]

It could be that wife beating was only considered wrong if it exceeded certain limits or resulted in specific injuries.

This is not to deny evidence for loving and mutually supportive relationships. A letter written by a man to his dead wife in the thirteenth century BC states how he cared for his wife when she became ill and grieved for her when she died.[35] Yet, in a society where women had less power than men, one must accept that not all relationships were so ideal.

WOMEN, THE LAW AND PROPERTY

In some ways, women had similar legal rights to men in ancient Egypt; the New Kingdom *Inscription of Mes* (sometimes written 'Mose'), a record of a protracted legal dispute, shows that women could inherit property, bring legal actions and stand as witnesses before a law court. However, not only were women entitled to less property than men on divorce, they also seem to have been less likely than men to bring court actions.

The *Inscription of Mes*, which dates from 1250 BC, recounts a long-standing dispute over some fields of about nine acres.[36] Two branches of a family were claiming ownership of these fields. The dispute dragged on for several generations with various courts awarding decision, appeals being made and decisions overturned. The vizier himself was involved. At one point, a delegation of judges travelled to the central archives in Piramesse, the capital at that time, to view the land registers. In this case, women were managing family holdings, contesting claims and being called as witnesses.

Women could also freely disinherit children, as is shown by the famous will of Naunakhte. This lady is known from several papyri as having been twice married. At a local court at Deir el-Medina around 1144 BC, she disinherits children by her second marriage who had not been good to her[37] – 'But see I am grown old, and see they are not looking after me in my turn'.[38] This suggests that in the New Kingdom, at least, women had similar rights to men and could dispose of their own property as they saw fit. However, if we actually compare the court cases brought by men and women and compare documents attesting property ownership by gender, it is clear that men hold more property than women[39] and were more likely to be claimants in court cases, while women were defenders.[40] During the Middle and New Kingdoms, women ran large estates, but these were under their husbands' control. The Rameside Wilbour Papyrus shows women holding only 10.8 per cent of apportioned plots, and it is possible that these women were specifically the wives of military men.[41] If we look at property other than land, the situation appears similar. When goods in tombs from men and women are compared in Deir el-Medina, women have significantly fewer items.[42] It seems that while there were certainly rich women, women were at a disadvantage when it came to wealth and property. Very often they were reliant on their husbands and a widow was as disadvantaged as an orphan; a similar position is not documented for widowers.

Women could inherit property and goods from their parents, and were entitled to one third of the conjugal property upon divorce (so long as they were the innocent party). This obviously puts them at a disadvantage compared to men.

This disadvantage extended into the third century BC; the Hermopolis Law Code of this date states that, where an executor existed, on death of parents, the estate was divided up into lots. Male children were allowed first pick of the lots. If the executor was male, he was allowed to claim parcels belonging to any children and heirs without issue who predeceased the father. Female executors were designated when there were no sons, but the code is specific in that, unlike male executors, women could not claim the parcels of any dead children.

However, there were ways of circumventing the usual property laws. From the Middle Kingdom onward, men could make a will – *imyt-pr* (imyt-per meaning 'house document') to allow their wives to obtain more or less of the joint property on a husband's death. A house document was basically a means of transferring property outside the normal lines of inheritance, but it was not strictly speaking a will since it could confer property during the lifetime of the donor. The existence of such documents suggests that at least some men were concerned for the weaker status of their wives and sought to ensure their security.

One such case comes from Kahun, around 1900 BC.[43] Ankh-ren, a minor government official, apparently without a wife or children, left all his property to his younger brother, a *wab*-priest called Wah. Five years later, the younger brother passed this property onto his wife, together with a house from which she couldn't be evicted. The younger brother's own property would pass to his children.

ADULTERY AND DIVORCE

Attitudes to adultery also indicate the extent to which a woman was considered the property of a man. When a man committed adultery, he wronged the husband, not his own wife. Additionally, while women could divorce their husbands, it is clear that they did not do so as often as men divorced women.

Adultery by either sex was certainly censured, although adultery cases were not taken to the courts. It is included in the Negative Confessions, a list of statements in the *Book of the Dead* in which the deceased claims, before the gods, that he has done no wrong. Papyrus BM 10416 shows angry public reaction to a married man committing adultery, yet the community threatens to beat the woman.[44] An official stops them and warns the man to correct his behaviour or else the beating will not be prevented.

In the Ptolemaic *Instructions of Ankhsheshonq* is the warning 'Do not take to yourself a woman whose husband is alive, lest he become your enemy'.[45] The idea that adultery was a crime of property may have been compounded by the paying of bride-price. Papyrus DM 27 from Deir el-Medina[46] recounts a complaint by a male servant who had 'carried a bundle' (paid bride-price) to the father-in-law's house and yet the woman had sex with another.

Furthermore, in literature, a lone woman is presented as a threat to a man's good name; she is the siren luring the 'innocent' man. The Eighteenth Dynasty *Instructions of Ani* urges men to ignore women who are not with their husbands:

> Beware of a woman who is a stranger,
> One not known in her town;
> Don't stare at her when she goes by,
> Do not know her carnally.
> A deep water whose course is unknown,
> Such a woman away from her husband.
> "I am pretty," she tells you daily,
> When she has no witnesses;
> She is ready to ensnare you,
> A great deadly crime when it is heard . . .[47]

Several tales present the wily ways of the lone woman entrapping her man, and the dreadful punishments that are justly meted out to the evil adulteress. These punishments are much more excessive than those known from court documentation. In Middle Kingdom Papyrus Westcar, the husband kills the lover by making a wax crocodile which comes to life and devours him; the woman is dealt with by the king.[48] The usual translation of her fate is that she was burnt to death. However, some scholars believe it is probable that she was merely branded. In the New Kingdom Egyptian *Tale of Two Brothers*,[49] the unfaithful woman is dismembered and fed to dogs by her husband. Thankfully, such punishment for adultery does not seem evident in real life; rather, it seems that adulterers were punished through divorce.

It is quite clear that women, as well as men, could divorce their partners, but the records show that it was much more common for the man to instigate the process. The ratio of male to female initiated divorces is 12:3. The public act of swearing an oath was required at the local or temple court and divorce could take place if a woman remained childless despite the fact that it was believed that men were largely responsible for procreation. It is also attested that some divorced men remarried and divorced the same woman.

An unusual incident from New Kingdom Deir el-Medina records a concerned father attempting to protect his daughter by getting his son-in-law to swear an oath stating dire consequences if he abandons his wife: 'As Amen endures, as the ruler endures, if I go back on my word and abandon the daughter of

Tener-Monthu in the future, I will receive 100 blows and be deprived of all the property that I will acquire with her'.[50]

It is not known what happened to divorced women who were thrown out of the home and who did not remarry. Sometimes their own family would take them back. In Nineteenth Dynasty Deir el-Medina, the workman, Horemwia, promised his daughter that if her husband threw her out, he would give her a room in his storehouse.[51] In the Eastern Necropolis at Deir el-Medina, there appear to be a group of graves of unmarried women, several of whom may have been divorced,[52] showing that at least some of these women were given suitable burials. There are instances from the Graeco-Roman Period where the divorced woman lives in her own home, in that of her ex-husband (who in this period may also be her brother), or returns to her family's home.[53] It is not known in these later instances if blame for divorce was said to lie with husband or wife.

CRIME AND PUNISHMENT

It is sometimes said that our own society is harder on women committing crimes than on men because the idea of women committing crimes is particularly shocking. While prison lists from ancient Egypt show the ratio of imprisoned women to be small compared to that of men, women were given the same terrible punishments as men for their crimes.[54] In one papyrus, a woman and three men are each given a hundred blows of a stick for making false accusations.[55] Like men, women could also be put to death for theft. So, for example, Ostracon Nash 1 (British Museum 65930) describes the woman, Heria, as having stolen goods. She denied it, her house was searched and stolen goods were found, including temple equipment. She was accused by the court of being a 'Great false one, worthy of death'. The woman was 'taken to the river bank' for execution.

HOUSEWIFE

Women certainly had professions outside the home, but generally a woman's work was in the home, running the household and caring for her family. While such work should be valued, it seems that it was not considered as important as men's work. The standard view was men hold office and women support them. 'In funerary epithets, a man is clever, useful, and admired by his peers; a woman is beloved of her man. Men are portrayed interacting with the public sphere, whereas women usually interact with their family members'.[56] In this volume, it is recognized that work in 'the home' may be more accurately described as work in the household, thus including work carried out in open courtyards, on roofs of houses, and in gardens and fields belonging to the home.

However, it is clear that women were not entirely restricted to work in the household, and men also spent some time working in the home, depending on their profession and status. As will be shown, women were not always confined to home work, although women's trading and weaving in workshops could be seen as an extension of their role in domestic production.[57]

The prevailing Egyptian social ideal of women as bearers and nurturers of children may have constrained the activities of women outside the home. It is often stated that an 'obvious' natural link between women and childcare is a reason for women's non-participation in activities outside the household. However, ethnographic evidence shows that such limitations are socially constructed. For Egypt, there are depictions of women in agricultural settings cradling children, and a scene from the New Kingdom tomb of Neferrenput shows children running around in a weaving workshop. It does seem, however, that in ancient Egypt women were usually idealized as perfect wives and mothers, and not as active participants in the world outside the home.

Generally, elite woman are shown indoors in the Dynastic Period. In tomb paintings of all periods, women are rarely depicted in roles outside the home. As throughout the ancient Mediterranean world, Egyptian women were shown with paler skin colour on statues and tomb painting than men. Men are usually painted red, and women yellow. The yellow colour, when applied in rare instances to males, seems to indicate indoor professions.[58] However, there were times, such as during the Amarna Period, when the colour convention was less rigorously applied. Perhaps these were periods when women were more outwardly active, or when colour symbolism was differently understood, but it is difficult to see a reason – other than the ideal indoor nature of women's work – for the general correlation of women with pale skin colour. Male figures might have been shown darker to draw attention to them;[59] however, one might then expect kings to be shown darker than their subjects, which is not the case.

Ethnographic parallels show that there are often attempts to limit women's financial reward for labour, or to confine women's work to domestic realms.[60] Production in the home is not as valued as work outside it partly because it is generally less quantifiable. Equally, activities in the home are carried out for love, not for money and prestige, and are therefore inferior.

We cannot know if this idea of the home always held true for the ancient Egyptians. We need to understand more of the constellations of ideas surrounding ancient Egyptian domestic life. However, as one might expect, the house is represented as a place of safety and seclusion for the man. That the house is private is suggested in the *Instructions of Ani* where a man is warned not to snoop around the house of another.[61]

It would be interesting to know how much control women had over domestic life. While Egyptian state religion was largely patriarchal,[62] there is some evidence that women had more control over domestic piety. Certainly, the high percentage of female-related religious items found in domestic homes might suggest that in household religion women were in charge. The Deir el-Medina seers are women and there is also a high preponderance of female deities (Hathor, Taweret and Meretseger) in the Deir el-Medina domestic cult. There is some evidence that women preferred female gods and men male gods,[63] so the high instance of female deities might suggest female influence. However, Deir el-Medina is perhaps unusual in that it is a place where men would have spent some time away from the home. Additionally, one might argue that in the West Bank the feminine in procreation is emphasised as opposed to the masculine on the East Bank.[64] Within New Kingdom homes, objects called 'ancestor busts' were set up, which, it appears, were used as a means of the living contacting the dead. The gender of ancestor busts is disputed,[65] but the only depiction we have of offerings being made to one shows a woman making the offering. On the other hand, most dedications of 'ancestor stelae', which appear to have functioned in a similar way, and were also set up in the home, were by men. It has been demonstrated that on private stelae and on votive cloths, women are shown directly before Hathor, without the male intermediary shown in tomb depictions.[66] This could either indicate that the tomb was the preserve of the male, or suggest that women did indeed have more control over certain spheres of religion.[67] Interestingly, while most votive stelae were dedicated by men, most votive cloths were dedicated by women.

We also cannot be sure that women's home work went unrecognized. The house was the place for bringing up children and fulfilling other domestic duties, but was also the centre for production of goods for barter. Women's transactions may have contributed no small amount to the family income. The Middle Kingdom *Instructions of Ptahhotep* claim the woman is 'a profitable field for her lord'.[68] The classical scholar Marilyn Goldberg[69] has described the importance of the house as the primary place of production in agriculturally based classical cultures. But, for ancient Egypt, we do not know how much a woman's work contributed to a family's income, compared to that of a man.

Despite all this, the role of the 'housewife' does not seem to have been particularly highly regarded. Domestic work is rarely shown in tomb scenes. While women are frequently titled *nbt-pr*, (nebet per, Mistress of the House), lists of members of households invariably begin with the male head of the household.[70]

The housewife was clearly secondary to the male head of the house. The New Kingdom *Instructions of Ani* contain a warning against ordering the woman about in the home, suggesting that women were not always true Mistresses of the House:

> Do not control your wife in her house,
> When you know she is efficient;
> Don't say to her: "Where is it? Get it!"
> When she has put it in the right place.
> Let your eye observe in silence,
> Then you recognise her skill.[71]

In the New Kingdom *Tale of Two Brothers*, it is clear that the husband expects the wife to be waiting to serve him when he gets home.

Women, with a few exceptions, did not receive the same education as men, meaning they were unable to become scribes and were unable to take on supervisory roles. With this went exclusion from the bureaucratic profession. The Middle Kingdom *Satire of the Trades*[72] explains what the Egyptians saw as aspirational professions; physical work was denigrated and bossing other people around was seen as good. The work of the scribe and the supervisor was to be desired.

Margaret Mead,[73] in identifying the phenomenon of denigrating women's work, states, 'Men may cook, or weave or dress dolls or hunt hummingbirds, but if such activities are appropriate behavior for men, then the whole society, men and women alike, votes them as important. When the same occupations are performed by women, they are regarded as less important.' In ancient Egypt too, women's labour was largely ignored or taken for granted.[74] The ancient Egyptian attitude to women's work is summed up in the New Kingdom *Instructions of Ani*: 'A woman is asked about her husband, a man is asked about his rank/profession/office'.[75] A man's job is important; a woman's is less so. Women were more reliant on moving between economic classes through marriage; men could do this through professions.

WAS ANCIENT EGYPT A MATRILINEAL SOCIETY?

Matrilineal societies are those which base succession or inheritance through one's female relatives, as opposed to patrilineal societies where succession or inheritance passes through the male line. It is still popularly believed that ancient Egyptian societies were matrilineal[76] despite the fact that academic Egyptologists have disproved this theory long ago. The idea persists because it explains the appearance of the high status accorded some ancient Egyptian women, and is attractive to those drawing a parallel between pre-colonial black African societies and those of ancient Egypt. However, not only was ancient Egypt clearly patrilineal, but matrilineal societies do not necessarily hold women in high regard in areas other than succession.

Various arguments have been put forward to support the idea that Egypt was matrilineal. First, the heiress theory is posited. This was the erroneous idea that kings could only succeed to the throne through marriage to royal women. As will be shown, this theory has long since been disproved.

Secondly, arguments for matrilineality usually state that Egyptian women, especially queen mothers, were accorded high status and that names of mothers are recorded rather than those of fathers. As previously discussed, the mother was even more important than the wife in the tomb until at least the New Kingdom, and some scholars[77] suggest that this state of affairs continued into the Eighteenth Dynasty. This, however, does not prove matrilineal descent. It can easily be explained by the fact that the mother was a necessary prerequisite for rebirth. In the Eighteenth Dynasty, filiation was often given to the mother and not the father to make inheritance rights clear where there were other children who were illegitimate; filiation to the 'Mistress of the House' – the legitimate 'wife' – would make clear the status of the son. Similarly, it is interesting to note that in the *Royal Annals* (an early list of kings) the pharaoh's name is preceded not by that of his father, but by that of his mother. Again, this could be to show that the king is the son of the legitimate wife (though the evidence for polygamy in the Old Kingdom is debatable). In the Eighteenth Dynasty, while the wife is given prominence in most tombs, in a significant number, the mother is the prominent female. However, such instances may be explained without recourse to the claim of the general importance of the mother. Alternative explanations include attributing such tombs to unmarried sons and sons with mothers who were particularly important (such as royal wet nurses). As an additional argument against the supremacy of the mother, while literary texts urge sons to care and love their mothers, it is also clear that texts urge sons to acknowledge their fathers.[78]

Bridewealth – the gifts given by the groom or groom's family to the wife or wife's family – is often said to characterize matrilineal societies. As will be shown in Chapter 4, this practice took place in ancient Egypt, though there is also some evidence for the giving of dowries. However, not all anthropologists agree that bridewealth is exclusive to matrilineal societies[79] and, indeed, in modern Egypt gifts may be given to the bride and her family, but no one would argue that this is a matrilineal society.

Similarities between Egypt and pre-colonial black Africa are used by some scholars[80] to support the idea of a matrilineal Egypt. This assumes that African societies were inherently matrilineal, and that this pattern was temporally and geographically uniform throughout Africa. While ethnographic parallels are useful, they can also be dangerous; it is arguably as wrong to assume that Egypt was like pre-colonial Africa as to assume it was like Europe.

Finally, there is, contrary to the claim of matrilineality, textual evidence that succession was decided through the male line. In the *Contendings of Horus and Seth*, Horus and Seth fight for the right to succeed to the throne of Osiris. Horus claims the right as the son of Osiris and it is he who is successful; his wife is not even mentioned in justification.

WERE WOMEN CONSIDERED TO BE SEX OBJECTS?

One could argue that ancient Egyptian women were denigrated through being considered 'sex objects'. Ostraca, and the Turin Papyrus, suggest that women's sexuality was of great interest to men, and women are shown as highly sexualized in the tombs of men. One might argue, as Lynn Meskell has done, that 'these images sexualize and commodify women through their constructions as visual subjects'.[81] Women appear as subservient because of their sexuality. They do not even take the lead role in reproduction, but rather are there to encourage and nurture male procreation.

Ostraca and the Turin Papyrus also show men engaged in sexual activity and furthermore, at New Kingdom Deir el-Medina, a place which was largely inhabited by women, front rooms of houses were also decorated with sexualized pictures of women. Are we to assume that these women had no voice in the decoration of their living space, or do we assume that women celebrated their own sexuality? If we agree that women's status was eroded through their role as sex symbols, we are forced to admit that occasionally, at least, women were encouraging their own secondary position. However, as will be shown in Chapter 6, sexuality was seen as a source of power. One might see a parallel in the modern west with the so-called post-feminist woman wearing sexually provocative clothing. This may be seen as either empowering or denigrating women.

The role of the woman in ancient Egypt does not, to our eyes, seem to be of equal status to that of the man. Women seem to have been expected to be passive and largely subject to male command. However, we should not think that women were therefore always quiet and demure. A woman in Twelfth Dynasty Gurob wrote to the king and there is no evidence of passivity, but rather of bragging.

She stated: 'I shall have myself boasted about because of them and not let fault
be found with me. It is advantageous that my Lord, l.p.h. [life, prosperity and
health], has had people sent to me to be taught and instructed how to perform
this important occupation (of weaving) . . .'[82] She tells the king he is lucky to have
her in charge. Elsewhere, in the Twentieth Dynasty, the wife of a priest complains
to a military commander in what would appear to us a demanding tone, 'Don't
make [. . .] complain to me again'.[83]

Egyptologists have shown[84] that in New Kingdom Egyptian literature, women
were certainly not more polite, nor did they phrase requests differently from men.
In stories, however, women often had to try much harder than men to get their
own way, to the extent of threatening suicide. There are no known stories of men
threatening suicide if they don't get their own way. It appears that while women
seem to be disadvantaged, this does not seem to have made them browbeaten or
verbally submissive.

Birth, life and death

In ancient Egypt, birth, life and death were significantly different for men and women.

In many societies, the birth of a boy is seen as more desirable than the birth of a girl, so much so that at times baby girls have been put to death while boys were celebrated. In childhood, it is common for boys to receive the best food and care, and in later life to be better educated than girls. This does not seem to have been the case in ancient Egypt, though it is true that boys could be educated as scribes, a high-status occupation, while women were rarely given this chance, if at all.

It is only in the Graeco-Roman Period that we have evidence of female infanticide, and, one might argue, this is due to Greek and Roman influence. Before this date, infanticide does not seem to have been practised in Egypt. Moreover, while there is evidence that male children were preferred – medical prescriptions, for example, ask for the milk from the mother of a male child – there is also evidence that the birth of a girl was at times celebrated. At New Kingdom Deir el-Medina, we have a reference to celebrations on the birth of a girl child at 'the place of hard drinking'.[1] We may assume that both men and women joined in these festivities.

Nor does it seem that female children were disadvantaged through diet. Scholars[2] have studied the dental enamel of males and females from the Old Kingdom to the Graeco-Roman Period as dental enamel can indicate levels of stress. The results showed no statistical difference between the sexes, suggesting that both were subject to similar amounts of childhood stress.

It is difficult to be specific about the lives of female children.[3] Both boys and girls enjoyed games and a number of artefacts have been discovered from Kahun which were interpreted as toys. These include wooden tip-cats and tops, a model boat and limestone hippopotami; baked clay models of animals and a man were also found. While girls and boys are often shown playing separately in tomb scenes, such as in those in the tomb of Mereruka, other evidence suggests that, at least in the Old Kingdom, children were not always separated by sex. A statuette from an Old Kingdom Giza tomb shows a boy and girl playing together.[4] There is also one instance of a game shown on a tomb wall where two boys stand upright and twirl girls around them.[5] Tomb scenes may simply be depicting the ideal of gender separation, something which is also shown to be practised by adults. Or it could be that, as in the west of today, boys and girls often choose to play in separate groups.

We may expect that there were specific games that were played by girls and others that were played by boys. True to the stereotype, girls are rarely shown playing aggressive games. In Old Kingdom scenes, only boys are shown doing balancing acts, and a Middle Kingdom limestone figurine from Kahun shows two boys wrestling. In Middle Kingdom tombs, in particular, girls are shown juggling balls. Although girls are not shown playing the rough games enjoyed by boys, in the New Kingdom tomb of Menna, there is a depiction of two girls pulling each other's hair!

EDUCATION, LITERACY AND SCRIBES

The childhood of women would have varied according to social status. Even for the wealthy, however, women were rarely trained to become scribes and, compared to men, their formal education, outside the domestic sphere, seems restricted. This meant that women could not usually take up male professions demanding high levels of literacy, such as scribes and other bureaucratic offices, nor could they become lector priests.

While we know that boys could be sent to school, references to girls' education are severely limited. Some have pointed to the scribal kit depicted in front of the Old Kingdom princess Idut as evidence of female literacy. However, this tomb was previously carved for a vizier called Ihy, and as his figure was replaced by hers,[6] the kit may have been intended for him. The evidence of scribal kits shown under the chairs of elite women in the New Kingdom (the wife of Menna in Menna's tomb in Thebes, for example) also need not suggest literacy. It may simply suggest status. It is true that there are letters sent from women, though it is possible that these were penned by men on their behalf. However, there were certainly some cases of literate women; four female scribes are known from the Middle Kingdom,[7] though some have suggested that this was only an honourific title. At Deir el-Medina, on one occasion, a pupil at school was a woman.[8] A Late Rameside letter implying a female student is also known.[9] By the Graeco-Roman Period, literate women were more evident, though still unusual.

One would think that in order to competently run a large household, women would have had to, at least, been able to read. If they were totally reliant on men to both read and write for them, they would have been wide open to unscrupulous practices. Additionally, one would expect female merchants, of which there appear to have been several, to have some ability to read. At the same time, this competence may not have been equivalent to that of a scribe.

AGE AND SEXUALITY

We now turn to the question of when the ancient Egyptian woman was considered an adult rather than a child, and whether or not this was marked by any coming of age ceremony, or outward form such as change in dress. But, before we study age demarcation we need to realise that many historians believe that childhood is largely a recent construction, and even if childhood was recognized in ancient Egypt, the age at which an individual would have been considered an adult probably occurred earlier than in today's societies.

In our society, girls under the age of 16, or even 18, are considered children. This is not the case in many other contemporary societies. Elsewhere, the onset of menarche or marriage may herald womanhood. A passage from the *Instructions of Ani*, urging a man to take a wife and teach her to be a 'human', suggests that women were only considered fully grown up once they had married.[10] Both marriage and menarche could well have taken place when the individual was around 12 years old. Thus, we should not be shocked by sexualization of adolescents in ancient Egypt.

The genre of the sexualized adolescent is particularly known in Egypt from the late Eighteenth Dynasty. Ritual spoons are shaped like youthful, swimming females. Ritual spoons and ring bezels show adolescent girls playing lutes. Their forms are also used as handles on mirrors, and they appear as servant girls in tomb chapels. All these girls are nude, or almost nude, and wear the heavy wigs associated with the erotic. These girls appear by their body shape to be immature, post-pubescent females, and are possibly those referred to in literature as *nfrwt* (neferut, meaning 'beautiful or youthful ones'[11]). The story of a boating party in Papyrus Westcar suggests that *nfrt* refers to a woman who has not given birth. An older women would be *st* (set) or *ḥmt* (hemet) and would often have a title, most notably that of *nbt-pr*, meaning 'Mistress of the House'.[12]

The symbolism of the spoons refers to fertility, birth and rebirth. Other decoration on the spoons can include Bes (a deity often considered erotic) and the lotus, a symbol of rebirth. Some spoons are in the shape of elaborate bouquets for which the word 'ankh', also meaning life, was given. Mirrors have a ritual aspect[13] and handles are often in the shape of Bes, a Hathor head or papyrus stem, all of which are rebirth symbols. In the tomb chapels, naked girls are shown pouring drinks for guests. The words for 'pour' and 'impregnate' were the same, *sti*. This, together with the fact that these depictions are shown on tomb walls – places highly charged with rebirth imagery – suggests a rebirth function for such motifs. In a more secular context, the Turin Erotic Papyrus shows adolescent girls with a 'sidelock of youth' participating in erotic scenes, where they are assisting sexual acts but are not themselves being penetrated. We may conclude that it does not appear to have been considered morally wrong to show adolescents in sexual scenes.

However, the contexts in which sexualized adolescent girls are shown are, with the possible exception of the Turin Papyrus, religious; therefore, they might not, reflect the everyday. There is little evidence for the sexualization of pre-adolescent girls; erotic scenes depict girls that appear at least pubescent (their body shape suggests this). Thus, sexualization may have been seen as an advertisement for marriage, and that once married, girls became respectable women who were then shown more fully clothed.

The Egyptians did recognize and mark differences between female children and adults. We have already discussed the textual differences between *nfrwt* and *st*. Tomb paintings include markers of women's age from childhood to adulthood in hairstyles and clothing, and indeed from adulthood to middle age and old age.[14] Young children of both sexes, and possibly adolescent girls, seem to have worn a hairstyle called the 'sidelock of youth'. Older, presumably married, women are shown with different hairstyles to younger women. Adolescent girls serving at banquets are shown wearing very little but a girdle, while older servant women appear more covered. It has also been suggested that the V-necked dress of the Old and Middle Kingdoms was largely worn by mature women.[15]

Some countries today practise genital mutilation of females and even attempt to justify it through appeal to tradition, claiming that the ancient Egyptians did the same. It is sometimes stated that it was a rite of passage for Egyptian females. However, there is absolutely no evidence for Egyptian female circumcision or genital mutilation from the pre-Roman Period. No evidence for it has been found on female mummies, though admittedly such evidence would not be obvious, nor is there any evidence in pre-Roman Egyptian literature. By the Roman Period, things may have been different, but even here there is room for debate. The Roman writer Strabo, in his *Geography*, said of the Egyptians: 'They circumcise the males, as also the females, as is the custom also among the Jews, who are of Egyptian origin ...' (Book XVIII). However, we may wonder just how accurate Strabo was, as he was certainly not accurate in all matters. Further evidence concerns a petition of 163 BC, suggesting that at this date circumcision was practised on girls prior to marriage.[16] Yet, the girl in question is associated with the Syrian goddess Astarte at Saqqara, and so her circumcision may be due to foreign influence.[17]

Thus, while we cannot be sure of any formal rite of passage, girls do seem to have been differentiated from women by their clothes, hairstyles and titles.

MENARCHE AND MENSTRUATION

As stated above, adulthood may well have been heralded by the onset of menarche. Menstruation in patriarchal societies, it is often claimed, is considered in a negative light and often associated with impurity. There is difficulty in understanding ancient Egyptian attitudes to menstruation, but it seems it was not considered entirely negative. Some of the confusion concerning Egyptian attitudes to menstruation results from the translation of the word *hsmn* (hesmen). While *hsmn* is usually taken to mean menstruation, it has been argued that the word may also mean purification. It may have covered a variety of meanings, including blood loss from menarche, menstruation, abortion or childbirth.

However, we can say that menstruation was identified with the Nile flood, an archetypal symbol of renewal and fertility for the Egyptians, although it was also considered to be a dangerous time. Thus, it had some positive symbolism. Menstrual blood seems sometimes to have been used in medicine for women; in Papyrus Ebers, menstrual blood smeared over the breasts is given as a remedy against breasts 'going down' (which could translate as sagging breasts[18]). Sanitary towels or loin cloths were worn and are mentioned in laundry lists,[19] and that they are included with other clothing suggests that they were not considered impure. Some believe the Isis knot, a form of amulet often made of red stone, represents female sanitary protection, though such an interpretation is only one of many. The use of such an article as an amulet again suggests a positive image.

However, other evidence suggests that menstruation was considered impure. In the *Satire of the Trades*, the washerman complains that he must clean the clothes of women soiled with menstrual blood, though one might argue that this does not mean menstrual blood was considered impure, but rather indicates a 'natural' disgust. There is possible textual evidence for a purification ritual following menstruation from Middle Kingdom Lahun. This occurs in a letter from the Mistress of the House, Ir, explaining her absence 'because this humble servant had gone into the temple on day 20 for monthly purification'.[20]

The need for purification might suggest her monthly period was considered impure. However, one might interpret the passage more positively as meaning that menstruation itself was a purification necessitating a celebratory trip to the temple.[21] It has further been suggested that women's monthly cycles excluded them from priesthood.

In some societies, menstruating women are sequestered from the rest of society. Again, this can be seen in either a positive or negative light. At times, women are separated because they are considered impure, while at other times seclusion might be seen as a time to rest from hard work, or a time of communing with other women and perhaps even celebrating this symbol of femininity. Ostracon OIM 13512 from Deir el-Medina has been seen as evidence for a place where menstruating women resided.[22] The relevant section reads: 'The day when these eight women came out [to/from the] place of women while they were menstruating'. However, the piece could alternatively be translated as 'place of women while they were being purified.' Whether this separation only took place at menarche, or each month, is debatable. As we shall see below, there is evidence for separation and purification following childbirth, and possibly following abortion. One might see the roofs of small houses being used for this purpose of seclusion, or, in large houses, rooms or suites of rooms may have been set aside. However, the text describing 'the place of women' seems to imply a place separate from the main house, and that eight women are involved suggests a substantial area. From a much later period, a document concerning the transfer of a house at Thebes, dated to 267 BC, describes an area to be used by womenfolk during menstruation.[23] The document seems to imply an area within the main home, rather than, as at Deir el-Medina, a place separate from it.

Also from Deir el-Medina, we have evidence that men were sometimes absent from work on account of a female relative's ḥsmn, and that in one instance food or gifts are brought to the woman.[24] While one might imagine that from time to time it would be necessary for men to either look after a woman with a particularly problematic period, or to carry out household duties while she was inactive, this may also be explained as an absence to carry out rites concerned with menarche.

Thus, menstruation, if only at menarche, would seem to be a time which was particularly important for women, probably marked by seclusion and other rituals. But we do not know if it was seen in a positive or negative light; following the inundation metaphor, it could well have been both a time of danger and a time to celebrate renewed fertility.

COMING OF AGE AND MARRIAGE

Given the desirability of having many children, women in ancient Egypt married young. The Egyptian name for wife was *ḥmt* (hemet) and some have suggested that the title *nbt-pr* ('Mistress of the House') also indicated marriage. We might assume that the onset of menarche heralded their marriageable age. During the Graeco-Roman Period, it seems the average age for women marrying was 10 years or older and even in nineteenth century Egypt, girls often married at 12 or 13 years of age.[25]

The *Instruction of Ani* advises:

> Take a wife while you're young,
> That she may bear a son for you;
> She should bear for you while you're youthful,
> It is proper to make many people.
> Happy the man whose people are many,
> He is saluted on account of his progeny.[26]

Nevertheless, there is some evidence that a large age difference between men and women was not uncommon, and Naunakhte from Deir el-Medina was some 42 years younger than her husband.[27] Such age discrepancies could be accounted for by the death or divorce of the first wife.

There was little virtue attached to being a virgin; indeed, there was no word for 'virgin' in ancient Egyptian.[28] Here again, the picture regarding morality is not clear. In Papyrus British Museum 10416, there is evidence that married men could not have sexual relations with unmarried women. This papyrus narrates how a group of men and women go to seek out and punish a woman who is accused of having an eight-month affair with a married man.[29] But the papyrus does not conclusively state that the woman was unmarried, and the punishment specifically relates to the fact that the man is married. Love poems are sometimes cited as evidence of premarital sex. While Egyptian sexual behaviour described in love poems appears to be between unmarried couples, we cannot take such works as proof that sexual relations before marriage were sanctioned or encouraged. Literary works very often portray events which are not normally sanctioned.

It could well be that marriage was arranged, or at least engineered, by parents, specifically the father. In the New Kingdom *Tale of the Doomed Prince*, a daughter refuses to accept her father's choice of groom. In the Graeco-Roman Period, a father is urged, 'Choose a prudent husband for your daughter; do not choose for her a rich husband'.[30] The process of choosing a partner is not clear, and Egyptologists disagree as to how common close kin marriages were in the Dynastic Period.

Certain phrases are generally seen as representing marriage: 'to make as a wife', 'bringing a bundle', 'to live with', 'to found a house', and 'to moor' [a boat]. The 'bundle' seems to have been given to the father of the bride by the groom;[31] such gifts are now usually termed 'bride-price'. There is also some, though slight, evidence of dowries, that is, transfer of property from the bride's parents to the bride.

It is generally agreed that there was no formal marriage ceremony, at least for the pre-Ptolemaic Period. The phrase 'spending a happy day' (ir hrw nfr) with the household and guests suggests some sort of celebration, and is attested from the Ptolemaic *The First Tale of Setne Khaemwes*.[32] There is one possible reference to an oath to solemnize a marriage,[33] though other Egyptologists see this as more an oath regarding property, and not essential to the marriage itself.

POLYGAMY

There is clear evidence that kings frequently took more than one wife. Given that there was no reproach against men sleeping with other women, unless they were the wives of other men, or servants, there remains the possibility that Egyptian men, other than kings, had more than one wife. It is sometimes stated that this is unlikely to have been the case, as it would have been expensive to take more than one wife; however, the earning power of women may actually have advantaged men with several spouses. Despite all this, there is no clear evidence that men commonly took more than one wife. There are a few examples of men being represented with several wives, but these can be explained as successive wives, each wife in turn being divorced or dead. Furthermore, house size generally would make it difficult for a man to have more than one wife. It therefore appears that if polygamy existed, it was a rare occurrence.

The few possible examples of polygamy outside of the royal family all concern the elite of Egyptian society. The four wives of the Old Kingdom vizier, Merefnebef, are shown playing harps for him.[34] There is also the First Intermediate Period example of Mery-Aha, whose tomb at Hagarseh shows six wives.[35] These may be evidence of polygamy, but could also be the result of bad luck, that is, a succession of wives dying. Both examples are unlikely to be the result of divorce, as surely divorced wives would not merit inclusion in tomb depictions.

Women's titles might give clues as to whether or not men had secondary wives.

The term *ḥbswt* (hebsut), as used in the Middle Kingdom, is sometimes translated as 'bride' or 'concubine', but some believe[36] this refers to a legal wife taken after another was divorced or had died. In the Eleventh Dynasty Letters of Hekanakht, there is an appeal not to mistreat a woman who is called a *ḥbswt*; the woman, Iutenheb, is being abused by the housemaid, Senen.[37] Hekanakht orders that the housemaid be turned out of the house and asks the family to respect his *ḥbswt*. The situation is understandable if we take Iutenheb to be a wife taken shortly after the death or divorce of another. Resentment by the family of a new bride is common in families of our own society.

The most common title for women, at least from the New Kingdom, was *nbt-pr*, 'Mistress of the House', designating the woman in charge of the household. This has been thought to be a title used for married women, although some Egyptologists raise doubts that it indicates married status, and suggest that, at Deir el-Medina at least, this was an honourific title indicating that the woman was in charge of household matters. For the New Kingdom, it has been claimed[38] that the main, or legitimate, wife was given the title *nbt-pr* to distinguish this wife from others.

There are several instances of men having sexual relations with women who were not their primary wives, and who bore them children. In some instances, the children are fully accepted in society. However, in the mythological *Tale of Truth and Falsehood*, a child is mocked for not knowing his father,[39] though goes on to become a member of the elite. The case of a childless couple is documented where the man did not divorce his wife, but the wife adopted the children of a female servant.[40] As the names of the children are not given, it is suggested that the husband was their natural father.

The mocking of the boy in the *Tale of Truth and Falsehood* suggests, however, that illegitimacy, even if not ostracised, was considered undesirable. The will of Wah from Kahun discusses the appointment of a male guardian for Wah's children, should he die. It seems it was recognized that children would have a better chance in life if a male was there to look out for them. By the Late Period, it seems that illegitimate children may have been 'given' to the temple.[41] It would seem likely that children without fathers would have been disadvantaged, hence the necessity of fatherless children entering the temple. If such children were accepted and protected by another man, there does not appear to have been any stigma. In some Eighteenth Dynasty tomb chapels, there is evidence of children whose mothers are not official wives.[42] The fact that these are shown in tomb scenes suggests no disgrace.

CONTRACEPTIVES AND ABORTION

Despite the fact that several children were the hoped for outcome of marriage, contraceptives were known; all of these were for application by the woman.[43] One wonders if, as in some modern societies, it was the women who were most desirous of family planning. Contraceptives include concoctions such as crocodile dung mixed in milk used as a suppository to be placed in the vagina. The crocodile dung may have represented Seth, who could take the form of a crocodile, and was credited with causing abortions.[44] Elsewhere, fermented vegetable paste is suggested, or a mixture of honey and natron. One would think that their contraceptive efficacy lay only in their being dissuasion from intercourse. However, some recipes may actually have worked[45] beyond simply blocking the passage of the seminal fluid; the recipe for fermented vegetables would have produced lactic acid, and lactic acid is used in contraceptive jellies today. Another papyrus records an oral contraceptive using celery. Celery, according to scientific reports, also has antifertility effects.

PHALLIC VOTIVES AND FERTILITY FIGURINES

There were also means to propagate children. The conception of children was believed to be essentially male, thus women were not entirely blamed for failure to produce progeny. Therefore, we may expect to see fertility-inducing artefacts and spells to be associated with men as well as women. Amulets, in particular, were used, though archaeologically speaking it is difficult to differentiate amulets to ensure women's fertility from those associated with safe delivery in childbirth. Taweret, for example, was a goddess associated with childbirth and the protection of the young. Amulets depicting her image may have been used to ensure pregnancy, to assist in childbirth or to protect the newborn.

Two types of material culture seem particularly related to human sexuality – phallic votives and fertility figurines. Model phalli of wood, stone or pottery were offered at many religious sites throughout Egypt. The phallus of Osiris is often mentioned in texts, and in the Graeco-Roman Period we have descriptions of its worship. While this may seem to denote a purely masculine aspect to religion, there were also phallic offerings to the cult of Hathor.[46] Such items may have been given to Hathor by couples desiring children.

Fertility symbols include figurines in clay and faience, as well as the Upper Egyptian and Nubian wooden paddle-shaped dolls of the Middle Kingdom.[47] In the past, clay and faience examples shaped in the form of nude women sometimes wearing girdles were called 'concubine figurines'; it was believed that such items were put in the graves of men to satisfy their sexual needs in the afterlife, and aspects such as the girdle do seem to have sexual connotations. More recent studies have stressed that they are also found in women's graves and on settlement sites, while those at Amarna were found in the same rooms as domestic altars. Clay figurines showing a nude woman on a bed, sometimes with a child, are also known from domestic sites. The addition of the child reinforces the suggestion that at least some were intended to ensure birth of children. However, other suggestions may be put forward for these, as well as for the faience figures and paddle dolls. They could have been made as votives to ensure menarche, as has been suggested[48] for naked and limbless 'dolls' from ancient Athens. They may have been given as votive offerings, or involved in other aspects of social actions where fertility would have been uppermost. One Egyptian text even suggests that these were used in healing rites: 'When he places his hands on the belly, his suffering will begin to be healed – to be recited over woman's statue of clay'.[49] Perhaps they had a variety of functions.

PREGNANCY AND CHILDBIRTH

The Egyptians even had pregnancy testing kits. Gynaecological texts in the Kahun Papyrus (1820), Berlin 199 and Ebers Papyrus (1500) and the Carlsberg Papyrus all suggest ways of telling if a woman is pregnant, and even determining the sex of the baby[50] – though this need not imply a preference for boys. The most quoted test is in Papyrus Berlin 199, with a damaged version in the Carlsberg Papyrus; this prescribes emmer and barley to be moistened with the urine of the woman. If it grows, she is pregnant; if only the emmer grows, she will bear a girl, if only the barley, a boy. A very similar test was also used in eighteenth-century Germany.[51] When put to the test more recently, there was some evidence it might show pregnancy, but it failed to correlate with the sex of the child.

As in many societies today, as well as in the past, childbirth was a dangerous time for both mother and child. A study of human remains from Gebelein and Asyut suggests that Egyptian women had a low fertility rate[52] and that women from Gebelein (as well as men) had particularly narrow pelvises.[53] This must have reduced the ability of women to give birth safely. Such problems are likely to have affected all classes of women. The body of Henhenet, one of these priestesses of Hathor in the Middle Kingdom 'harem' of Mentuhotep II, has been studied.[54] It is said that Henhenet must have suffered a terrible death – she died in childbirth at around 23–24 years of age – as her narrow pelvis would not allow her child to be born. The evidence is said to demonstrate a vesico-vaginal fistula – a tear running from her bladder to her vagina, often a result of birth complications. It might be argued that this tear was due to mummification procedures, which means we still need to account for her early death.

Other birthing complications are known. Some scholars[55] discuss the birthing history of Queen Mutnedjmet, the second wife of Horemheb, last ruler of the Eighteenth Dynasty. Her remains show that she had had a number of pregnancies resulting in severe blood loss. Her last pregnancy, in her mid-forties, was fatal to her and her child. While these examples show that birth complications were not limited to the non-elite, the poor nutrition of non-elite women can only have exacerbated their problems.

Various measures were taken to ensure a successful delivery and the safety of both mother and child. After giving birth, women underwent a period of rest and purification in a special area set aside for this purpose. Apotropaic wands, birth amulets, dance and 'women's beds' all seem to have played their part. The mysterious 'apotropaic wands' appear in the Middle Kingdom to Second Intermediate Period and it is possible that they continued into the New Kingdom as they are depicted in the tomb of Rekhmire. The wands are usually made of hippopotamus tusk, split in half to produce two curved objects with one side convex and the other flat. The material possibly invoked Taweret, a hippopotamus goddess of childbirth. The wands are usually roughly engraved with deities associated with the protection of young infants, such as the frog goddess Hekat, the hippopotamus goddess Taweret and the dwarf Bes. These deities often carry protective knives or snakes. The inscriptions, too, bear witness to the fact that these 'wands' are intended to be protective: 'Cut off the head of the enemy when he enters the chamber of the children whom the lady . . . has borne' and 'Protection by night, protection by day'.[56]

Inscriptions also usually name the mother and the child. The child is invariably a boy. There could be several reasons for this. The first might be that these items were only made for boys. The second might be that most of the tombs in which the wands were found belonged to men, which does not necessarily mean that girls did not have them in life. The preponderance of male names may also be a result of putting names on tusks before the birth of the child, and indicate that male children were usually hoped for.[57] However, the fact that these items were repaired, and spells thereon suggest several children, seems to imply that these were used for girl as well as boy babies.

Egyptologists usually claim these wands were used to protect women in childbirth, though most have been found in tombs. The fact that the points of some wands are worn away on one side has suggested to some that they were used to draw a magic circle around the child. Some examples have perforations at each end with a cord running through perhaps to carry or move other objects. On tomb walls, wands are shown being carried by nurses, but here their presence shows that they had a secondary function of protecting the deceased at the time of their rebirth.

More rarely, a similar type of item, the 'birth rod' of bone, steatite or ivory, was used.[58] Similar rods are known from outside Egypt.[59]

Texts from New Kingdom Deir el-Medina show that the villagers purchased 'birth amulets' to aid in delivery.[60] We do not know what form these took, though there are amulets from Egypt depicting the hippopotamus goddess Taweret, 'The Great One', who was a goddess of pregnant women. Taweret is often shown pregnant with pendulous breasts and her fearsome teeth bared. She may also carry a knife. Female hippopotami are fiercely protective of their young. Other amulets may have been in the form of apotropaic deities such as Bes and functioned to ensure a safe delivery for mother and child. Charms for childbirth are certainly known for the Graeco-Roman Period.[61] It is difficult to separate fertility amulets from those intended to ensure successful childbirth and it is possible that some amulets were used for both.

Acacia seed-pod beads were also worn as amulets by women of childbearing age.[62] The acacia contains tannin and phenol. Tannin acts as an astringent and phenol is antibacterial and would thus be useful in preventing haemorrhages and infection. In the recent past, Egyptian women bathed in water steeped in acacia pods in the hours following childbirth;[63] it therefore seems possible that acacia was also used by ancient Egyptian women after childbirth and amulets worn by them were associated with protection in childbirth.

There is some evidence that women unbraided their hair in readiness for childbirth[64] and men wore their kilts disordered (as described in Papyrus Westcar 10, 2[65]). It could be that both these actions were a sort of sympathetic magic with the undoing of knots of both hair and kilts leading to a loosening of the womb and successful childbirth. Dance also played a part but whether as an aid to childbirth, or in celebration, is not clear.

Several ostraca are known from ancient Egypt showing nursing women seated on beds, often with convolvulus in the background and sometimes with snakes depicted. Women may be shown having their hair done and a mirror may be evident. Similar scenes also appear in the front rooms of some houses at Deir el-Medina. These scenes, which seem to indicate some special area for birth or post-parturition recuperation, are termed by Egyptologists, 'Wochenlaube' scenes (the term was coined by Brunner-Traut in 1955 to mean 'birth arbour' or 'maternity bower'). On some 'Wochenlaube' scenes, and on the clay model beds showing women nursing children, there are small black figures, sometimes shown dancing.[66] These are difficult to explain but the figures could be apes or monkeys (indicating eroticism), or perhaps Nubian dancers.

At New Kingdom Deir el-Medina, 'women's beds' appear to have been purchased along with birth amulets.[67] Unfortunately, we don't know what such beds were like, though there are clues in the 'Wochenlaube' scenes and in model clay beds.[68] On both, snakes are shown. On the clay models, the bed legs may take the form of Bes, and a snake is depicted on either long edge of the bed.[69] But only one complete bed exists which depicts snakes; it is that of Sennedjem.[70] Here two snakes are shown painted on the bed frame, one on each side. Depictions of Bes on actual beds are, however, much more common.

The snake, which is either shown as red or red and black, has been identified[71] as the protective ḳrḥt snake, a guardian of fertility. The pottery beds on which such serpents appear are dated as Late Eighteenth Dynasty to Third Intermediate Period.[72] There is also evidence paralleling the 'Wochenlaube' scenes where Isis and baby Horus are flanked by protective serpents.[73] Although no definite 'women's beds' have been found, the Egypt Centre at Swansea, however, has a pair of bed legs probably from the same bed (accession number W2052). One leg depicts Bes and the other Taweret; a snake is also apparent. Perhaps this is the remains of a 'woman's bed'.

It seems probable that 'women's beds' were not used for the birth itself, but rather for nursing. The evidence suggests that in ancient Egypt, women gave birth squatting over two birth bricks, with one foot on each brick. One text describes a man being chastised by the goddess Meretseger; he says, 'I sat on bricks like the woman in labour'.[74] An actual example of such a brick has been found from Middle Kingdom Abydos[75] near fragments of an apotropaic wand. The brick was decorated with a woman holding a baby boy; she is shown with two other women and the scene is flanked by Hathor standards. Protective deities decorate the other sides of the brick.

'Wochenlaube' scenes also show women nursing babies with a backdrop of convolvulus. It has therefore been suggested that women gave birth in a pavilion, or birth arbour, constructed in outdoor buildings or perhaps erected on roofs of houses. Given the cold nights in Egyptian winters, one would expect that such arbours would be enclosed. Separate areas for women to give birth and in which women were confined after childbirth are well known ethnographically.[76]

The post-parturition period is likely to have involved some element of rest, as well as purification, and it is perhaps this that is depicted on the arbour scenes. Papyrus Westcar[77] states that the woman Redjedet had 14 days of purification after her delivery. On 'Wochenlaube' scenes, women are often shown having their hair done, and a mirror is frequently included. This may suggest that after having loosened her hair prior to birth, the woman is ensuring she is now prepared to resume her everyday life. The mirrors and hairdressing could also relate to purification, or a celebration of the end of the post-parturition period.

In many societies, women are given special treatment shortly after birth, not only with rest, but also with gifts and a special diet. A letter from Deir el-Medina gives information on arrangements for a servant woman who has given birth.[78] She is to be provided with bread, meat and cakes, sgnn-oil, honey, etc. as well as wood and water. There is also another example from Deir el-Medina where a husband is given three days off as his wife is in labour.[79] Whether this was to help his wife in childbirth, help with the child or to celebrate is unknown.

MOTHERHOOD

Fear of the death of the newborn was all too real. Generally, in ancient societies 10–20 per cent of babies died in their first year.[80] Berlin 3027, a New Kingdom collection of spells for mother and child, gives a rather chilling indication of this fear, suggesting a spirit 'who comes in the darkness and enters furtively' might steal the soul of the child through a vampiric kiss.[81] The New Kingdom *Instructions of Ani* warn:

> Do not say, "I am too young to be taken",
> For you do not know your death.
> When death comes he steals the infant
> Who is in his mother's arms . . .[82]

Papyrus Ebers 838 states that, if on the day a child is born, it says 'ny', it will live, but if it says 'mebi', it will die.[83] Other unlikely indications of death include whether a newborn bends its face down or not.

It is sometimes said that in cultures of high infant mortality children were not considered fully human, or mourned like adults. This is seen as a mechanism to stop parents getting too attached to short-lived offspring. Others see this idea as a rather patronising view of other cultures, and believe that the death of children was usually considered devastating for those involved. What was the case for ancient Egypt? While there were cemeteries including young children, and at Deir el-Medina separate cemeteries were set aside for them, burials of young children have also occasionally been found under the floors of houses.[84] Flinders Petrie noted that, at Middle Kingdom Kahun, burials of newborns were found.

His journal of 8–15 April 1889 records:

> Many new-born infants were found buried in the floors of the rooms, and, strange
> to say, usually in boxes made for other purposes evidently, by their form. In short,
> unlucky babes seem to have been conveniently put out of the way by stuffing them
> into a toilet case or clothes box and digging a hole in the floor for them ... I fear these
> discoveries do not reflect much on the manners and customs of the small officials
> of the Twelfth Dynasty.[85]

Contrary to Petrie's opinions, burials in homes need not suggest that young
children were considered unimportant. Protective beads and amulets buried with
these babies show they were certainly not casually discarded. Many formal burials
of adults contain as few grave goods. Home burials could simply represent the
desire of the parents to keep the child close to its family. In recent times, Egyptian
peasants would bury very young children under the threshold or inside the house
wall in the hope that their spirits would re-enter their mothers' bodies.[86] It is
clear from depictions of mourning following the death of a child shown in the
royal tomb at Amarna (EA26) that the deaths of royal children were met with
outpourings of grief. We should expect that other children too were mourned.

As stated above, the ancient Egyptians did not practise infanticide, and
attempts were made to rear deformed children.[87] At Deir el-Medina, several
children probably died from their severe deformities. An unnamed boy who
suffered from scoliosis, a condition involving an abnormal curving of the spine,
was buried with bread, dom-fruit and jewellery, and another child, Iryky, who
had an enlarged torso, head and stunted limbs was buried in a decorated coffin.[88]
That such children survived, even for a few years, suggests that they were cared
for. Mothers very clearly loved their children.

Women are shown nursing children, while continuing to work at their jobs.
In the tomb of Menna, a woman picks fruit while she carries a baby in a sling. In
the Fifth Dynasty tomb of Niankhkhnum and Khnumhotep at Saqqara, a mother
suckles a baby and tends a fire. Young children seem to have been carried in slings
in front of their mothers, on their backs, or in their mothers' arms. That other
members of the family aided the mother in caring for the child is shown by small
girls carrying babies in slings.

Ideally, mothers were expected to breastfeed their children. A Late Ptolemaic
Period text instructs: 'Do not give your son to the wet nurse and so cause her
to set aside her own' (The *Instruction of Ankhsheshonq*[89]). There is a suggestion
in the literature (the New Kingdom *Instructions of Ani*) that children were only
weaned after they were three years old. Such long suckling periods would act as

a contraceptive and offer protection to the child from food-borne diseases.

However, despite the ideal, it is usually the lower classes who are depicted breastfeeding.[90] Women are shown breastfeeding on the 'Wochenlaube' ostraca, but the status of these women is unknown. If, as has been suggested, the 'Wochenlaube' scenes mark the end of the immediate post-parturition period, wet nurses may not have been immediately available. Where elite children are shown being suckled, the feeders are either deities or wet nurses, not their own mothers.

One may wonder why elite women were not shown breastfeeding. Several explanations are possible; breastfeeding may have been associated with 'primitive' behaviours as has been suggested for the Graeco-Roman world; use of wet nurses may have allowed elite women to engage in other activities, or alternatively, use of wet nurses may have reduced the risk of ruining one's own figure. The prominence given to the slender, youthful body in ancient Egypt suggests that sagging breasts were not considered beautiful. Cessation of breastfeeding would also enable women to conceive more quickly. One would expect that, generally, wealthy women would be able to care for more children, and it is possible that the pressure upon women to produce male heirs was greater in wealthy families than in poorer ones. Of course, wealthy families would also be more able to provide for a wet nurse.

It was believed that the qualities of the mother could be passed on to children receiving her milk.[91] Breast milk was thought to have had magical properties, especially if the mother had borne a boy. It was used for wounds, eye ailments and burns. Spells and amulets were used to ensure its supply (Papyrus Ebers 113, XCVII).

From late in the reign of Thutmose III to early in the reign of Amenhotep III, several pottery vessels were manufactured in the shape of nursing mothers, often with an inverted crescent around their necks. It has been suggested that these were mothers or wet nurses with lives governed by monthly cycles, and that the vessels contained breast milk.[92] It has also been suggested that these may represent foreign women, Asiatics.[93] However, this does not argue against these being receptacles for mothers' milk. These vases are usually associated with magic or medicine and midwives and that liquids placed therein, like mother's milk, would have rejuvenating properties.[94] Whether the vessels were normally used by wet nurses for everyday purposes, or for magical or medicinal purposes, is debateable, though the fact that some of these were found in tombs suggests a more than everyday use for several of them.

The magical nature of breastfeeding, in particular its revivication properties, is highlighted by a study[95] which showed that the motif of the king being suckled by a goddess specifically occurs in relation to his birth, coronation and death.

The milk of goddesses was important to assist the king in crucial stages of his life. It has also been suggested[96] that, in the Amarna Period, the role of the wet nurse, as shown in royal scenes, may have had a cultic function. Not only would royal wet nurses have been important because of their closeness to the divine royal household, but also may have been portrayed in imitation of goddesses.

While the virtues of breast milk for the health of the child are recognized by us today, other means of ensuring healthy children appear more fantastical. Papyrus Berlin 3027, the New Kingdom collection of *Spells for Mother and Child* cited above, recommends knots, garlic and honey, as well as spells.[97] The elite may even have employed a 'Magician of the nursery' (*ḥkзy n kзp*) mentioned in this same papyrus.[98]

Ideally, at least, mothers were held in high regard. The reason for the prominence of the mother, as discussed in Chapter 2, is probably due to ideas of rebirth. While a sexual partner is necessary for birth, the mother is the first, most obvious and direct link with the formation of a child. Additionally, the importance of the mother is given mythic value by the elevation of deities such as Isis and Nut (although both were also sexual partners). The importance of the mother in myths concerning royalty is discussed in a later chapter.

Children were expected to repay their mothers for bringing them up, though as we shall see below, this ideal did not always work out. The New Kingdom *Instructions of Ani* read:

> Double the food your mother gave you,
> Support her as she supported you;
> She had a heavy load in you,
> But she did not abandon you.
> When you were born after your months,
> She was yet yoked (to you),
> Her breast in your mouth for three years.
> As you grew and your excrement disgusted,
> She was not disgusted, saying "What shall I do!"
> When she sent you to school,
> And you were taught to write,
> She kept watching over you daily,
> With bread and beer in her house.
> When as a youth you take a wife,
> And you are settled in your house,
> Pay attention to your offspring,
> Bring him up as did your mother.

Do not give her cause to blame you,
Lest she raise her hands to god
And he hears her cries.[99]

WIDOWS AND OLD AGE

We have very little information on older women in ancient Egypt. They are rarely shown in art, and there is little documentary information concerning them. While the aspirational lifespan was 110 years, few would have lived to old age. The wife of Sennedjem was one of these exceptional people, dying aged 75 years.[100] There are several estimations of average lifespan, varying from period to period and place to place.[101] However, generally it seems that more women than men would have died before the age of thirty. Women would have been considered old in their thirties, though, as is the case in most societies today, rich women would have lived longer than poor women. However, after age thirty, more women than men lived into old age.[102]

What contributed to the short lifespan? Ancient Egyptian sources for women's ailments are largely contained in the Ebers Papyrus and the Kahun Gynaecological Papyrus. Unlike the Greeks, the Egyptians do not seem to have prescribed to the rather strange later Greek view that women's ailments were largely due to the wandering of the womb, that is, hysteria.[103] Instead, other ailments of women are listed, such as diseased breasts or lack of menstruation.

Examination of human remains, however, tells us more about ailments, and the percentages who suffered. Many ailments were common to both women and men, such as tuberculosis and anaemia. The average height of adults is at least partly due to nutrition, and thus the height of ancient Egyptians shows that both men and women were malnourished. In the Middle Kingdom, average height for men was 160 cm and for women, 150 cm. At Amarna, the average height estimate for females was 152 cm and 157 cm for males.[104] In Europe, height reached its nadir at the beginning of the nineteenth century; the average height in Napoleon's army, for example, was about 152 cm. Average height in modern Egypt is 175 cm. Needless to say, mortality rates suggest that the most common cause of death of women was childbirth.

Youth and beauty were desirable, particularly in women, and thus several preparations were available to reverse the process of aging. The Ebers Papyrus (c.1550 BC), for example, gives recipes to stop greying of hair, and to prevent sagging breasts. There are very few depictions of aging women in tombs, but this can surely not be put down to the efficacy of Egyptian beauty products. Rather, since representations in tombs were designed to ensure an afterlife existence, few women, or their families, would want portrayals of older women. If you are going to live through representations of yourself on tomb walls, most people would want to be shown as youthful and beautiful. Additionally, tomb depictions of women served at least partly to sexually arouse the male, and one would assume a male preference for young, healthy females.

Deborah Sweeney[105] has sought out those few depictions of older women. Where aging women are shown, they are generally of low status, with examples including the Middle Kingdom depictions of emaciated women with drooping breasts called Neferet and Samut.[106] These women are shown working at a grindstone. Female foreign captives are also portrayed as elderly, in keeping with the general Egyptian practice of showing foreigners in an unflattering light. Occasionally, individuals with white hair or wigs are depicted in tombs (such as the tombs of Pashedu TT3; Ipuy TT217 and Irinefer TT290), and it has been suggested that these show aging individuals, despite the fact that, apart from the hair, they are shown as youthful.[107]

Certain signs of aging are considered appropriate for men but not for women.[108] Men may have vertical lines of concentration between the eyes, lines across the forehead and multiple folds of fat on the lower torso. Women may, however, be shown with white hair or sagging breasts. They may be portrayed as gaunt or display a wrinkle from nose to mouth. Women can also be shown with bags beneath the eyes. Which signs of aging were used varies from period to period; gauntness, for example, more often occurs in the Old Kingdom, while white hair dates from the New Kingdom.

Remarkably, during the reign of Akhenaten, it seems to have become accepted, or perhaps even desirable, to show royal women aging, and not simply through hair colour. Some statues of Tiy and Nefertiti show the royal women with down-turned mouths, lines at the corner of their mouths, heavy eyelids, lines from nose to mouth and drooping cheeks, bottoms and breasts. It has even been suggested[109] that the famous bust of Nefertiti, said in popular literature to be the most beautiful woman in the world, when shown in a certain light displays the beginning of a nose to mouth wrinkle and bags under the eyes. Another scholar[110] suggests that such signs of physical aging are the equivalent of males depicted in wise old age. During the Amarna Period, other non-royal women adopted the fashion of depicting their signs of aging. It is also noticeable that, during this period, royal women seem to have become particularly powerful. Dare we imagine that such powerful women sought to use physical signs of aging to show wisdom, rather than, as was usual in Egyptian art, to portray the female body as only desirable if youthful and fruitful? Unfortunately, this fashion did not last.

Some Egyptologists believe that the ancient Egyptians respected the elderly.[111] Rosalind Janssen, who has made extensive studies of aging at Deir el-Medina,[112] does not believe that this was entirely the case, but rather that the status of the elderly depended very much on their gender, wealth and earlier status. Status may also have varied from period to period.

So what type of life did the elderly woman in ancient Egypt enjoy? While literature hints at the desirability of a restful old age, there was no retirement age, and there are depictions of elderly women carrying out physically demanding tasks such as grinding grain or winnowing. An overseer of weavers at Gurob was clearly elderly as she had worked not only for the living king, but also for his grandfather (Papyrus Gurob III.1[113]). It may be that a leisured old age was something only obtainable by the rich, or those with supportive children. Certainly, children were expected to support their elderly parents. The Stato Civile Papyrus fragments in Turin show that in one instance an elderly woman lived in her husband's house and in another she had moved in with her son and daughter-in-law.[114]

However, texts from Deir el-Medina make it clear that children did not always support their aging parents. There are instances of older women disinheriting such ungrateful offspring[115] and we have already seen how the widow Naunakhte famously disinherited four of eight children. It is also clear that at times old people were mocked. An ostracon in the Petrie Museum in London reads: 'Do not mimic an old man and an old woman when they are decrepit; beware lest they place a curse on your old age'.[116]

The life of the widow (*ḫꜣrt*) was not always easy.[117] The ancient Egyptians themselves considered widows disadvantaged. The First Intermediate Period *Instruction to Merikare*, for example, urges 'do not oppress the widow'. *The Instruction of Amenemope* reads:

> Do not be greedy for a cubit of land,
> Nor encroach on the boundaries of a widow.
>
> . . .
>
> Do not pounce on a widow when you find her in the fields[118]
> And then fail to be patient with her reply[119]

The fact that officials boasted that they were kind to widows and orphans[120] shows that widows were considered a generally disadvantaged group, like orphans. There is no equivalent in literature of disadvantaged widowers. The disadvantaged nature of women without husbands is borne out archaeologically at Deir el-Medina, where it has been shown[121] that Eastern Necropolis, the area where poorer people tended to be buried, contained several burials of lone women.

There is a documented court case at Deir el-Medina where the widow ḥri3 (Heria) was accused of stealing a mirror and a chisel which were found in her house.[122] This shows that she at least had a house of her own. When her case came before the vizier, he was told of another instance where a woman committed a crime of theft. The vizier was asked to make an example of ḥri3 so that 'there shall be no other women like her, again to do likewise.' It is suggested that this shows that thieving women were separately categorized from thieving men, something which is borne out by other texts. This text also asks the question of whether the woman was stealing because of the dire economic straits in which she found herself. We will, of course, never know.

On a more positive note, the elderly did not lose their rights to the law; an older woman could be an executrix of her husband's will and could own property. At Deir el-Medina, at least, older women received a state pension in the form of a grain ration of one and a half sacks of grain, compared to the four given to the workmen.[123] Widows' pensions could also be transferred from one woman to another. A man writes: 'Now as for the message you had sent about your mother, stating she had died. You said: "let the wages that used to be issued to her be given to my sister, who has been a widow here for many years until today". So you said. Do so, give it to her until I return'.[124] We do not know if this was the norm.

The ancient Egyptian word for 'widow' is written with the hieroglyph of a lock of hair. According to Plutarch's version of the Osiris and Isis myth, the first act of Isis, on hearing of the death of Osiris, was to cut a lock of her hair.[125] This perhaps relates to the sexuality surrounding hair. Women's hair was necessary to stimulate their husbands, though when they became widows, this need ceased.

Women's work

Women's work was often in the home, collecting and preparing food, building and maintaining the home, taking care of children and so on. Such work included creative aspects such as production of clothing, basket-making and decorating the home. Part of the problem in looking for women's labour is that it is very difficult to equate women with specific tasks from archaeology alone, though one might argue that objects found in graves with specific genders are particularly useful. Iconography may help, but although women do not appear on tomb walls engaged in activities such as metalworking etc., this need not necessarily mean that they did not do such jobs. It may simply mean that, among the elite, it was not considered desirable that women carry out such tasks. In addition, the activities shown on tomb walls do not reflect all the activities carried out in everyday life, but are mainly high-status and/or ritual activities.

Women worked in the home, running the household and caring for children. Some did have professions, but these seem to be restricted to midwifery, textile production, mourning, priestesses of Hathor or priestess musicians. However, it also true that there were few male midwives and mourners, so it may not be the case that men had more opportunities than women, but simply that their opportunities were different.

The roles women held were not only influenced by gender, but also by their social class. While elite women could become Chantresses of Amun, and would spend much of their time running large households, non-elite women might be household servants, hairdressers and wet nurses, as well as homemakers.

Roles also varied from period to period. During the Old Kingdom, women were priestesses, buyers and sellers, gleaners and possibly even doctors. In later periods, it appears that women's roles became more restricted, with only elite women holding prestigious posts in the priesthood. From a feminist viewpoint, one could see this as a gradual usurpation of women's roles by men, though one would have to question how this came about. It is possible that the increase in specialization, and demands of literacy made by a bureaucratic state, meant that women, excluded from the realm of scribal functions whether by social or religious factors, were also increasingly excluded from other realms.

Women's trades were certainly not insignificant. For much of ancient Egyptian history, they were the chief producers in Egypt's second most important industry – textile manufacture. Throughout Egyptian history, they were vital to the running of the home and in the care of children critical to social reproduction.

While the home workplaces of women varied according to status and period, invariably the structure of the house was made of mud-brick, even if it were a palace. Sizes and arrangement of buildings varied considerably, but generally the front room/s seem to have been the public area. Behind the front rooms was an open courtyard or columned hall used communally by the family, with stairs leading to a roof area. Living quarters and store areas were at the back. One might expect that much work was carried out on the roof tops of houses, which would have the advantage of daylight. Indeed, at Amarna, spindles were found by excavators on top of roof debris, suggesting that spinning was carried out there.[1]

At the New Kingdom settlement of Deir el-Medina, the average house covered 80 m², the smallest flats about 50 m², and the largest, probably those belonging to the foremen and village administrators, 160 m² (the average semi-detached house in the UK is about 60 m²).

It has been suggested that houses contained rooms intended specifically for women and others for men.[2] At Deir el-Medina, the front rooms, replete with pictures of Bes, a deity associated with women and other female orientated scenes such as nursing or grooming women, were used by women. A similar arrangement was found at Amarna. The second room with divan was probably a male-centred room. However, it seems unlikely that small houses could have had these divisions. Scenes of nursing women in front rooms could be celebrations of childbirth and would have been enjoyed by both men and women. Besides which, given the general ideological association of women and home, we need not be surprised that the home was decorated with scenes relating to women. Unfortunately, excavations of Egyptian domestic sites have not been able to differentiate between areas of women's work and men's work by activity. Perhaps one might use the fact that most of the decoration relating to women as evidence that women had the upper hand in domestic cult activity and hence really were 'Mistresses of the House'.

What type of work did women carry out in these buildings? Unfortunately, scenes of women doing household activities were not normally put on tomb walls. Duties within the household would have varied according status. Within the smaller household, not only would the woman be responsible for the young child, but also for cleaning, weaving, cooking and grinding of grain.

From the First Intermediate Period on, it is usually women and female goddesses who provide nourishment for the deceased,[3] perhaps mirroring the gendered activities of everyday life. Women both baked and brewed in their own homes, though there was a certain amount of baking and brewing done on a larger scale in elite homes, and servants, including men, would be brought in to do this task. While in the Old Kingdom, men may be shown as bakers,[4] women have the back-breaking task of grinding corn. It is estimated[5] that it took between fifty-five minutes to one hour and twenty minutes to grind enough flour for one adult per day. At Deir el-Medina, housewives appear to have had other women carry out this task for them. Other food preparation is shown in tombs as being carried out by men, though the Eleventh Dynasty Theban tomb of Djari shows women servants engaged in food preparation.

Tomb models suggest that in large households it was men who did the brewing, but in the Middle Kingdom *Tale of the Eloquent Peasant* the merchant tells his wife, 'Look, you have twenty gallons of barley as food for you and your children. Now make for me these six gallons of barley into bread and beer for every day in which [I shall travel]'.[6] Scenes also show that in large households, men did the cooking. It seems unlikely that this was so for smaller households, where men would have been out during the day.

At Deir el-Medina, households seem not to have been large, usually consisting of fewer than five individuals.[7] Perhaps older children moved away in their teens. Additionally, there is evidence that workmen had property outside the village and may have farmed elsewhere. Family members could have worked and lived on these estates outside the village. Houses such as those of officials at Amarna and Kahun could well have contained more people. Middle Kingdom Heqanakht had a household of more than 16 people.[8] In addition to Heqanakht, the household contained the following members: five other men, his mother Ipi, her maidservant, Iutenheb, Heqanakht's wife, a maid called Senen, two women named Nefret and Satweret, the daughter of a person called May, and Nakht, the son of a person named Heti.

Within larger households, elite women would have supervised servants in cleaning, weaving, food production, grinding of grain and apportionment of domestic produce and rations. Here one would expect the woman to take on important administrative duties. In the Middle Kingdom, women could be seal bearers,[9] which seems on the surface to indicate an administrative function which was perhaps part of the state bureaucracy. However, the actual distribution of women's seal impressions at Lahun, at least, appears confined to their own homes.[10] There is a possible known exception to a household sealer in the form of lady Ib-Neith, a 'Trustworthy Sealer' of the Hathor temple in Sinai.[11]

Some activities were conducted outside the home, though they may have largely involved women whose primary role was that of housewife. These include trading, cultic singing and dancing, wet nursing, gleaning, flax-pulling, looking after animals, and so forth.

WOMEN SERVING WOMEN

Servants did not constitute one class. The title *wb3yt* (webayet, meaning 'house-maid' or 'housekeeper') was a common title in the Middle Kingdom.[12] Her authority would have depended on the size of the household, but could at times have been prestigious. Such women often lived in the family's household. At the lower end of the social scale, women appointed to grind corn for households at Deir el-Medina were probably paid very little and would have lived elsewhere, conceivably running their own households.

It seems that generally women served women and men served men, though this rule was not hard and fast. In the Old Kingdom, there were exceptions where women employed male scribes and stewards.[13] In the early New Kingdom, male and female servants wait on guests of both sexes.[14]

The general rule may be a facet of the tendency to separate men and women in ancient Egypt, at least for the purpose of tomb paintings. Dancers are usually shown performing in segregated groups, and men and women are shown mourning separately. In New Kingdom drinking parties, men and women sit separately, although husband and wife are shown together.

CONSCRIPTED LABOUR

Women, as well as men, could be conscripted into work for the king.[15] Old Kingdom papyri unusually list a group of men and women involved in temple construction work.[16] In the Twelfth Dynasty, women were brought to Thinis to work as servants. When Teti, daughter of Sa-inheret, fled from doing agricultural work, her family was conscripted in her stead. She was eventually found and her family released.

AGRICULTURE

Elite women are sometimes shown in tomb scenes working in fields. But the fact that these are upper-class women in their 'Sunday Best' suggests that this is not everyday harvesting, and was probably part of a ritual activity or intended to show an afterlife idyll. However, women were certainly involved in working the land. Elite women could be holders of agricultural land, though it is possible that men administered them,[17] while non-elite women carried out manual agrarian tasks.

In the Old Kingdom, sowing, gleaning, winnowing, sieving of grain and pulling of flax are carried out by non-elite women, but in later periods women are rarely shown doing such tasks. It is possible that women did perform such jobs later, but were simply not shown doing so. Most of the evidence relates to men. However, in the New Kingdom tomb of Nakht, women are shown carrying out agricultural tasks.

As noted in Chapter 3, women are never shown cutting, using sickles or knives. Perhaps a taboo on showing women using sharp implements existed. This would explain the lack of depictions of women in the kitchen preparing food, despite the fact that women must have cooked food for their families and women were called 'cooks', at least in the Old Kingdom.

TEXTILE PRODUCTION

Cloth production was the most common employment of ancient Egyptian women, both within the home and outside it. Oddly, perhaps, throughout Egyptian history, it was men who were professional launderers. Some have suggested men did the laundry because it was a dangerous occupation due to the threat of crocodiles along the Nile. We tend to forget that doing the laundry was an outdoor occupation, and therefore ideologically better suited to men.

Cloth was a valuable commodity, so valuable that ancient tomb robbers would often take it in preference to items of stone or metal. Cloth was needed for temple use, for furnishings, for provisioning the dead, as well as for clothing. It was at times used as a medium of exchange.[18] As a valuable source of income, it seems that in some instances, it was accumulated and traded by elite women.

In the Old Kingdom and later, women were involved in harvesting flax, pulling up the plants which provided the raw material for linen.[19] Men do not seem to have carried out this role. Likewise, throughout Egyptian history it seems that it was women who did the spinning. Spindle whorls have been found in domestic debris at Middle Kingdom Lahun and at New Kingdom Amarna. Spindle whorls and spinning bowls at New Kingdom Deir el-Medina also suggest that women spun their own thread at home. However, it was also possible to buy ready-spun flax.[20]

As discussed in Chapter 2, in the Old Kingdom, in contrast to later periods, women's textile production was recognized as particularly important. In the

Old Kingdom women not only manufactured cloth, but oversaw its production. Several women are even overseers in 'the house of weavers' (presumably a
workshop), though men also hold the same title. Women seem to have also been
primarily responsible for weaving until at least the late Middle Kingdom, though
with less prestige.

By the New Kingdom, the vertical loom had been introduced and from this
date on, tomb paintings usually show men weaving.[21] The New Kingdom tomb
of Djehutynefer shows men and women preparing thread, spinning and weaving.
However, texts from Deir el-Medina suggest that contrary to what is depicted
in tomb paintings, it was largely women who wove;[22] one of the charges against
Paneb, a foreman at Deir el-Medina, was that he ordered the wives of workmen
to weave for him. In the New Kingdom story of the *Tale of Two Brothers*, the wife
of Bata offers to make clothes for Anubis if he will sleep with her. There is other
evidence for the continued employment of women in weaving long after the
New Kingdom.[23] It is possible that women wove at home, while men tended to
carry out workshop tasks, though workshop production by women took place at
Mi-wer. We may assume, however, that women's production was largely domestic.
At Amarna, loom materials have been found in one of the large houses.[24]

One might ask why men are shown weaving from the New Kingdom onward.
While women certainly continued to make cloth, it seems unlikely that tomb
paintings do not reflect some change. It may be that the introduction of the
upright loom was somehow the impetus. Introduction of new technologies does,
at times, seem to be equated with a change in roles. For the most of the twentieth
century, women were employed as typists, using keyboards, but with the advent
of the word processor, male office workers also assumed the role of keyboard
operator. One might ask if the upright loom, as a more complex tool, perhaps
attracted men who would not have wanted to carry out such simple, though
admittedly skilled, tasks such as weaving. Alternatively, it may simply have been
the appearance of the new machine, so different from that which had gone before,
which was not quite so closely associated with women.

Excavations at Graeco-Roman Period Ismant el-Kharab, ancient Kellis, show
strong evidence for workshop textile production in the hands of both men and
women.[25] Spindles, spindle whorls, loom weights and unspun yarn indicate that
textile production was of major importance at this site. Loom weights show that
warp weighted vertical looms were used, in contrast to the non-warp weighted
types used in Pharaonic Egypt. Texts show that a weaving business was carried
out from House 3, under the direction of a woman, Tahet, and her husband
Hatres. Some of these garments were sent to the Nile Valley. Based on archaeological remains, it seems possible that other houses carried out a similar trade.

While, at times, men were involved in textile production, the feminine nature of weaving is underscored by goddesses such as Neith – albeit a goddess also associated with the less stereotypically female pursuits of hunting and warfare – who are associated with weaving (see Chapter 8). The goddess Tayet was also associated with weaving. Because women's work frequently revolved around weaving, it is apt that woven cloth was an important votive offering to Hathor, a favourite goddess of women. The textiles of the Eighteenth and Nineteenth Dynasties were offered to this goddess by both men and women[26] although women are the primary donors.

It is sometimes assumed that women's work was largely domestic production, implying that women made a little 'pin money' from a part-time job. Yet, even if such domestic production was the norm, this need not mean that it was carried out merely to augment the household income. Rather, it could have been a major, or even the major, contributor to family income. There are many societies in which items produced in the home contribute to the main income. Unfortunately, it is archaeologically difficult to differentiate between low-level production for the household and specialization in such tasks as textile production.

WOMEN AND TRADE

As we have seen, Herodotus claimed that in Egypt, 'women attend market and are employed in trade, while men stay at home and do the weaving.' As is usual with Herodotus, it is likely that he exaggerated to show how strange the Egyptians were. Even in the Roman Period, women were involved in weaving. Yet, it does seem that for much of Egyptian history women were indeed engaged in trade, unlike other contemporary regions of the ancient world.

In the Old Kingdom, women are shown selling cloth and freely engaging with men in trade, but once again, it seems men were more active in this area. There is less evidence for women's trade in later periods. The Eighteenth Dynasty tomb of Kenamun, Mayor of Thebes in the reign of Amenhotep III, shows a harbour scene.[27] Here two men and one woman seem to be selling cloth and sandals. In the Deir el-Medina tomb of Ipuy, men are shown emptying grain into women's baskets.[28] Women appear to be holding out food and one woman is perhaps selling beer. Finally, there is textual evidence that women also sold produce, such as honey,[29] from their gardens.[30]

Again, this production, being centred round home and garden, may be seen as an extension of domestic production[31] and thus, as in many other societies, not given as much value as men's production. However, it was not only women who were involved in domestic production. Workmen were likely to have taken private commissions, indeed it is estimated[32] that they could have made as much from private commissions as from state work. One might wonder how much a woman earned compared to a man.

The problem is that while we know the costs of finished goods, it is difficult to guess how much each item cost to make, and thus how much profit was made. A *mss*-garment might cost five deben,[33] while other garments might cost as much as 25 deben. (For comparison, a coffin was worth 25 deben[34] and an ivory comb two deben. Workmen made 11 deben a month[35]). However, we know that the produce of women could be considerable. A Middle Kingdom male head of a household, Heqanakht, was able to rent fields with income from cloth woven in his household and presumably also supply the household with cloth.[36] In the New Kingdom, one woman accumulated enough surplus to buy goods such as slaves[37] and when the wife of a Twentieth Dynasty tomb robber is asked where she got the money to buy slaves, she answers, 'I bought them in exchange for produce from my garden'.[38] Another woman states that she received silver 'in exchange for barley in the year of the hyenas when there was a famine'.

THE 'WISE WOMEN'

The *t3 rḫt* (ta rekhet, 'the woman who knows') is mentioned in several ostraca from the village of Deir el-Medina, and seems to have been able to identify the gods which brought misfortune, look into the future, and diagnose illness.[39] Such women were consulted by both men and women, with there being only one ta rekhet at any one time. Such women had a deep knowledge of the realms between the living, the gods and the deceased[40] and in one text the wise woman is consulted concerning the cause of death of a child.

These mysterious women are only known from New Kingdom Deir el-Medina and have no known male equivalents. It is possible, however, that they are referred to elsewhere. On the Thirtieth Dynasty Metternich-Stela, Isis is described as saying, 'I am a daughter, a knowing one (*rḫt*) in her town, who dispels a poisonous snake with her oral powers. My father has taught me knowledge'.[41]

PROSTITUTION

There is very little information concerning prostitution in ancient Egypt. In the Pharaonic literary sources, the only two people who offer to pay for sex are women, not men. In the Westcar Papyrus, the wife of the high priest sends a box of clothing to a man in the town to engage his attention and in the *Tale of Two Brothers*, the wife of Anubis offers to make her brother-in-law fine clothing if he will sleep with her. This was in a period when textiles would have acted as currency.

While there is evidence of undesirable, and possibly sexually promiscuous, women, clear evidence for female prostitution before the Graeco-Roman Period is absent. In the Nineteenth Dynasty Papyrus Anastasi IV, a father berates a scribe, 'Now you are still seated in the house and the harlots surround you; now you are standing and bouncing ... Now you are seated in front of the wench, soaked in anointing-oil ...'.[42] However, the word for harlot here is *msyt*,[43] which although usually translated as 'prostitute' or 'harlot', is never used in circumstances clearly relating to the exchange of goods for sex.[44] Papyrus Turin, discussed in Chapter 6, is often cited as evidence of a brothel. However, depictions of people having sexual intercourse cannot alone be taken as evidence of such institutions. There is also the view[45] that at least some of the love poems may refer to brothels, though again the evidence is debatable.

Evidence for payment for sex is much stronger from the Ptolemaic Period. *The Instructions of Ankhsheshonq* state, 'Man is even more eager to copulate than a donkey; his purse is what restrains him'.[46] The same papyrus suggests that prostitutes were women who wandered the streets.[47]

To the fictional Setne Khaemwes, son of Pharaoh Usermare, one hour with Tabubu, the daughter of the prophet of Bastet, was worth 10 pieces of gold:

> Setne said to the servant: "Go, say to the maid, 'It is Setne Khamwas, the son of Pharaoh Usermare, who has sent me to say, "I will give you ten pieces of gold – spend an hour with me ..."[48]

In the story, Tabubu was less offended by the proposition itself than the fact that she was being treated like 'a low woman of the street', though it may be doubted that a streetwalker would have been remunerated in such a handsome way.

It is sometimes said that in ancient Egypt prostitution was connected with female musicians and dancers. But does this supposed connection say more about Egyptologists than ancient Egyptians? There certainly was an association between music and sexuality and music for Hathor had a strong erotic element.[49] In Egyptian art, female lute players are often displayed in a sexualized way, wearing heavy wigs and accompanied by monkeys. In Mereruka's mastaba, Mereruka's wife plays a harp on their bed.[50] This has sometimes been seen as a sexualized scene. Mereruka himself holds a fly whisk of three fox skins – the hieroglyphic symbol for birth.

In the Old Kingdom, the frequency with which women are shown playing the harp suggests that this was an important role of elite women.[51] That this is not purely sexual may be suggested by the fact that it is not only the wife, but also the daughters of the deceased, who are so depicted, as can be seen in examples such as the tomb of Pepiankh at Meir.[52]

It is sometimes said that the Bes tattoo on women dancers' thighs is a symbol of prostitution, with Bes being a symbol of sexuality. However, there is no evidence that dancers were prostitutes, and Bes was associated with fertility and protection of women in childbirth. As such, he would have been important to all women. It is possible that all classes of Egyptian women were decorated with Bes tattoos (if indeed these are tattoos rather than painted symbols), but they can only be seen on the thighs of dancers due to their unclothed nature.

In Papyrus Anastasi, a contrast is drawn between the desirable life of a scribe taught to sing and chant and the undesirable life of being surrounded by prostitutes.[53] Singing was not, it seems, associated with loose living.

DOCTORS AND MIDWIVES

The stela of Lady Peseshet of the Fifth and Sixth Dynasties is known from the Giza tomb of Akhet-hotep, who was probably her son. Astonishingly, the stela names her as either a 'female overseer of female physicians' or a 'chief woman physician',[54] depending on the translation. If she is the former, this need not suggest that she was a physician, but does suggest that there were other female doctors at this time. No other female physicians are known until the Ptolemaic Period.

By contrast, midwifery appears to have been a solely female profession in ancient Egypt. That this was so is suggested by medical texts, which include gynaecological information, but do not discuss obstetrics. Additionally, men are never shown in birthing scenes, and in Papyrus Westcar, the mother is assisted in birth by four goddesses. It has been suggested that the Old Kingdom title *in't* implies a midwife and is related to the word *mnat*, meaning 'nurse'.[55] This title is not known after the Old Kingdom. In fact, there is no word for midwife after this date,[56] but this does not mean that midwives ceased to exist. The midwife may have been a friend, neighbour, or maidservant. Such women were possibly not professionally trained – there is certainly no evidence for a school of midwives – but women may have handed on their knowledge more informally.

NURSES AND TUTORS

The word *mn't* (menat, meaning 'nurse') is used from the Middle Kingdom onward, and as it is written with the breast determinative hieroglyph, it is sometimes assumed to mean 'wet nurse'. There are occasional depictions of the female title holders suckling children, such as the fragmentary statue of Hatshepsut with her nurse Sitre,[57] so at least at times a wet nurse was intended by the term *mn't*. However, this is a title also given to men, and so probably encompassed the professions of both tutors and nannies.[58] A second term, *3tyt* (atyt), can also mean nurse. One interpretation of the verb *3tyt* means to suckle, but as *3tyt* is usually written with the 'child on the lap' determinative rather than the breast, this probably means a dry nurse.[59] Besides which, male counterparts are again known. Finally, in the New Kingdom, the word *ḫnmt* (khenmet) refers to a nurse, who is usually divine.

In the New Kingdom, at least, the royal nurse was an important person, being so close to the king. Despite the fact that women's occupations are rarely shown in the tombs of their male relatives, tomb owners often show their female relatives in the role of nurses to the king.[60] Hatshepsut's nurse, Sitre, was important enough to be buried near her queen. Nurses also seem to have been held in high regard by the non-royal elite, as they are shown in private tomb chapels and on stelae with the family.[61] In the early Eighteenth Dynasty, where a man's mother held this title, she might often be given a prominent place in his tomb.[62]

Children are only shown being nursed in tombs where the wives or mothers of tomb owners are royal nurses.[63] This might suggest that either there was some ritual importance to showing nursing of royalty, or simply that being related to a royal nurse was prestigious.

With the probable likelihood of high mortality of mothers, wet nurses would have been particularly important, although of course such women would also have been invaluable for those who were unable or unwilling to feed their own children. A wet nurse at Deir el-Medina is paid in one instance as much as a doctor, though it is possible her work was provided over a much longer period of time.[64]

Legal agreements between wet nurses and parents are known from the later periods of Egyptian history. These stipulate that a wet nurse was to have a trial run before being hired; she was obliged to provide milk of a suitable quality, not to nurse any other children and not to fall pregnant or enter into sexual activity. Her employer was to pay the nurse and provide oil for massaging the child.[65]

HAIRDRESSERS AND PERFUMERS

While today we usually associate those involved in beautifying the human body with women, in ancient Egypt, several male manicurists are known. However, those associated with hair and perfume were often female. A female 'Overseer of the Wig Workshop' is known from the Old Kingdom. This lady was a high-status woman who also held the titles 'Royal Acquaintance' and 'Royal Ornament'.[66]

TREASURERS

Female treasurers are occasionally found in the Old Kingdom and in the First Intermediate Period attached to private households; sometimes, there was more than one in a household. One such woman was Treasurer Tchat.[67]

VIZIER

Viziers were second in importance to the pharaoh. In the Sixth Dynasty, the Lady Nebet, wife of Huy, was remarkably appointed by Pepi I as both judge and vizier.[68] In light of such unusual activities for a woman, it has been suggested that her husband undertook the responsibilities on her behalf.[69] Female viziers are not known again until the Ptolemaic Period when Berenice II and Cleopatra I held the titles.[70]

WOMEN AND THE COURT

There is a rare instance[71] of two women possibly acting as judges at Deir el-Medina, although it is possible that they were actually witnesses rather than judges. The other persons listed are workmen and thus not of particularly high social standing.

WOMEN DEPUTIZING FOR THEIR HUSBANDS

If husbands were unable to carry out their allotted tasks, it seems to have been acceptable – in at least some instances – for their wives to deputize. When the scribe of the Necropolis at Deir el-Medina, Nesy-su-Amen-em-ope, was absent from Thebes, it seems his wife stood in for him and supervised and checked the receipt of grain he had sent.[72]

WOMEN AND THE TEMPLE

'No woman holds priestly office, either in the service of gods or god; only men are priests in both cases'.

(Herodotus)

This may have been the case for Egyptian women in the time of Herodotus, but Herodotus contradicts himself elsewhere in texts by referring to women priests.[73] Certainly, it is true that, with a few exceptions, men held the administrative posts in the temples. This could in part be due to the fact that these roles were full-time, but is also probably predicated upon the fact that men were generally the literate ones and literacy was the key to office. However, for most of Egyptian history, women held a variety of priestly posts. In the Old Kingdom, they seem to have taken similar roles to men as 'Servants of the Gods' and were involved in providing for the cult statue. While it is true that women gradually lost such roles, for most of Egyptian history they held the important function of providing music and dance with which to revive the gods and the deceased. This task was largely, though not exclusively, carried out by women. Additionally, from the New Kingdom on, two important female sacerdotal roles emerge from the royal family, having the titles, 'God's Wife of Amun' and 'Divine Adoratrice'. Women with these titles become particularly powerful in the Third Intermediate Period, so that postholders are almost rulers of Upper Egypt in their own right.

In understanding the function of women priests, we need to realize that the role of ancient Egyptian priests was not the same as that of modern priests. In ancient Egypt, priests did not preach or care for groups of people, nor were they 'messengers of God'. The term 'priest', when applied to ancient Egypt, is a modern term covering a variety of religious offices connected with the temple or with funerary practice. There is a further problem in understanding the role of women in religion, in that while a number of women were connected with the temple, we cannot always be sure that their roles were similar to those of men, even when they appear to have held similar titles.

SERVANTS OF THE GOD

A female *ḥmt nṯr* ('Servant of the God'), would be responsible for looking after the cult statues in the temple; she would give offerings, perform liturgies, dress, anoint and feed the god. As far as we can tell, this title appears to be a female equivalent of a male role, which in the Old and Middle Kingdoms was not necessarily a full-time occupation. It is possible that some of the women seem to have kept the night vigil in the same way as men. At the Temple of Min at Akhmim, both men and women kept the night vigil.[74] The male equivalent, *ḥm nṯr*, is somewhat rarer than the female title and women seem to have been under the authority of men.

In the Old Kingdom until the Middle Kingdom, a large number of elite women were servants of the gods.[75] Usually, ladies were servants of female gods, rather than male gods, and particularly of Hathor. Less often, they were priestesses of the archer goddess, Neith. At Beni Hasan, a priestess of the lioness goddess, Pakhet, is known.[76] Even less frequently, there are occasional priestesses of male gods. Queen Meresankh was known to be a priestess of Thoth, the god of wisdom.[77] At Sixth Dynasty Akhmim, there was a lady who was a priestess of Min,[78] a god of fertility, and another who was a priestess of Ptah, a god of craftsmen.[79] There were also female priests of the mortuary cult of King Khufu.

HENUT

Other types of priesthood were also open to women. Generally *ḥnwt* (khenut) are female, though male equivalents called *ḥnwt* (khenu) are known in the Old Kingdom.[80] In the Middle Kingdom, henut were attached to the temple of Osiris at Abydos.[81] Both male gods and female gods had henut and henu. On Hatshepsut's Red Chapel in the Karnak, there are female priestesses called henut. The chief female henut was often the wife of the High Priest. So, for example, the wife of Pepiankh, nomarch of Qusae and High Priest of Hathor, was khenut of Hathor.[82]

GOD'S WIFE OF AMUN AND DIVINE ADORATRICE

As we have seen, for most periods of Egyptian history, the status of women was not equal to that of men, and it was rare for women to rule as kings. However, in the Twenty-fifth and Twenty-sixth Dynasties, we have evidence of individual women of such power that they practically ruled Upper Egypt in their own right, with the blessing of both Egyptian society as a whole and the traditional institution of male kingship. These are clear and rare exceptions to the lack of women in administrative roles. These women were the 'God's Wives of Amun'. They also took the title 'Divine Adoratrice', and were powerful individuals whose status included the cultic and the administrative.[83]

The importance of the Divine Adoratrice can be traced back to the early Eighteenth Dynasty at Karnak. Records show that it was a position held by high-status women, such as the daughter of the High Priest of Amun in the reign of Hatshepsut, or sometimes, royal women. In the reign of Thuthmose III, the title was held by the King's Principal Wife. Although we do not know what the role entailed at this date, it has been suggested that use of this title was an attempt to enhance the general power of the monarchy.

The domain of the Divine Adoratrice was an important administrative centre, with its own personnel and property. The institution of pr dw3t, 'house of the adoratrice', as shown in a Papyrus of Amenhotep II, had land and palaces in various parts of the country, including Middle Egypt. Texts show that the domain had its own treasury and produced food.[84] Administrative duties of the God's Wives were largely carried out by stewards.[85]

In the Third Intermediate Period, the title 'Divine Adoratrice' became associated with the title 'God's Wife of Amun' (ḥmt-nṯr n ʿImn), which appears to be an even higher rank. The earliest divine consort appears to have been the 'God's Wife of Min', first attested in the First Intermediate Period as a title given to non-royal priestesses.[86] The title 'God's Wife of Amun', however, does not appear until the Eighteenth Dynasty, and is confined to Thebes. It is said to refer to the impregnation of Amun's mother by the god himself.

The first royal God's Wife of Amun appears on the Donation Stela at Karnak. The same stela also records the institution of Divine Adoratrice. The title, God's Wife, appears to have been elevated by Ahmose I, along with the elevation of the city of Thebes, Amun being the most important of the Theban deities. The Donation Stela records the bestowing of the title 'God's Wife of Amun' on Ahmes Nefertari, wife of King Ahmose and mother of Amenhotep I, and also transfers the title of 'Second Priest of Amun' to her and her heirs without challenge. The title seems to have been used by this powerful woman in preference to other important titles such as 'King's Principal Wife', or 'King's Mother'. From then on, it was a royal prerogative. Ahmes Nefertari passed the title to her daughter Meritamun. It was then passed on to Hatshepsut. When Hatshepsut took on kingly titles, she gave the title 'God's Wife of Amun' to her daughter, Neferure.

The title 'God's Wife' goes out of use with the reign of Thuthmose II. Reasons for its decline are unclear, but it may be that Thutmose II deliberately reduced the importance of the title to prevent other women using it to gain power. It is reinstated in the Nineteenth and Twentieth Dynasties, and held, for example, by the daughter of Rameses VI, Aset (Isis), though when at first reintroduced, it seemed to have little importance.

By the reign of Rameses VI, it is often stated that the God's Wives had become celibate, or at least unmarried, daughters of kings or high priests of Amun. Rameses VI's daughter, Aset (Isis), is credited as being the first celibate postholder, and also with holding the title, 'Divine Adoratrice'. The practice of postholders adopting their successors is used to support the argument for celibacy; the suggestion being that as the title was hereditary, celibate postholders could only adopt successors.

However, some question the celibacy of the God's Wives. The case of Princess Maatkare-Mutemhet of the Twenty-first Dynasty has sometimes been used to support the idea that the God's Wives were not celibate. It has been claimed that she had a child which died at birth.[87] A mummified bundle found in her coffin was believed to be a child, and speculation abounded as to who the father could have been. However, the 'child' was later discovered to be a mummified baboon! The swollen abdomen of her mummy is sometimes attributed to her pregnant state; however, others claim that this is merely an effect of the embalming materials.

Moreover, adoption need not mean childlessness, but can simply be a way to pass on property or rights. Additionally, that a woman does not mention a husband or offspring on her coffin does not mean she is childless; the lack of a husband in a high-ranking woman's tomb should not be taken as unmarried status. Furthermore, there is evidence that the God's Wife, Amenirdis II, was married to a vizier called Montuemhet, and that they had a son, Nasalsa.[88] There is also a reference to Shebenwepet II, another God's Wife, also being a King's Wife. Teeter[89] concludes that if celibacy existed among any of the God's Wives, it was more concerned with politics than cultic purity, that is, it functioned to stop ambitious nobles gaining influence through marriage.

At the end of the Twentieth Dynasty, Thebes and the south were ruled by the chief priest of Amun and kings ruled the north. The title 'God's Wife' was therefore used by the female relatives of kings to retain some royal power in the south. From the Twentieth Dynasty, the titulary (formal titles and names) of the God's Wife imitated the king's double cartouche (the prenomen usually contained the name of Mut, the consort of Amun). Such women, paralleling the king, are also called 'Mistresses of Upper and Lower Egypt'. From the Twenty-first

Dynasty on, it was the king's unmarried daughter or sister who was given the title. Karomama, of the Twenty-second Dynasty, was the first God's Wife to enclose her name in a cartouche[90] like that of a king. Under Libyan rule, the God's Wife, Shepenwepet I, officiated at the Temple of Osiris, and is shown in the temple of Osiris Heqa-Djet at Karnak being suckled by a goddess, paralleling the way kings could be depicted.

Rulers from Kush, the black pharaohs, then took over. When Piankh invaded Thebes and instituted the Twenty-fifth Dynasty, he persuaded Shepenwepet I to choose his sister, Amenirdis, as successor. Amenirdis was the first Nubian God's Wife and the first to combine all three titles of God's Wife, Divine Adoratrice and God's Hand.[91] She was probably a child when she took the title, which she held for thirty or forty years. Amenirdis I then adopted Shepenwepet II as the next God's Wife. These two were the first to also adopt queenly titles such as 'Mistress of the Two Lands'.[92] It is in the Nubian Period that the role of the God's Wife was at its zenith. The God's Wives of the Twenty-fifth and Twenty-sixth Dynasties left Osirian Chapels at Karnak and unusual funerary monuments at Medinet Habu.[93] Certain elements such as the pylon façade are paralleled in temples, not tombs.

The idea that the title 'God's Wife' allowed the king some control over the south is supported by the adoption stela of Nitocris (Cairo JE 36327). Psamtek I had his daughter, Nitocris, adopted by Amenirdis II.[94] The stela states: 'I have given to him my daughter to be a God's Wife and have endowed her better than those who were before her. Surely, he will be gratified with her worship and protect the land who gave her to him.' The stela describes the vast endowment given to the postholder. It also shows that the God's Wives at this date were not always free to name their successors. The Kushite Kings may well have been required to spend time in the Sudan, and appointed God's Wives to act as government in their absence.

Persian rule finally put an end to this title in the Twenty-sixth Dynasty. The last God's Wife was Ankhnesneferibre, who was also the first woman to take the title 'High Priest of Amun'. The post then disappears, perhaps because the high status now obtained by the God's Wife threatened that of the king.

The cultic roles of the God's Wives often closely related to, or mirrored, those of kings, though presumably varied in detail over time.[95] It has been argued that the God's Wife acted, in her religious role, to sexually stimulate the male god, Amun-Re, so that he could recreate life.[96] The title, 'God's Hand', is also sometimes used as an alternative to 'God's Wife' and refers to the act of masturbation whereby Atum produced Shu and Tefnut. The word 'hand' in Egyptian was feminine. Sexual stimulation of the god was perhaps carried out through music and dance. However, this function is perhaps overplayed, as earlier 'God's Wives' also played music for goddesses.

Scenes on the Hatshepsut Red Chapel show the God's Wife of Amun, possibly Hatshepsut's daughter Neferure, performing various rituals. She is shown with a male priest burning the image of the king's enemies (on fans). She is also shown washing in the sacred lake at Karnak, worshipping gods and following the king into the temple sanctuary, the holy of holies.

From the Twenty-second Dynasty on, God's Wives are also shown presenting maat to the gods,[97] an activity usually only carried out by the king. This honour was bestowed on only one other woman, Nefertiti. In the funerary chapels at Medinet Habu, the God's Wives oversee other rituals associated with kingship, such as foundation ceremonies. The funerary chapel of Amenirdis I shows the God's Wife driving the four calves, again a ritual usually associated with the king. The God's Wife in the Twenty-fifth Dynasty Edifice of Taharqa at Karnak is shown firing arrows at four balls, possibly showing Amun's sovereignty over the four cardinal points.[98] In the same room, she is shown elevating four gods.

The costume worn by the God's Wife distinguishes her from other women. On the Eighteenth Dynasty Red Chapel at Karnak and the Twenty-fifth Dynasty Edifice of Taharqa, she wears a distinctive outfit of a sheath dress sometimes tied at the waist, a hairband knotted at the back and a short wig. The hairstyle possibly links her with Isis and Nephthys.[99] This special outfit is reminiscent of those worn by priestesses in the Middle Kingdom. After the Eighteenth Dynasty, queenly dress was also sometimes used. Later still, the God's Wife wore the vulture headdress and uraeus, with shwty plumes or falcon-tail feathers worn by Amun and Min, or alternatively the sun disk and Hathor crown on modius. Sistra, *menit*-necklaces, or flagella were carried.

PRIESTESS SINGERS AND MERET

The goddess Meret has been called 'the personification of the priestess as singer' and the goddess is usually depicted as if she were clapping. It seems that several classes of music-making priestesses, including chantresses, were identified with her.[100] Meret figures adorn the barques of kings and welcome them. They are also associated with the *sed*-festival and the role of priestesses therein. It seems likely that the term, meret, covered a wide variety of musician priestesses.

Women seem to have been employed to imitate Meret; from the Fourth Dynasty on, women called 'meret singers' are known under the male overseers.[101] Their role was to hail the king with handclapping and cry, 'he comes who brings, he comes who brings'. These women of the Old Kingdom are associated with Hathorian cults.[102] In the Ptolemaic Period, they play sistra before the gods.[103] It is possible that women with the title 'Meret' also had responsibilities towards estates, and that they looked after property and fields of the cult place.[104]

THE CHANTRESS

By the New Kingdom, the title 'Mistress of the House' is the most common for elite women; the second most common title is *šm'yt* (shemayet, meaning 'Chantress'). Such elite, though non-royal, women are shown carrying the *menit*-necklace and sistrum associated with Hathoric rituals, and appear to have been lay priestesses attached to temples. The term, 'Chantress', is usually used in a religious context. In the New Kingdom tomb of Kheruef (TT192), the Chantresses appear shaven,[105] like male priests, though later postholders wear the fashionable cloths and hairstyles of the day. Similarly, in the New Kingdom tomb of Khonsu, two Chantresses are shown bald, while others are not.[106] While there are both male and female chanters, women increasingly take the role.

A further change concerns the status and geographical origins of 'Chanters and Chantresses'. In the Middle Kingdom, the title is held by the middle classes, though by the New Kingdom, it is largely the preserve of the Theban elite. By the Rameside Period, the postholders are more socially diverse, though still largely Theban. One Chantress of Wepwawet, at Asyut, had a husband who was a lowly boatman.[107] When the Asyut women are shown in the presence of men, they are occasionally depicted of greater size (size equating with status), despite the fact that the husband may be of high status.[108] While the position was not hereditary, family connections, as well as personal piety, seem to have played some part.[109] After the Twenty-second Dynasty, the title of Chantress appears to have been in decline.

This title was not merely honorific, but demanded a service to the gods, who could be either male or female. By the New Kingdom, Chantresses were organized, like male priests, into a phyle system working in rotation in groups, one month in four. Each group would have an overseer. Chantresses in the Third Intermediate Period acted under the direction of the God's Wife of Amun.[110]

The role of the 'Chantress' appears to have been to provide music to the gods. As such, these women would accompany the king in offering to the gods in the daily liturgy; they functioned to announce the king in the *sed*-festival – perhaps taking the role of Meret – and provided music for the Beautiful Festival of the Valley. They also provided singing at private funerals.[111] That the 'Chantress' was allowed close to the king and the gods suggests that they were considered ritually pure.[112] The term 'Chantress' appears to be based on the word *šm'* (shema) which means 'to sing' or 'clap hands',[113] and indeed such women are primarily depicted as vocalists associated with percussion instruments or, less commonly, stringed instruments.

SINGERS IN THE 'INTERIOR'

Around one hundred women have the title *ḥst ḥnw n ʿImn* (Singer in the Interior of the Temple of Amun), a title known from the Twenty-second Dynasty until the Twenty-sixth Dynasty. It is assumed that these women were under the patronage of the God's Wives of Amun,[114] and at least some attained their titles in their youth. Like the God's Wives, such women are sometimes said to be celibate, although some see no evidence for this,[115] and some women, at least, had children. The interior of the temple was not open to all, so unsurprisingly many 'Singers in the Interior of the Temple' were known to come from the finest families of Thebes. Some of them served as valets or stewards to members of the ruling family. Women who held this title were the elite among a complex bureaucracy of many other women who held the title 'Singer in the Temple of Amun'.

KHENER AND DANCING

It has been said that the word *ḫnr* (khener) is related to the word meaning 'to confine', or 'constrain', and is thus associated with harems. This is, however, a mistranslation.[116] Rather, the term refers to groups, usually of women, who were singers and dancers who performed temple and funerary cultic roles, and possibly, purely entertainment roles. The translation as 'harem' is shown to be particularly inappropriate by the fact that goddesses, such as Hathor, and the female nome personification, Bat, could also have khener, and wives of elite men were known to have had roles as overseers of khener.[117] Although groups of musicians and dancers are shown in earlier times, they are not labelled as 'khener' until the Fifth Dynasty.[118] Increasingly, women performed this role.

Wealthy families and palaces, as well as temples, would have had their own entertainers.[119] In the Old Kingdom tomb of Djau at Deir el-Gabrawi, the funeral cortege includes khener dancing.[120] Khener troups were sometimes attached to funerary estates[121] and involved in Hathoric rites for the deceased. 'The Golden

One', that is, Hathor, is described as 'coming out'. An inscription above the dancers in the tomb of Nebkaure proclaims 'beautiful dancing for your *ka* every day'.[122] Khener troups seem to have been used to entertain the living king until the First Intermediate Period, but as well as providing 'pure entertainment', their role probably had religious overtones.[123] The king was, after all, also a god. In the Middle Kingdom tomb of Antifiqer's mother at Thebes, dancing is associated with the harvest. Women seemed to have played a part in khener groups belonging to temples, as is shown on the Red Chapel of Hatshepsut in the depiction of the Beautiful Festival of the Valley. Here women sing and shake sistra and hold *menit*-necklaces, accompanied by a male harpist and three men designated as a 'choir'. Other women are shown performing acrobatic dancing.

Khener troups probably provided music for women in childbirth.[124] This theory is based upon the similarity of a tool, perhaps used in cutting the umbilical cord, and the determinative for the word 'khener' (a determinative is a classifying sign written after the main body of the word to clarify its meaning). In the Sixth Dynasty tomb chapel of Princess Watetkhethor at Saqqara, female dancers are portrayed accompanied by a song which refers to childbirth; the top register is translated as, 'But see, the secret of birth! Oh pull!' Additionally, Papyrus Westcar, from the Second Intermediate Period, describes the birth of Fifth Dynasty kings accompanied by four goddesses who have disguised themselves as dancers.[125] Until recent times, in several parts of Africa, friends and relatives of a birthing mother would dance to aid delivery. One would expect that dance would also be carried out for celebration.

In early scenes, such as those in the Fourth Dynasty tomb of Debeheni at Giza, and the later Fifth Dynasty tomb of Nefer at Giza, dancers are dressed as ordinary women with cropped hair. From the Sixth Dynasty on, they wear shorter skirts and crossed bands across their chests. A Libyan origin for these outfits has been suggested[126] and so these bands are often referred to as 'Libyan bands'. Indeed, a group of dancing women wearing bands across their chests is captioned in the New Kingdom tomb of Kheruef as 'women who have been brought from the oases'.[127] In some scenes, such as in the tomb of Ibi at Deir el-Gebrawi, women are shown with a round object attached to a pigtail which they appear to be whirling around as part of the dance. A statue of such a dancer has been found at Naga-ed-Deir, from which it is clear that the circular object is a disk. However, another Middle Kingdom statue in the Berlin Museum shows a dancer wearing a ball.[128] Seated female harp players, daughters of the tomb owner, are also shown wearing such ponytails and disks/balls at the tomb of Pepiankh at Meir.[129]

WOMEN AND FUNERALS

As well as providing music for funerary rituals, for example as khener members, women also acted as mourners and 'Servants of the *ka*' at funerals. Often, it is not clear if such actions were paid, or whether they were carried out by the friends and relatives of the deceased gratis.

Women, as well as men, seemed to have performed cultic roles in funerals in the role of *ḥmt-k3* ('Servant of the *ka*'), at least during the Old Kingdom. They are also occasionally overseers of such. Servants of the *ka*, maintained offerings at tombs and, according to some, were paid for their work.[130] However, such titles held by women[131] may well have been honorary. By the New Kingdom, both men and women were engaged in performing the mortuary cult, by giving offerings and libations.[132] Women are shown in tombs offering sistra and *menit*-necklaces to the deceased. This work, however, may not have been paid. There is also one possible instance of a female *sem*-priest. (Her Twentieth Dynasty coffin is in the Metropolitan Museum of Art in New York City[133]). *Sem*-priests were responsible for the 'Opening of the Mouth Ceremony', whereby the mummified body of the deceased was brought to life. However, women were never lector priests responsible for ensuring the transfiguration of the deceased, perhaps because this would have involved maintaining maat (cosmic order), which was a masculine role, or because the lector priest read written spells, and women were not formally taught to read or write.

Importantly, women are often shown as mourners. Cross culturally, the display of grief seems to be the preserve of the female and there is some evidence that this was so in ancient Egypt. Show of emotion seems to have been frowned upon by the scribal elite with cool-headedness and reservation preferred.[134] Grieving individuals are shown throwing dust upon their heads, weeping, scratching their faces and adopting poses which we would recognize as those of grief. Such gestures are usually displayed by female relatives, though there are some instances of males doing the same.[135] For example a mourning man is shown in the Eighteenth Dynasty tomb of Kenamun (TT162).[136] It should be added that shows of emotion by men may be artificially rare as Egyptian tombs are usually those of men; therefore, their wives are shown mourning them.[137]

Men, as well as women, are however, depicted singing laments,[138] particularly in funeral processions. Textual evidence for laments shows women as more emotional;[139] they are also credited with some of the more beautiful laments. A touching lament from Merytre, mourning her husband Neferhotep at the end of the Fourteenth Dynasty says:

> ... You have gone far away;
> how can you do it?
> Alone I shall walk,
> Yet I will always be behind you.
> The one who loved to converse with me,
> You have fallen silent;
> You do not speak.

There is the possibility[140] that, in the Eighteenth Dynasty, a number of these women were singers in the divine cults, and thus may have written their own laments.

Mourning was not simply an outpouring of emotion, but seems to have been an important part of funerary ritual. Women impersonated Isis and Nephthys in funerary rituals, at least as early as the Old Kingdom,[141] acting as professional ḏrt (djert, meaning mourners or kite – the goddesses and Isis and Nephthys became kites plaintively mourning the death of Osiris) so that the deceased would be identified with Osiris. These women had to be pure and their body hair removed.[142] Other female mourners are called m3t̠ rt, but it is not known how these differ from ḏrt.

By the Thirteenth Dynasty, women acting out the cult drama of Isis and Nephthys not only mourned, but also collected the bones of Osiris, allowing him to become whole. Such women, dmḏ(y)t, are usually called 'mourners', but it has been suggested that 'bone collector' might better describe their role.[143] Women also danced in their capacity as mourners.[144] Indeed, dancing was an important part of funerary ritual and was carried out by khener troups. The role of such mourners could be hereditary.[145]

THE ROLE OF MUSIC AND DANCE

As we have seen, the role of women in religion was often to provide music and dance for religious ceremonies. Not only priestesses, but also women in general were associated with music. Wives, daughters and mothers are frequently shown shaking sistra for the deceased in the Eighteenth Dynasty.[146]

The heavy smell of incense, the rhythm of the menit-necklace and the sistra, the chanting of the female priestess musicians in the semi-gloom of the Egyptian temple are sensual experiences which we can only imagine today. While the ingredients of the incense and even the words of songs survive, the musical rhythms and their pitch and melody are all lost to us. It has been suggested that the music of the Coptic Church best approximates that heard in the Egyptian temple, though this assumes an unchanging tradition. What can be said is that the sensuality provided by the priestess musician was considered essential in soothing and reviving the gods and also in serving the deceased. There are also hints that music and dance were at times part of the ecstatic religion of ancient Egypt, and that the goddess Hathor was particularly associated with such direct communication with the gods.

The role of music and dance in the temple was essential.[147] Music was necessary in maintaining order and restoring balance. The sistrum was shaken to drive away hostile forces and revive the gods. By the Hellenistic Period, it is recounted that the Egyptians sang to the gods three or four times a day. Private stelae show individuals shaking sistra in front of the gods. Music also accompanied gods in processions and was very much associated with festivals of revival.

Music and dance were also important at the *sed*-festival, a time of renewal of the king's vitality. In the tomb of Kheruef, acrobatic female dancers are overseen by priests as they dance for King Amenhotep III, at his *sed*-festival. The king is accompanied by Queen Tiy and 'Hathor, Mistress of Dendera'. Processions such as the Opet festival, a festival of the renewal of the king's *ka*, at Luxor, show women and men accompanying the barque of the god and providing music. Music and merrymaking was an important part of the Beautiful Festival of the Valley, an apparently colourful festival which allowed the relatives of the deceased to eat and drink at the tombs in order to honour the dead.

IMPERSONATING HATHOR

Earlier, we saw how singers impersonated the goddess Meret. The production of music and dance in ancient Egypt was also heavily connected with the goddess Hathor, and hence performers would at times impersonate her.

In Fifth and Sixth Dynasty tombs, dancers singing and clapping invoke Hathor by name, or her epithet, 'The Golden One'. Texts invoking Hathor are placed above several scenes depicting khener troups as part of funerary rites.[148] Individuals are shown with lion-masked figures, possibly imitating her,[149] and the early Sixth Dynasty tomb of Mereruka, Saqqara, shows girls playing 'games', holding mirrors and hand shaped rattles and playing 'Hathor's dancing game'.

Both the *menit*-necklace and the sistrum, commonly carried by female priestesses, are instruments of Hathor. The *menit*-necklace is a heavy bead necklace, with a counterpoise at the back, which could be rattled as part of religious ceremonies. *Menit*-necklaces are given as votive offerings to the goddess[150] and in certain cases are decorated with the head of the goddess. Hathor, in her form as a cow, is usually shown wearing the *menit*-necklace counterpoise. The sistrum was also a type of rattle. Sistra are very often decorated with the head of Hathor, and the sound of the sistra was said to imitate the sound of the Hathor cow walking through the reeds of the marshes. The Egyptian word for sistra was *sesheshet*, an onomatopoeic word mimicking the rustling of reeds. In the late Old Kingdom, we have the first attestation of women offering the *menit*-necklace and sistrum to revive the deceased.[151] In the Middle Kingdom *Tale of Sinuhe*, the princesses do the same in order to welcome the prodigal back to his life in Egypt.

At Heliopolis, priestesses were referred to as Hathors.[152] In Rameside text, Hathors of the temple of Atum rejoice and play drums on account of seeing the king. In the Ptolemaic Period, female musicians playing frame drums wear horned headdresses like Hathor. 'It is quite possible to suppose that priestesses of all periods, even when they are not called Merets or Hathors, were engaged in representing the activities of the goddesses'.[153]

In the earlier periods of Egyptian history, it seems that women played similar roles to those of men in the state religion. This state of affairs seems to have altered with time so that women no longer served in the same way as men. However, throughout Egyptian history, women were particularly associated with religious music and dance, which should not be trivialized as mere entertainment, but rather seen as essential to state religion and to domestic piety. One might more controversially venture that music and dance were at times used in the service of gods, particularly of Hathor, in order to commune with the goddess. This aspect is discussed more fully in the chapter on goddesses.

6

Sexuality, art and religion

Sexuality has often been seen as unworthy of study, not simply because of prudish notions that it should not be discussed in polite society, but also because it is seen as identical across societies. The argument goes that if it is the same everywhere, why study it? However, sexuality is not only differently expressed, and has different effects and influences from culture to culture, but also invariably shapes our identity. It is thus essential in understanding other societies. Before exploring ancient Egyptian sexuality, there should be a word or two on definitions. In this book, the terms 'fertility' and 'sexuality' are often interchanged since it is very difficult to differentiate between what would have been considered 'sexual' in the sense of encouraging procreation or fertility and what would have been considered purely 'pornographic' in the ancient world. However, to us, the two concepts have different connotations. Fertility concerns sexual practice with the addition of the notion of procreation. Sexuality concerns beliefs and practices which revolve around gender.

Evidence for ancient Egyptian sexuality is far from straightforward. On the one hand, we have explicit 'erotic cartoons', probably manufactured for private amusement. Since these show little more than the sexual act itself, they do not explain the wider social and religious meanings surrounding sexuality. On the other hand, we have the coded 'high art' of temple and tomb, and because sexuality is not obvious here, some Egyptologists have even labelled the Egyptians 'prudish'. Further problems are posed by different media of evidence. Textual evidence includes sensuous love poems, comparable to the Biblical *Song of Songs*, myths and stories of gods, goddesses and human affairs, letters and medical papyri. But this evidence largely pertains to the elite, and most of it only describes the ideal or mythical. Archaeological finds including 'votive phalli' and 'concubine figurines' can all have so many different, sometimes opposing, interpretations.

However, all evidence points to the idea that Egyptian gender was basically dualistic, depending upon the opposites of male and female. In exceptional circumstances, gender fluidity was possible; homosexuality was recognized but frowned upon; androgyny among the gods was largely a means of explaining primeval creation. Men were considered the lead actors in procreation, with women acting as Hathoric enchanters, stimulating and nurturing the male seed. Sexuality could be the subject of bawdy humour, or a sacred activity embedded in beliefs of creation and rebirth.

Sexuality was essential to religion and to human rebirth, which is perhaps a strange concept in the Twenty-first century west. Mothers, wives and daughters are largely portrayed in tombs as erotic symbols, that is, beautiful and powerful sexual stimulators, mirroring the allure of the goddess Hathor. In order to be reborn, men and women had to identify with the male god, Osiris, and Osiris' sexual stimulation by his sister and wife, Isis, was a necessary component of afterlife existence. But where does this Osirian identification leave the woman in her desire for rebirth? How can a woman be reborn and retain her sexuality if she must identify with Osiris? As we shall see, the Egyptians employed various means to solve this conundrum.

SEXUALITY AND THE EROTIC

If sexuality is defined as a group of biological and mental entities including fantasy, reproduction and gender identity, this complexity makes it difficult to prove that sexuality as a distinct categorization existed for the Egyptians. It has even been argued[1] that sexuality is a recent construct, and certainly there is no Egyptian word for it.[2] However, we can still discuss the ideas and practices which the ancient Egyptians related to gender and reproduction, and which we would call 'sexuality'.

We need to be careful, however, not to impose our own ideas when interpreting the past. Eroticism outside our own society is difficult to study. In the modern west, the act of childbirth is rarely seen as erotic, though it is closely connected with sexuality and, of course, fertility. In our society, see-through clothing may be considered erotic, but does not necessarily imply fertility. The Egyptians, however, appear not to have separated out the erotic and procreative in the same way that we do. The Bes deity was associated with young children and with women in childbirth, but he also appears on the thighs of semi-clad, beautiful girls. Was he an erotic stimulator, or a symbol of fertility? He seems to have been both. Hence, in this book, words such as 'sexuality', 'erotic' or 'fertility' are only used loosely.

SEXUAL IDENTITY

It has been suggested that, in ancient Egypt, individuals were not defined by their sexuality.[3] However, categorizations of people did exist based on gender and sexual activity, and as we have seen, gender shaped people's lives, including their professions and social relations. Among living humans, two genders were recognized, male (s) and female (ḥmt), though some Egyptologists would also include eunuchs (sḫt). Homosexuality, or at least same-sex relations, were recognized, but abhorred. Among the gods, androgyny was also a factor, and for human females a certain amount of gender fluidity was essential for rebirth. This gender fluidity extended to rulers. However, Egyptian society and the world of the gods was largely dualistic and heteronormative. The male was aggressive and active; he was a person who produced children through taking the active role in intercourse.[4] Women were there to encourage, support and nurture the male lead.

THE CREATIVE POWER OF THE MALE

In most societies, procreation is considered to be in the hands of women, and in the west this is apparent in the terms 'Mother Earth' and 'Mother Nature'. For some, this aspect of femininity is at the heart of women's power. There is also a negative side: cross culturally, women tend to be considered at fault if couples cannot produce children. One study concludes that over 50 per cent of societies under consideration had negative attitudes towards women who did not bear children,[5] and it is women who are subject to treatment to correct such faults. Unusually, in Egypt, it was men who were central to procreation.[6] This has given rise to the idea that Egyptian society was phallocentric.[7] Some see the importance of the male in fertility as mirroring the Egyptian landscape and agricultural cycle.[8] For the Egyptians, both the earth and the annual inundation that fertilized the land were male.

The ancient Egyptians clearly realized that sperm was necessary for birth and believed it to be the creative aspect. They also knew that semen was connected with the testicles, though did not understand how it got there and assumed it came from the bones.[9] In comparison, the reproductive anatomy of the female was much less understood, perhaps because it was considered less vital. The word for 'to conceive a child' in ancient Egyptian was the same as the word 'to receive' or 'to take', showing the role of the woman as simply a vessel for the already created child. Thus, although childless women could be divorced, failure to conceive was not laid entirely at the door of women. The creative power of the human male, though mythical, is demonstrated in the New Kingdom *Tale of Two Brothers* (Papyrus D'Orbiney British Museum EA 10183[10]). Bata, the hero, transforms himself into a tree. He then impregnates his wife when a splinter of the wood from the tree flies into her mouth. This causes her to give birth to Bata. In a text relating to actual people, the scribe Nekhemmut from New Kingdom Deir el-Medina is berated for being unable to make his wife pregnant: 'You are not a man since you are unable to make your wives pregnant like your fellow men' (Ostracon Berlin 10627[11]). This idea of the procreative male could also be extended to the animal world; all scarab beetles, for example, were believed to be male.[12] It is only in the Graeco-Roman Period that the female is given credit for the forming of a child. While, as stated below, the male god Khnum, the potter, is credited with creation and birth of children through spinning his wheel, by the Graeco-Roman Period, Hathor is sometimes credited with spinning the wheel.[13] Another text from this period states that the bones of a child are formed by the father and the soft body parts by the mother.[14]

The creative power of the male extended to the world of the gods. In order to be reborn, the deceased Egyptian needed to become identified with the male god Osiris. The reborn individual, regardless of gender, was for most of Egyptian history known as 'The Osiris N' ('N' standing for the name of the once living person). The identification of the female with the male Osiris gave rise to what might be seen as bizarre depictions of female rebirth. A necessary part of the rebirth process, for example, is the resexualization of the god, Osiris, frequently displayed as the mummiform Osiris lying upon a bed while Isis, his sister and wife, hovers in bird-form (as a kite) above his phallus, stimulating it into life. For this reason, the body of Tutankhamun was mummified with his penis in the erect position.[15] The inert form of Osiris, despite his erect phallus, and the bird-form of the female, preserve the decorum of religious art, keeping the gods dignified. Surprisingly perhaps, this motif was also used for the revival of the deceased female, with the female bird hovering above the genital area. However, there are no depictions of deceased women displaying an erect phallus.

Creation myths, many of which mirror ideas of human birth and rebirth, also privileged the male role. In the cyclical rebirth of the sun-god, Re-Atum sails across the sky in his boat to enter the mouth of the goddess Nut, and be reborn daily from her vulva (*Pyramid Text* 1688b). He thereby impregnates her in the west and is reborn from her body in the east. Re-Atum is the active participant; Nut does not affect the sun.[16] This was mirrored in human rebirth, where the coffin was associated with Nut. Coffins were painted with depictions of this goddess so that she cocooned the deceased prior to his/her rebirth. The deceased was seen as Re-Atum, with Nut as the mother.

From at least as early as the New Kingdom, Khnum, a male god, is credited with creation and the birth of children through spinning his potter's wheel.[17] A Late Period to Graeco-Roman rite, called the 'Transmission of the Wheel to Female Beings',[18] asks for the wheel of Khnum to be established in the body of all female beings. Since Khnum is male, creation remains essentially male. The centrality of Khnum's work is described: 'May you model on the wheel in heaven, making potter's work on earth, so that children are brought to life within the wombs of their mothers by the action of your arms'.[19] The female womb is paralleled with the kiln.[20]

Eunuchs, of course, were incapable of reproduction. As most references to them come from myth and legend rather than actual living people,[21] it is believed they were rare in Egypt. So, for example, self-castration appears in the *Tale of Two Brothers* (Papyrus D'Orbiney British Museum EA 10183[22]). However, this is a fantastical story in which the hero at one point becomes a bull and in another point a woman is made pregnant by swallowing a splinter of wood; it is not a factual tale of real people.

HOMOSEXUALITY

The living together of man and wife and production of children was the norm for Egyptian society. This does not mean that same-sex relationships did not exist.[23] Homosexuality was recognized, though frowned upon.

Egypt may lay claim to one of the earliest known examples of a socially acceptable same-sex couple. Dating to the third millennium BC, the Saqqara tomb of two manicurists, Niankhkhnum and Khnumhotep, it has been claimed, depicts the first 'gay kiss'.[24] Certainly, the two men are shown in close affectionate embraces, and Khnumhotep appears to be portrayed using motifs usually reserved for women, such as smelling lotuses and standing at the left of the male. However, while this tomb may, in its construction and decoration, show acceptance of same-sex relationships, later texts show that males who were sexually penetrated by other males, were termed 'backturners' (*ḥmiw*) or 'fucked man' (*nkkw*). The word *ḥmiw*, which can also be understood as 'coward', is probably related to the word for woman, underlining the essentially passive nature of women. In the story of *Contendings of Horus and Seth* (Papyrus Chester Beatty I, Recto[25]), Seth claims to have taken the active role in their homosexual intercourse. Horus is spat upon by the other gods, while Seth appears proud of his actions. It seems that Horus' transgression lay, not in homosexual activity, but in being the passive partner. Elsewhere, a Middle Kingdom story (the *Tale of Neferkare and Sasenet*[26]) recounts how Pepi II visited the house of a general 'in whose entire house was no woman'. In this story, the whole incident is seen as a joke.

In contrast to male homosexuality, there appears little evidence of female homosexuality. There is a reference in a Late Period dream manual (Papyrus Carlsberg XIII b 2, 33) to the effect that dreaming of one's wife copulating with another woman is bad.[27] Kasia Szpakowska sees this as an admonishment of infidelity – sleeping with another man's wife – rather than an admonishment of lesbian acts.[28]

ANDROGYNY

Androgyny is here defined as gender ambiguity, rather than display of dual sexual characteristics. The Egyptians, in their essentially dualistic categorization of gender, did not have a word for androgyny; nevertheless, there is blurring of gender boundaries, particularly in areas concerning creation. As rebirth required both male and female, androgyny was essential where creation was attributable to only one entity, such as a primeval god without a partner, or a king wishing to identify with a primeval god. It was also necessary for female rebirth where the woman needed to become the male god, Osiris.

Primeval gods – gods at the beginning of time – existed alone, without partners. This created a paradox for the Egyptian mind. How could creation occur without male and female? The solution was androgyny,[29] though many androgynous gods were still essentially male or female.

The earliest texts, the *Pyramid Texts*, were first written down in the Fifth Dynasty, though may well have been used orally much earlier. Here creation is a male act by a lone god, and thus, one might say, an androgynous god. In *Pyramid Text* Utterance 527, 'Atum is he who (once) came into being, who masturbated in The On [Heliopolis]. He took his phallus in his grasp that he might create orgasm by means of it, and so were born the twins Shu and Tefnet'.[30] In the Late Period–Early Ptolemaic Papyrus Bremner-Rhind, Atum says 'I acted as husband with my fist, I copulated with my hand'.[31] In the New Kingdom, the god Amun comes to the fore. Amun bears the title 'bull of his mother', he is the god who creates all, including himself. In the Memphite Theology of the Rameside Period, the male god Ptah creates through his heart and his mouth.[32]

Essentially, male gods are difficult to portray as androgynous in sculpture or two-dimensional representations, and hence are depicted as dual-gendered, either by titles such as 'the mother and father', or by bizarre stories of birth through vomiting, sneezing or spitting (for example, *Pyramid Text* 600). The sun-god Re was said to have created humankind from his sweat or tears. The Egyptian word for people, *rmṯ*, comes from the word for tears – humankind was created from the tears of the god.

It is noticeable that several male creator gods employ organs which are both creative and feminine. This makes creation essentially the product of a male god. While 'hand of Atum' *ḏrt* (djeret) is female, masturbation by the god is essentially a sexual union with himself. By the Eighteenth Dynasty, the hand of the god is an epithet for goddesses, frequently Hathor,[33] and is a title given to priestesses.[34] Similarly, during the New Kingdom Amarna Period, the sun's disk, the male Aten, had rays which were understood as female, sometimes ending in hands. The king, Akhenaten, referred to this god as 'father and mother of his creation'.[35] However, one Egyptologist has suggested that there may be less androgyny in both the Aten and Akhenaten than is usually claimed.[36] Finally, the Eye of Re/Horus is the female creative aspect of a male god, though shown in art as a separate being.

While kings were essentially masculine, as divine and creative beings, androgyny could be extended to them.[37] This can be demonstrated in several ways. The king's titulary (all kings were given a series of titles) included his two ladies name. A Middle Kingdom hymn to Senusret III described him as the goddess Sekhmet.[38] The feminized shape of Akhenaten, as shown in art of the Amarna Period with pendulous breasts and wide hips, is sometimes considered to be a representation of disease or genetic disorder. Others have seen this as indicating androgyny[39] – his self presentation as the 'mother and father' of his people. Certainly, the fact that not only Akhenaten, but also the rest of his court display the same feminized traits, suggests something other than a genetic disorder or disease. Androgyny presents the king as a divine creator, a role which Akhenaten particularly stressed, taking several epithets of the creator god.[40] This androgynous trend in ideology of kingship is earlier evident under his father, Amenhotep III, who was also sometimes depicted in a feminine manner.[41]

Only one well-known creation myth, the Hermopolitan creation myth, suggests a more equally male and female creation. The earliest text of this dates to the Middle Kingdom and describes the uniform substance at the beginning of time (the Ogdoad), characterized by eight gods, four male and four female. In this text, neither male nor female is seen as pre-eminent.

So what is the role of the female god? Goddesses such as Hathor and Isis are sometimes considered 'fertility goddesses'. However, they are not;[42] rather, their role is to arouse the male god, to act as a vessel and to be a nurturing mother. Female goddesses rarely, in themselves, create and where they do, these are primeval goddesses and/or very often an aspect of a male god. The idea of an explicitly androgynous, but essentially female, goddess does not appear until the Eighteenth Dynasty and becomes particularly salient in the Late Period.

The creative power of the Eye of Re/Horus (the two could be interchanged), symbolized in the uraeus and the crown, and personified as the daughter of Re, includes goddesses such as Hathor, Mut and Sekhmet. The Eye as an agent of renewal, and thus creativity, as well as aggression, is apparent from the Old Kingdom.[43] Its character becomes increasingly explicit, and may have encouraged the emergence of the androgynous female creator goddesses, which are apparent from the New Kingdom. Very often, these goddesses are shown with the head of a lioness, probably symbolizing their aggressive characteristics. To what extent they were considered separate entities, or a part of the male god, we shall never know, though they are depicted in art as individuals detached from the male god.

Female gods may easily be portrayed in art as androgynous by the addition of an erect and overlarge phallus, not only a symbol of the ability to procreate, but also a symbol of power.[44] Examples include the ithyphallic goddess Mut from the *Book of the Dead* 164, dating from the Twenty-first Dynasty.[45] At the Graeco-Roman Temple of Hibis, Mut is depicted as an ithyphallic lioness-headed goddess[46] similar to an unnamed god/goddess in the temple of Khonsu at Karnak. Mut may at times be considered a primeval goddess, and is even given the name of Atemet – a primeval female version of Atum, the god who creates through masturbation. A text on the propylon of Khonsu at Karnak names her as 'the Mother who does not have a mother' and 'the Mother who gave birth to her father', that is, Mut is self-creating.[47] The goddess Neith, another primeval goddess, is given androgynous characteristics from the New Kingdom onward and a Roman text at Esna describes her as two thirds male.[48]

Female rulers are given the attributes of essentially male kingship such as false beards (the beard is also false when worn by male kings) and kilts. But depictions of female queens, such as Sobekneferu or Hatshepsut, wearing male attire should certainly not be seen as evidence of transvestism or mythical androgyny. Female kings were rather taking on a male persona, given the essential masculinity of kingship.

Some have seen the pendulous breasts and stomach of the Nile deity Hapi as androgynous. This is not, however, a sexual androgyny, but more an aspect of fecundity; Hapi is portrayed as an overweight male, symbolizing the fruitfulness and plenty brought by the Nile.[49] Likewise, there is debate over depictions of the usually male Bes-type deities, who occasionally seem to have breasts. Bes depictions with breasts are accepted as female for the Graeco-Roman Period, but Egyptologists dispute the belief that earlier depictions of Bes are female, preferring instead to see a fecundity aspect.[50] However, at least two wooden figures with

Bes faces are known from the Middle Kingdom,[51] and these are clearly female, as shown by their slim waists, breasts and lack of phalli. There is no evidence to support the idea that these are women wearing male Bes masks. Why should such magical items show a person with a deity's mask rather than the deity itself?

WERE THE EGYPTIANS PRUDES?

The idea that the Egyptians were prudish is suggested by the general lack of sexually explicit scenes in 'high art', that is, the art of the elite usually displayed in temples and tombs. However, sexually explicit scenes certainly do occur, and tales of penetrative sex are extant in elite literature. It seems unlikely that the Egyptians were any more embarrassed by sexual activity than other cultures.

The earliest known pharaonic Egyptian depiction of a couple engaged in sexual intercourse occurs in the tomb of Khety at Middle Kingdom Beni Hasan.[52] Here, a hieroglyphic sign shows a couple on a bed, with the man lying atop the woman. Presumably, as this was a standard hieroglyph, we may assume that this scene was the way the ancient Egyptians imagined typical sexual intercourse. The position, with male on top, is referred to in the *Coffin Texts* (Spell 576). However, depictions on the Turin Erotic Papyrus, as well as on ostraca and graffiti, show less conventional poses.

OSTRACA AND THE TURIN PAPYRUS

While the depictions on tomb walls may be classed as idealized, and largely for religious purposes, there are ostraca from New Kingdom Deir el-Medina which appear more informal in execution. Those depicting sexual activity are explicit, not coded. Since it is likely that these were crafted by the men of the village, they presumably show the male viewpoint.

The several hundred ostraca from Deir el-Medina have been found in houses, chapels and tombs. Not all examples could be classed as erotic. Some borderline erotic scenes depict naked servant girls, musicians and dancers, but it is unclear if these had sexual meaning in the past. Others are more obviously satirical erotic pieces showing fat, old, bald men coupling with young women. The women are replete with erotic motifs such as heavy wigs and hip girdles, and invariably take a passive pose in couplings. Frequently, intercourse is depicted as penetration from behind, though whether anal or vaginal is unclear. Finally, some pieces simply show genital organs, or nursing mothers.

On some of these ostraca, as on other objects showing scenes of an erotic nature, such as a dish showing a semi-nude lute player, a monkey or an ape is depicted. It is also noticeable that on some ostraca the woman shown engaged in sexual intercourse may be shown with an ape-like muzzle.[53] Such a depiction, but with both male and female shown with ape-like faces, is also evident on an inscription from Wadi Hammamat. Egyptologists generally agree that the ape or monkey is an erotic symbol. Elsewhere, apes and monkeys are displayed as though mimicking human behaviour such as at Amarna, where small limestone groups of monkeys are shown grooming their young, it is sometimes said, in satire of the royal family. Perhaps the depiction of women with ape-like muzzles is also satirical, indicating a bawdy sense of humour on the part of the Egyptians.

One may wonder quite why these ostraca were produced. Were they merely for entertainment or male fantasies? Or, were they produced with some magico-religious end in mind, or even given as votive offerings to gods and goddesses, especially since some were found in chapels? It is possible that different ostraca had different functions. Only one example includes a child adjacent to a coupling scene,[54] which might suggest that these pieces were not produced with the aim of magically inducing fertility, but rather that the sexual act itself was important. Interestingly, many examples show little differentiation between the male and female,[55] unlike formal art of the period. This enforces the idea that with this class of object, it was not social ideals, but the act of sexual intercourse, which was important.

The sexual acts depicted on the ostraca mirror those in the famous Turin Erotic Papyrus (Papyrus 5501), the only extant Egyptian papyrus showing explicit sexual activity. It is believed to have been painted in the Rameside period (1292–1075 BC) by a professional scribe.[56] The fact that this work is on papyrus, and well drawn, suggests it was intended for an elite audience. The papyrus scroll, which is about 259 cm long, consists of several vignettes; some vignettes are of animals carrying out human tasks and some of people in sexual poses. The men have enlarged genitals and balding heads, they are unshaven, and generally appear unkempt and older than the women. The women are young, elegant and naked except for bracelets, necklaces, lotuses in their hair and girdles around their waists. Sexual poses are varied, and three of seven sexual scenes show coitus from the rear. In one, the male is standing holding the female while she has her legs around his neck. The women are not inactive, and in one vignette the woman appears to mock an exhausted lover, who has apparently fallen out of bed and is crawling away. She asks, 'Am I doing anything wrong to you?' One wonders if this reflects a male fear of female sexuality, ridiculing the dominant ideas of male superiority and sexual prowess. Certainly, the idea of the femme fatale discussed in Chapter 3 would suggest that the Egyptians had such a fear.

Most Egyptologists agree that neither the Turin Papyrus, nor the ostraca, had any sacred significance, though this option need not be entirely ruled out. It has been suggested that the Turin Papyrus, in particular, was a humorous satire on human behaviour. In some ways it is similar to the so-called 'Satirical Papyrus' in the British Museum, which shows animals engaged in the human activities normally shown on tomb paintings, such as a lion mummifying a corpse. And indeed, part of the Turin Papyrus shows animals engaged in human activities. However, any humour in the ostraca and Turin Papyrus need not necessarily be satirical, but may indicate that the Egyptians also understood the bawdy humour which can surround human sexual acts. This idea is also suggested in the story of Re's laughter at witnessing Hathor expose herself, which will be explored later.

HIGH ART AND CODED MESSAGES

Many Egyptologists believe that eroticism is displayed in Egyptian 'high' art through coded imagery and word play.[57] This hidden coding makes sexual imagery difficult to identify; indeed, one sometimes wonders if Egyptologists' identifications of sexual interaction between couples are over-interpretations. Other Egyptologists disagree that there are encoded messages in Egyptian art.[58]

Certainly, gestures of affection between couples who appear lost in one another's gaze, with the woman embracing, supporting or affectionately touching, do not necessarily have a purely erotic meaning. Such interaction may be alternatively interpreted as display of power relations. Kings are shown acting in such an affectionate manner toward gods,[59] with the lesser partner embracing the more powerful.

The 'coding', at first glance, is as well hidden as the phalli of the male elite. In tombs and temples and upon papyri, the male elite are almost invariably shown with covered genitalia, though attention might be drawn to this area through strangely sticking out, voluminous kilts. Those males shown naked are usually field labourers, boatmen, or children, and all non-elite exposed males are shown with a flaccid penis.

Sexual activity by gods is only subtly hinted at, though there is one extraordinary instance of Geb auto-fellating, which appears on the Third Intermediate religious papyrus of the Chantress of Amun, Henuttawy[60] (British Museum EA 10018). In temples and on coffins, representations of the reanimation of the phallus of the reborn Osiris, through the stimulation of his sister/wife, is depicted by a small bird hovering above the genital region of the god. While the phallus is frequently displayed, it is usually unnaturally large, and frequently testicles are not depicted, as with Egyptian art generally, a symbolic rather than lifelike representation. Moreover, depictions of ithyphallic gods are confined to the realm of the religious, where they would be seen by only a few, usually elite, males.

Several ancient Egyptian words use the phallus hieroglyph as the determinative (the glyph indicating the categorization of the preceding word), but the glyph for female genitalia is used infrequently. Perhaps decorum inhibited explicit reference to female sexuality.[61] The erect phallus, however, was not simply a symbol of male sexuality, but also of power. Rather than suggesting a taboo on female sexuality, it is possible that the male member was considered particularly important. Perhaps it is hidden though suggested on depictions of male elite because it is powerful. In Egyptian art, gods are frequently hidden from view by a cloth or shrine.

In tombs and temples, women are often shown semi-naked. However, these are rarely elite women, but rather adolescent servant girls. Elite women are almost always clothed, though their bodies may be depicted in outline. Even the pregnant female form of the elite is underplayed, despite the fact that fertility was highly desirable. In Birth Houses connected to temples, buildings in which the conception and birth of kings is subtly indicated, the pregnant mother does not proudly display her rounded belly, but only sports a tiny bump. This clothed nature of elite women extends to deities. With the exception of Nut, the sky goddess, female deities are rarely shown naked. Even Hathor, goddess of love and sexuality, is depicted clothed. However, the clothing of elite women, the settings in which they are depicted, and the roles in which they are shown, frequently convey a coded eroticism.

In art, elite women, while clothed, are heavily sexualized. They wear diaphanous or gaping outfits or tight-fitting clothes, in contrast to the loose clothing in which men stride forth. In tight clothing the woman is forced to be passive, and in the case of both restrictive clothing, and diaphanous dresses, the shape of the female body is clearly suggested. However, clothing found in tombs suggests that the more common form of female Egyptian clothing was loose-fitting and opaque.[62] Elite women may also be shown with the symbols of Hathor, particularly the *menit*-necklace, a symbol of her sexuality. The shape of the *menit* counterpoise arguably imitates and emphasised the female uterine form.

Women are usually shown as young and slender in ancient Egyptian imagery, but men can be shown as fat. It seems that, for the tomb, it was important for women to appear desirable and youthful, whereas for men, fat was perhaps associated with wealth. There are occasional exceptions. An old woman is depicted as thin with sagging breasts on an Eighth Dynasty false door from

Busaris, although at the top of the door she conforms to the stereotype of the slender young woman, as we saw in Chapter 2.

Several activities have been decoded to imply sexual interaction between elites, including scenes of shooting arrows or pouring liquids. A queen pouring liquid into the hands of a king, as for example on the small golden shrine of Tutankhamun, suggests ejaculation; the word meaning 'to pour' is the same as the word meaning 'to ejaculate' (*sti*). The same word is used to describe the shooting of an arrow, as carried out by the king.

In Chapter 4, the marking of age by hairstyles was mentioned. Elite women may be shown wearing heavy wigs or have their hair dressed by servants.[63] This is a symbol of status, as well as an erotic signifier. It is often assumed that in ancient Egypt, both men and women shaved their heads and wore wigs. However, at least at New Kingdom Deir el-Medina, both sexes had their own hair and women's hair was long.[64] At Deir el-Medina, only one tomb among several hundred contained a wig.[65]

In many cultures, hair is highly eroticised and the same seems to have been so for the ancient Egyptians.[66] 'Don your wig for a happy hour' is a loose quotation from *The Tale of Two Brothers* (Papyrus D'Orbiney, British Museum EA 10183[67]). In the story, a woman accuses a man of seducing her, and claims he had asked her to put on her wig (or an alternative translation is 'loosen braids') so that they may spend time lying together. The motif of the heavy wig appears in scenes of an erotic or sexual nature, such as the Turin Erotic Papyrus, and widows cut a lock of their hair, perhaps symbolizing their loss of sexual activity. Naked adolescent girls may be depicted swimming while wearing heavy wigs. The fact that such wigs would be totally unsuitable swimming attire suggests they had a symbolic importance.

Servant girls, dancers and musicians are more explicitly sexualized. The association of sexuality and music was discussed in Chapter 5. Not only do servant girls and dancers wear heavy wigs, they may also be shown as naked or semi-naked save for a girdle or other jewellery. This girdle was only worn by males until the Twelfth Dynasty, but is later associated with women. Cowrie shell bead girdles are found in the tomb of queens of the Twelfth Dynasty,[68] and it has been suggested that such shells were particularly popular because their shape mimicked female genitalia. The genre of the adolescent servant girl, often with hip girdle and heavy wig, makes an appearance in the Eighteenth Dynasty. The hip girdle appears on the women on the Turin Erotic Papyrus and upon dancers. Some girdles had metal pellets which would have rattled (seductively?) with movement, plausibly linking the sound with Hathorian sistra.[69] All of this might suggest an erotic coding. However, the girdle is also worn by respectable noblewomen such as Senebtisi.[70]

In art, the lotus is associated with both the elite and the non-elite, while the mandrake, which is particularly evident from the Eighteenth Dynasty, is largely a plant associated with the elite. Both seem to have similar erotic associations. In the Old Kingdom, it is usually the woman who is associated with the lotus, though later men are shown holding the plant. By the Twenty-first Dynasty, while lotus flowers are only attested for women on statuary, on Twenty-first Dynasty coffins men may wear them.[71] In the New Kingdom, mandrake fruit are shown being held and sniffed by women, and in love poems are compared to a woman's breasts:

> The mouth of my beloved is like a lotus bud
> Her breasts like mandrake fruits . . .[72]

While one would assume that, as both men and women wore make-up, both sexes would have needed mirrors. Mirrors, however, were predominantly associated with women.[73] They were included as funerary goods for men, but mirrors are rarely shown held by, or in front of, a man. Also, most mirrors were inscribed for women. Mirror dances are portrayed in tombs as being carried out by young women. It has been suggested that women may have been associated with mirrors because of the link between mirrors and Hathor.[74] However, we cannot associate all things to do with women as sexual, and the link between women and mirrors may have been related to the more general link between women and grooming.

There are several depictions of women having their hair arranged, but none of men. While men and women both used eye make-up, there are no depictions of men applying make-up, but many of women doing so. This, together with the depiction of application of make-up in the Turin Erotic Papyrus, has led to the suggestion that make-up for women had sexual overtones.

The climbing or trailing plant usually identified as convolvulus appears to be associated with both women and fertility. It appears in the Turin Erotic Papyrus, and on depictions of women nursing young children on 'Wochenlaube' scenes. It is also shown on women's coffins, such as on the Nineteenth Dynasty coffin of Iset, where it is held by the deceased (the coffin of Iset in Cairo Egyptian Museum JE 27309).[75]

Sexual coding also includes Bes, a deity, or rather group of deities, depicted as a dwarf with a leonine face and tail.[76] In the past some Egyptologists have even associated Bes with prostitutes[77] despite the fact that, as shown in Chapter 5, there is little evidence for prostitution in Pharaonic Egypt. While Bes may not necessarily have had erotic overtones, and the history of the group of deities shows various guises, usually Bes deities are protective and related to women and young children. In a limestone relief of c.2400 BC, a male figure is shown with a lion head in a register called 'dancing with children'. In the Middle Kingdom, a leonine dwarf appears with the label Aha 'the fighting deity' on carved 'magic wands' used in childbirth. In the Eighteenth Dynasty and later he appears in amuletic form. These amulets were worn in life, mainly by women and children, but also appear in the tomb. He is shown on scenes of royal birth on the walls of temples, and is associated with bedroom furniture, appearing on beds, headrests, chairs, mirror handles and other cosmetic items. It is, however, not until later periods that the lion-maned dwarf god and his female counterpart are named as Bes and Beset.

In the New Kingdom, Bes is often shown connected with domestic buildings, such as at Deir el-Medina. In the houses he is painted on walls. Bes is also depicted as a tattoo, body paint or scarification (the medium is not certain despite the fact that these decorations are usually said to be tattoos) on the thighs of swimming girls and on reliefs depicting dancers, and musicians. Some Egyptologists have suggested that the Bes mark was only worn by dancers, but others[78] have shown that this was not the case.

TATTOOS, SEX AND DANCING GIRLS

In 1891, two ancient Egyptian female mummies were uncovered from Middle Kingdom Deir el-Bahri; they bore tattoos of geometrically arranged dots and dashes. Their burial places were adjacent to those of a number of ladies who held the title 'King's Wife' and thus, the tattooed ladies were considered to be members of the king's harem. A few years later, another two female mummies were discovered in the same region. The decorations on the bodies bore striking resemblance to faience and wooden figurines of barely clothed women of the same period. Egyptologists noticed that from the New Kingdom on semi-clothed women were frequently depicted sporting depictions of the deity Bes, and suggested that these were tattoos, the marks of dancing girls – or even prostitutes.[79] One might suggest that tattooing in Egypt was therefore associated with prostitutes and was erotically charged. Reality is a little more complex and as is often the case, ideas of the past are strongly coloured by modern preconceptions. In our own society the wearing of tattoos has been negatively associated with immorality and low social status and this preconception seems to have influenced an understanding of ancient Egyptian tattoos. In the late 1920s, for example, the conviction of a rapist was overturned because a small butterfly tattoo was found on the female victim. The tattoo was considered to have sexual implications and thus the woman was thought to have misled the man who raped her.[80]

Much confusion also arises from the conflation of New Kingdom depictions of Bes on dancers' legs, with Middle Kingdom marks on the bodies of elite women and 'fertility dolls'. All the evidence suggests that the only Egyptians in Dynastic Egypt to have tattoos were women, and that these women would be elite court ladies and priestesses of Hathor, perhaps decorated to ensure fertility, but not for the simple amusement of men. The origins and precise meaning of the tattoos remain unclear.

Much of the textual evidence for tattooing in Egypt comes from the Graeco-Roman Period, when it is clear that tattooing and branding were considered negative.[81] Slaves were branded and tattooing was used as a punishment. Cultic tattooing, however, is also mentioned. Sextus Empiricus says that the majority of Egyptians were tattooed,[82] and evidence suggests that both men and women were indeed tattooed in this period. However, the extent to which this took place was probably exaggerated by Classical writers to support their ideas of the 'weird' nature of the Egyptians. Evidence from bodies themselves suggests a less ubiquitous practice. Maspero's excavations at Akhmim in Middle Egypt 'yielded several female mummies of the Graeco-Roman period with tattoo marks on the chin and sides of the nose.'[83] While the discolouration and partial decomposition of mummified bodies means that we would not expect evidence of tattooing on every mummy, one might expect a little more available evidence than merely the Akhmim bodies.

Prior to the Graeco-Roman Period, evidence for tattooing is largely archaeological. One of the few possible textual references comes from the Bremner-Rhind Papyrus (British Museum EA 10188). This papyrus is dated to the fourth century BC, but the archaizing language suggests an earlier prototype. The relevant phrase can be translated as 'their name is inscribed into their arms as Isis and Nephthys . . .' The problem is that this may represent scarification rather than tattooing, and like all textual evidence, may suggest an idea rather than a reality.

Firm evidence for tattooing must ideally come from the bodies themselves. As with the Graeco-Roman Period, the evidence does not suggest ubiquitous practice. In fact, only four mummified bodies are known, and these all from the Middle Kingdom, all from Deir el-Bahri, and all female.

Perhaps the most well known tattooed lady is that of the Eleventh Dynasty (c.2055–2004 BC) Priestess of Hathor, Amunet,[84] discovered in 1891 in a tomb at Deir el-Bahri. Unfortunately, there appear to be no pictures of Amunet's tattoos.[85] The body often shown as Amunet in publications is actually that of her companion, an unknown lady from the same tomb who was also tattooed.

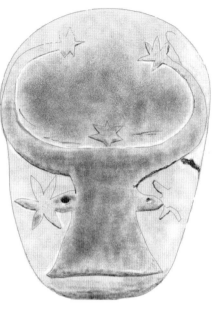

left: 1. The Gerza palette. (Drawing by the author)

below left: 2. King Menkaure in the centre with Hathor, right, and the nome deity Bat, left. (Egyptian Museum, Cairo)

below right: 3. Taweret, 'The Great One', in amulet form, perhaps used to protect women in childbirth. (Accession number PM19. Copyright Egypt Centre, Swansea University)

4. Pottery fertility figurines. (Accession numbers EC446 and EC447. Copyright Egypt Centre, Swansea University)

5. The chapel of the Divine Adoratrice Amenirdis I at Medinet Habu. (Photograph author's own)

6. The God's Wife of Amun, Shepenwepet I being suckled by Hathor at the Chapel of Heqa-Djet at Karnak. (Photograph author's own)

7. Male priests (left) and the God's Wife of Amun, possibly Neferure (right), engaged in rituals. From Hatshepsut's Red Chapel at Karnak. (Photograph author's own)

8. A male harper, male and female dancers and female sistra players. From Hatshepsut's Red Chapel at Karnak. (Photograph author's own)

9. Isis in the form of a bird hovers over the erect phallus of the recumbent Osiris. From the temple of Seti I at Abydos. (Photograph author's own)

10. A graffito at Wadi Hammamat. Note the monkey-like faces of the couple. (Photograph author's own)

left: 11. A scene from the Turin Erotic Papyrus. (Drawing by the author)

below left: 12. The deity Bes at Dendera. (Photograph author's own)

below right: 13. The colossal statue of Meritamun (consort of Rameses II) at Akhmim. The queen wears the modius and double plume. (Photograph author's own)

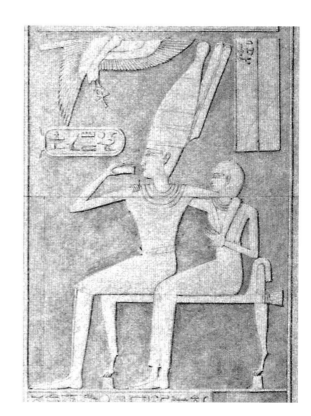

right: 14. Mentuhotep II embracing his wife Sadeh. (From XIth Dynasty Temple at Deir El-Bahari II by Edouard Naville 1910)

below: 15. The rock-cut temple built by Hatshepsut to Pakhet at Speos Artemidos. (Photograph author's own)

16. Osirid statues of Hatshepsut at Deir el-Bahri. The queen is shown as Osiris, the 'king of the dead'. (Photograph author's own)

17. Cleopatra VII and her son Caesarion. She wears the sun disk with cow horns and her son, shown at smaller size, stands in front of her. From the back south wall of the temple at Dendera. (Photograph author's own)

Amunet had tattoos on top of the abdomen, above thighs and breasts and on lower legs and arms in a geometrical pattern of dots and lines. Her titles 'Sole Lady in Waiting, Priestess of Hathor' showed that she was a high-status lady of the court. Although, the title ḥkr.t nsw wʿt.t had been translated in the past as 'Sole Royal Ornament', and connected with concubines, a better translation may be 'Sole Lady in Waiting'.[86] Ladies holding the title 'Sole Lady in Waiting, Priestess of Hathor' were often wives of important officials. The much published tattoos of Amunet's companion were very similar to her own.

Amunet and her companion were buried close to the temple of King Mentuhotep Nebhepetre, in an area which seems to have been given over to other royal ladies, several of whom were priestesses of Hathor, and which are sometimes considered a harem. Even if these women were royal wives, we should not equate this with prostitution or low status. Indeed, there is even doubt that these ladies were married to the king.

Two other female mummies, again from the Eleventh Dynasty and from Deir el-Bahri, were found by Herbert E. Winlock in 1923 near the Mentuhotep temple. These bodies appear to exhibit scarification, as well as tattooing, and the pattern of designs is like that of Amunet with geometrically arranged dots and dashes.[87] Winlock[88] identified them as 'dancing girls', apparently as their tattoos were the same as the patterns on the faience figurines which he believed to be dancing girls. However, the titles of these women, if they had any, remain unknown and they were buried with few objects, though it is possible that they had been moved from a former grave. Winlock states that their graves had been robbed during the building of Hatshepsut's Temple. Thus, their status is unclear.

It has been argued that elite women were not tattooed[89] but the case of Amunet and her companion, and perhaps also of the two other Deir el-Bahri women, would suggest otherwise. Amunet's title shows she was a court lady and she was buried near the king wearing bead collars and necklaces. Her companion in the same tomb, given its situation, appears also to be of high rank. As for the other two, the fact that they were buried on such an important site suggests that they may have been court ladies, and like many women buried here could have been priestesses of Hathor. Such women may have danced, though they are not shown doing so, and have no titles suggesting that they did so. They may or may not have been sexually intimate with the king, but they were certainly of high status.

It has been suggested on the basis of the actual skulls, and from iconographic depictions, that some of these women were black Nubians.[90] While representation of skin colouring as black is now known to have religious overtones, associated with Osiris, and with fertility and rebirth, rather than depicting skin colour in life, the evidence from the shape of the skull is harder to dismiss. However, the skull identification was carried out some time ago and so was possibly not as accurate as might be expected today. One scholar[91] identifies Amunet and the two tattooed ladies found later, as light-skinned, but another,[92] suggests that the mummification process may have reduced the melanin in the skin. Interestingly, an archaeological study has shown[93] that some of these women had extremely narrow pelvises, a trait associated with at least some ancient Egyptian women. A new examination by a modern physical anthropologist may help resolve the matter.

As well as these four tattooed bodies, a number of Middle Kingdom figurines have been found which not only have similar decorations, and possible Nubian origins, but are also sometimes considered concubines. These figurines fall into two main groups: faience fertility figurines, classified by the British Egyptologist Geraldine Pinch as type 1, and wooden 'paddle dolls'. Both are Middle Kingdom. There are, of course, other types of fertility figurines, but it is these two types which most approximate to Middle Kingdom mummified bodies.

Pinch's type 1 fertility figurines,[94] faience 'dolls' decorated with geometric patterns strikingly similar to those on the mummified tattooed ladies, are discussed first. These figures date to the late Middle Kingdom–Second Intermediate Period and many are made of faience, stone, wood or ivory. Most are found in tombs, though one was found in a domestic context at Kahun.[95] They are found in both male and female burials, as well as in votive deposits to Hathor, with the bands around their bodies being similar to the 'Libyan bands' worn by priestesses. While Pinch,[96] the authority on these artefacts, is doubtful of accepting the idea of their Nubian origins, the connection does seem difficult to refute. While not identical, examples of Nubian pottery dolls of the same date do exhibit similar patterns, and like the Egyptian figures, are without feet. The similarity of design does suggest a cross-fertilization of ideas surrounding them, particularly as Nubia was at least partly under the control of Egypt at this time.

The decoration on the mummies, and also on the type 1 fertility figurines, bears some similarity to the decoration on paddle dolls, common in the Middle Kingdom.[97] Such dolls, with emphasized pubic area and long hair, appear to symbolize the feminine erotic, and are usually considered fertility figures rather than children's playthings. Interestingly, at least one of these paddle dolls sports a depiction of Taweret[98] who, like Bes, is associated with women and childbirth. The two seem closely linked and Keimer[99] illustrates an example of Taweret with a Bes face. We have seen that, in the New Kingdom, Bes was depicted on the thighs of some women. These paddle dolls are common in Upper Egypt and Nubia.

The geographical distribution of paddle dolls, the possible Nubian origins of the faience and pottery figurines, and the possible Nubian origins of the

Mentuhotep Nebhepetre ladies have all been linked to evidence of a Nubian connection for tattooing. In each individual case, the evidence is not clear, with the paddle dolls being the most convincingly Nubian. It is probably going too far to claim that these dolls are somehow depictions of the tattooed ladies; the paddle dolls wear long hair, while our ladies are shown on their chapels with short hairstyles. However, perhaps together, the paddle dolls, faience dolls and Deir el-Bahri women, provide some support for a relationship between female body decoration and Nubian influence, at least in the Middle Kingdom.

In support of Nubian origins for our ladies, Nubian women were decorated with similar tattoos between the Sixth and Eighteenth Dynasties,[100] that is, they were contemporary with the Deir el-Bahri ladies. C-group women (2000–1500 BC), in cemeteries near Kubban discovered in 1910, also had tattoos, like those of Amunet and the other three women. Moreover, the Nubian women were buried with pottery dolls exhibiting the same tattoos.[101] Other C-Group tattooed women have also been found[102] exhibiting similar dot and dash patterning. One expert[103] states that all the tattoos found in Nubia are on females, but there is at least one instance of a tattooed male from the later period in Nubia.[104] A Nubian connection may be accepted with caution.

An alternative suggestion is that the origins of Dynastic Egyptian tattooing may be sought in Egyptian prehistory. There are several depictions of female Predynastic figurines patterned as though tattooed.[105] However, we do not know if this practice continued unbroken into Dynastic Egypt, or again if these patterns represent tattoos, body paint or scarification.

We may ask how the tattoos were executed. An early Dynastic flint flake set in a wooden handle, found at Abydos, was said by Petrie to be a tattooing instrument. Petrie writes, 'The flint set in wood did not seem capable of bearing any strain, but it was explained by my friend Prof Giglioli as a tatuing [sic] instrument of usual form . . .'[106] This suggests that Professor Giglioli had seen similar contemporary items. Another instrument, consisting of wide, flat needles found together, was uncovered from Eighteenth Dynasty Gurob. The latter is now deposited in the Petrie Museum.

Interestingly, tattooing seems to have either continued, or been revived, in more recent times in Egypt. At least one drawing of an Egyptian woman is known, as well as bone figurines, a lusterware dish and other artefacts of the Fatamid Period (AD 969–1171), apparently showing tattoos.[107] Of course these could also indicate body paint.

Ethnographic evidence shows that, at times, tattooing may be associated with the elite, and at other times, subordinate groups.[108] It is frequently practised as a means of healing and protection, and thus is not always intended as mere sexual ornament. For ancient Egypt, it is certainly evident that tattooing in the Middle Kingdom was associated with some high-status women. As to the meaning of the tattoos, all that can be said is that there is some suggestion that the body decorations are associated with fertility. The faience dolls and paddle dolls are very clearly fertility figures and these have designs which appear similar to the tattooed mummies. As for the later Bes body decorations, Bes, if not an erotic symbol, was associated with women in childbirth, and hence fertility and/or protection. This, of course, need not rule out a connection with eroticism, as the fertility and eroticism are difficult to untangle. What can be ruled out is the association of tattoos and low-status women. Additionally, the paucity of tattoos suggests it was not common practice.

The positioning of the tattoos on the abdomen and upper breasts and thighs of these mummified bodies, and also on the dolls, has suggested to some an erotic connection. However, some of the tattooing also occurred on the lower legs and arms; and besides, positioning near female genital areas may be associated with either fertility or protection. It is also possible that the tattoos may be marks of devotees to Hathor, given that these dolls are often given as votive offerings to Hathor, and that Amunet, and possibly the other mummified ladies, were Priestesses of Hathor.

By the New Kingdom, women are sometimes shown with depictions of Bes upon their thighs, often assumed to be tattoos. These appear in a different tradition to the geometrical designs of the Middle Kingdom, though the difference may be superficial. The Bes 'tattoos' are sometimes cited as supporting the link between tattoos and eroticism in ancient Egypt. However, this link is open to question for three main reasons. First, we do not know if these were tattoos, scarification, or body paint. The suggestion that these may have been tattoos is supported by the interpretation of a dotted design on a Nubian Meroitic female mummy from Aksha as a Bes figure.[109] However, the Meroitic Period is equivalent to the Ptolemaic Period of Egypt, that is, it is much later than the Egyptian New Kingdom. Secondly, Bes was associated with women and childbirth, and had an apotropaic role, thus to assume a mere erotic role limits, or even twists, the nature of Bes. Thirdly, it is possible that all Egyptian women had depictions of Bes painted upon their thighs, though they are not shown on higher status women because such women were usually depicted clothed.

We need to consider the link between Bes and the erotic. Certainly Bes is sometimes shown on the thighs of women who are holding musical instruments, wearing hip girdles and sporting long flowing locks. The presence of a small monkey[110] appears to enhance the erotic feel. The problem is to disentangle the erotic from the fertility aspects, which is probably largely impossible for an ancient society. It is very likely that such a distinction simply was not made in ancient Egypt.

DAY BEDS AND PUBLIC CELEBRATION OF SEXUALITY

The front rooms of houses at Deir el-Medina show scenes of almost nude nursing mothers, the so-called 'Wochenlaube' scenes. Similar motifs to those on the Wochenlaube scenes can also be found on more explicitly sexualized scenes, where, for example, make-up is being applied and hip girdles are worn, as on the Turin Erotic Papyrus. Within the front rooms, artefacts and paintings associated with childbirth and fertility were also found – depictions of Bes and Taweret. In addition there are also the so-called 'lit clos' (enclosed beds). There were also more conventionally domestic items such as mortars. Similar sexualized or fertility paintings occur in the front rooms of houses at Amarna.[111] Such artefacts and paintings show that items associated with fertility or sexuality were not hidden, but rather celebrated, in the front rooms of houses.[112] As stated in Chapter 5, the front room in New Kingdom houses tended to be for use of women and the middle, divan room, for men, though it seems likely that all rooms, especially in smaller houses, would be used by both sexes.

The 'lit clos' structures of Deir el-Medina were initially so christened by the French Egyptologist Bernard Bruyère,[113] who considered them as day beds. At the time of Bruyère's excavations, the 'lit clos' was, in France, a type of day bed used for short naps which took the form of a divan usually hidden by a cupboard when not in use. Ancient Egyptian 'lit clos' structures date to the Nineteenth and Twentieth Dynasties. One house even contains two such structures. They consist of a brick elevated area approximately 1.7 m long, 80 cm wide and 75 cm high. Steps go up to them and some appear to have been enclosed by side walls. A number were decorated. The most common scene was that of Bes, but others show a woman at her toilette, a dancing girl, a person on a papyrus skiff in the marshes, and a possible scene of a nursing mother. One structure was found to contain a limestone headrest, part of a statue and a fragment of a female statuette.[114] Similar items were found in other 'lit clos'.

The purpose of these structures remains highly debatable. The 'lit clos' are unlikely to be casual sitting areas, as the Deir el-Medina houses had sitting areas in the central room of the house. One suggestion is that these were used for ritual intercourse, with the motifs intended to be erotic. However the enclosing walls and restricted area would seem to inhibit such activity. Alternatively, based upon the motifs therein, they may have been places for childbirth. However, use as a birthing area seems unlikely given the evidence for women giving birth squatting and the fact that 'lit clos' are enclosed might have caused problems for midwives. Similar, though not identical, structures were found at Amarna, and it was suggested by some that these were household altars. Some[115] see the Amarna structures, like those at Deir el-Medina, as functioning to celebrate successful childbirth.[116]

Alternatively, given their size and motifs, these elevated areas may have functioned as a safe place for babies or toddlers, while mothers were engaged in work around the house. The motifs would then be a celebration of childbirth and have an apotropaic function. This would not preclude 'lit clos' from also being used as storage areas.

As we have seen, display of sexuality also appears common in tombs and temples. Ostraca showing sexual activity are apparent in chapels and houses. That sexuality, including scenes of semi-nude women, was not tabooed, but rather considered part of everyday life to be celebrated in front rooms, does not mean that all sexual acts were considered acceptable. Extra-marital sex seems to have largely been frowned upon.[117] In Victorian society, depictions of nude women in classical poses were on display in houses, while Victorian women themselves retained a modest dress code. We need not assume that sexuality was totally embedded in Pharaonic culture, anymore than in Victorian society. What we can say is that it is apparent that sexuality was important, both in the everyday, and in the reanimating environment of the tomb and temple.

THE EROTIC BODY

In different cultures, different parts of the body may be considered erotic. We may assume that the young women illustrated by men in Egyptian tomb paintings and temples depicted sexually desirable women. We might also assume that the desirable women of Egyptian love songs and tales had some relation to male fantasy. Of course, in both cases, men are those who are executing the art, and so we have problems in deciphering what Egyptian women may have found sexually attractive in their men.

Egyptian ideas of sexual beauty for men and women varied over time. In the New Kingdom, the ideal of the adolescent girl appears, and at times such figures seem almost androgynous. In the Amarna Period, older women are also occasionally celebrated and in the Third Intermediate Period, women are depicted as almost voluptuous.[118] The Middle Kingdom Papyrus Westcar[119] gives a male fantasy of the female form. Pharaoh asks to go sailing 'with twenty women with the shapeliest of bodies, breasts and braids, who have not yet given birth. Also let there be brought to me twenty nets and give these nets to these women in place of their clothes'. Generally, the feminine ideal is shown two-dimensionally by slim, usually long-haired, youthful beauties. Smooth skin is clearly desirable in ancient Egyptian love poetry and it has been suggested[120] that hairless bodies were the ideal.

The fact that elite, mourning women are sometimes shown with revealed breasts, and in other contexts both goddesses and human women are shown with one breast revealed, suggests that breasts were not highly sexualized. The pubic area of elite women, while often suggested, is not usually explicitly shown. The hiding of this area might suggest that, for the Egyptians, this was taboo and hidden from view. The problem is, of course, that it is quite difficult to tell what was hidden and what was not in everyday life, and if the hidden was necessarily the sexualized.

Women's sexual needs are apparently ignored in tomb paintings, and even in love poetry, so it is difficult to know what an ancient Egyptian woman would have found desirable in her man. This is particularly problematic as art and literature were created by men, and so at best, only describe what Egyptian men may have thought women desired. Funerary and temple images of men are largely made by, and often for, a male audience, though one may argue that these too are sexualized.[121] These often show muscular men in the prime of life with naked V-shaped torsos, or occasionally, and especially in the Old Kingdom, older men with some body fat. Muscular males are described[122] as inducing a woman's desire in the *Tale of Two Brothers*. Further clues to male imagining of women's desires are to be found in love poems, such as: 'He grants me the hue of his loins. It is longer than it is broad'.[123]

LOVE POETRY

'Love poems' are often cited in evidence for sexuality. Most were found at Deir el-Medina, and date to the Nineteenth and Twentieth Dynasties. Hence, these were only short-lived phenomena and may be atypical of usual Egyptian ideas of love. Although usually taken at face value and considered 'secular',[124] as with other areas connected with sexuality, there is a strong case for considering them religious.

Mystic love poetry abounds across cultures. Examples include the *Song of Solomon* in the Judeo-Christian tradition, or the love poems of the Islamic mystic Rabiya al-Adawiyya. Papyrus Harris 500 includes several love songs along with the *Song of the Harper*. Usually harper's songs are written on tomb walls, a place where one would expect to find religious texts.[125] Against the idea of the religiosity of these poems, deities are only rarely mentioned.

Since it seems likely that these poems would have been written by men, it is difficult to know if they truly reflect female sexuality or are a male fantasy. The women are portrayed as beautiful, exotic and intoxicating figures of desire. While they are obtainable, they appear with no personality and are, in some ways, the archetypal male fantasy. There is no mention of the femme fatale stereotype which appears elsewhere in Egyptian literature, or of the sexually active powerful male. It has been pointed out[126] that the women are not portrayed as passive, but as active in seeking out and 'catching' their lovers, while the males are the passive partners; 'the boys in the Egyptian Paraclausithyra just pout'.[127] This contrast with the dominant discourse does not appear to be considered in a negative light.

There is little direct mention of genitalia, but the songs are steeped in desire, and describe the sexual act without dwelling on detail. There is mention of naked or semi-naked limbs clothed in diaphanous garments:

> Just for you I'd wear my Memphis swimsuit,
>   made of sheer linen, fit for a queen–
> Come see how it looks in the water![128]

Flowers, fruit and scent are portrayed as intoxicants. The settings are gardens and water:

> When I hold my love close
>   (and her arms steal around me),
> I'm like a man translated to Punt
>   Or like someone out in the reedflats
> When the whole world suddenly bursts into flower.
>   In this dreamland of South Sea fragrances,
> My love, you are essence of roses.[129]

It appears that 70 per cent of lovers' trysts described in the poems take place near the house of the woman.[130] Her house is metaphorically her body and entry to the house is metaphorically possession thereof. It has been suggested that the sequence of events described in the poems mirrors the real-life courtship process. The man makes a request to the girl's mother. The girl is then his wife, but stays for a time in her own home. She then enters the house of her mother-in-law. These poems show no sanctions on sex before marriage. However, anthropological studies clearly show that often the reality of social life may be very different from ideals expressed in other spheres.

WOMEN AND REBIRTH

The means to existence in the afterlife and conceptions of life after death were largely male centred. This is not surprising in a society where life and the afterlife revolved around the king, intrinsically and essentially male. Additionally, the afterlife mirrored human reproduction, which was again, for the Egyptians, essentially male. Women, whether wives, daughters, sisters or mothers, are apparent in men's tombs to enable the deceased male to regenerate through sexual activity, thereby mirroring the activity of the gods. How, then, did the female ensure an afterlife? While concessions were certainly made to femininity, for most of Egyptian history the process of rebirth and existence in the afterlife was essentially male. Women, in order to achieve the afterlife needed an extra transformational step that required attaining gender fluidity.[131] Women needed first to identify with the male Osiris and then regender themselves.[132]

The woman has an importance in the tomb of the male beyond being her own means of achieving an afterlife existence through association. The woman's role is important as the man metaphorically impregnates her with himself as 'bull of his mother'. This need not be the wife, but at times may be the mother or even the daughter.

Ideas concerning the part played by the wife in the tomb vary from period to period. In the Early Dynastic Period, spouses did not appear in the tombs of their partners, and children were not depicted.[133] By the Fourth Dynasty, however, in the private tombs of Meidum, an emphasis on the family appears, perhaps related to the emergent sun cult. Such cults stressed fertility and sexual reproduction. However, by the end of the Fifth Dynasty, wives begin to be omitted from their husbands' tombs,[134] a situation preceded by a marked decline in illustrations of affectionate gestures from wives toward husbands. By the Sixth Dynasty, wives reappear in tombs, but are omitted from Theban tombs of late Eleventh to early Twelfth Dynasties even though in several cases it is clear that the tomb owner was married. In the New Kingdom, there are several tombs of men where women are omitted. Perhaps such men served powerful women and it would be considered unseemly to mention the name of one's wife. It should also be noted that in several tombs where wives are omitted, the mother is shown as important.

It is difficult to know if sexualized tomb paintings were created to provide the means of rebirth,[135] or as a means of ensuring that sexual activity continued in the afterlife.[136] Some Egyptian inscriptions state that apotheosis replaces lovemaking in the afterlife; elsewhere it seems that it was intended that sexual activity continue. However, it is clear that human reproduction, divine creation and attaining an afterlife existence were very much paralleled.[137] The term for divine creation was the same as that for birth (*msi*). Just as Atum created life through sexual activity, so rebirth required sexual activity. The cyclical birth of Re-Atum from the vulva of Nut and its parallel with human rebirth was discussed above. It must also be noted that human rebirth and creation were paralleled in the act of creating a cult statue, particularly within the Memphite creation myth of Ptah.

Several implements connected with the rebirth of the deceased parallel implements used in childbirth. The *psš-kf* and *ntrwy* blades are both stone instruments used in the 'Opening of the Mouth' ceremony, a ritual used to ensure the rebirth of the deceased. It is also a ceremony carried out on cult statues to ensure that they function as a dwelling place for deities. Both the *psš-kf* and *ntrwy* blades have parallels in artefacts used shortly after the birth of infants, with the *psš-kf* knife being used in childbirth to cut the umbilical cord.[138] The *ntrwy* blades mirror the little fingers used by the midwife to clear the mouth of the newborn. In the 'Opening of the Mouth' ceremony, two jars were presented, one full and one empty and were called the breasts of Horus and Isis (*Pyramid Texts* 41 and 42). Hard and soft food was also offered, perhaps mirroring weaning.[139]

Other childbirth instruments are used in funerary ritual. Apotropaic wands appear to have been used primarily to protect living children, though several have been found in tombs. On the rear of wall of the Eighteenth Dynasty tomb relief of Bebi at Elkab, two figures called *hnmt* (khenmet meaning 'nurse') raise an amuletic knife, while others hold knife and serpent staffs.[140] The four magic bricks placed in tombs from the New Kingdom parallel the bricks upon which women squat when giving birth.[141] On scenes of the weighing of the heart depicted in the New Kingdom, wherein the deceased heart is weighed against the feather of truth to ascertain their suitability for the afterlife, a birth brick is also depicted. Containers apparently meant for milk for the newborn have also been found in tombs of adults.

Rebirth images also make use of Hathorian images of motherhood. In the Old Kingdom, images of cattle 'coming forth' from the marshes were popular. These include references to the mother cow and to the feeding of calves. Such scenes herald the later motif of the Hathor cow in the papyrus thicket, and Hathor coming out of the western mountain at Thebes. The later scenes of Hathor coming out of the hillside at western Thebes at times make the rebirth concept explicit by the inclusion of Taweret, a goddess of women in childbirth and protector of young children.

Other evidence suggests that the reason for sexual images in tombs was to ensure sexual activity in the afterlife. Because of the importance of afterlife sexual activity, enemies of the deceased were to be rendered impotent. In some renditions of Spell 39 of the *Book of the Dead*, the arch enemy of order, Apophis, will be made impotent: 'You shall not become erect, you shall not copulate, O Apophis . . .'[142] Temple scenes show that the enemies of Egypt had their phalli removed. While this was an effective means of counting dead enemies, it was also a means of ensuring that these individuals could not achieve an afterlife.

Whether sexualized elements of funerary artefacts are intended as a means of rebirth, or of providing a sexualized afterlife, the archaeology surrounding funerary monuments makes it clear that the sexual needs of the male, not the female, are paramount. Or at least, it is not that women's sexual needs are ignored, but rather that the woman needs to become a man with male sexual needs in order to achieve the afterlife.

In the New Kingdom, both the male and female were, like Osiris, fragmented before being reborn.[143] By the Dynastic Period, this did not take the form of actual dismemberment, but rather is implied by the mummiform coffin, mirroring the mummified Osiris, a male. Anthropoid coffins are, in the large part, male, though some concession to femininity may be made by showing stylized breasts. However, the reborn person is often shown gendered on inner mummy boards, as an *akh*, a transfigured one, one who has been dismembered and then reborn complete. Similarly, on the exterior sides of later coffins, the reborn deceased is clearly gendered. The Egyptians obviously believed in the revival of the self in some form after death, and so, transfigured deceased females retained their female forms, and deceased males retained their masculinity. The deceased needs to become male Osiris to reach the afterlife, but once the journey is complete, a woman may become fully feminine again. But, who acted as the female vessel in the tombs of women?[144] The answer must be the woman herself. She was her own husband, wife and mother.

Shabtis (servant figurines or substitutes for the deceased) are largely male and like Osiris, are shown mummiform. Very occasionally, female shabtis have breasts, but otherwise they are masculine. One female shabti of the Eighteenth Dynasty[145] has a masculine, red skin colour, not the typical yellow skin colour of women. Additionally, even the text on the shabti may use the male pronoun.

From the Eighteenth Dynasty on, penises in the form of amulets provided for procreation after death.[146] These amulets were provided for both women and men. Similarly, fertility figurines, once considered concubines for the dead, have sometimes also been seen as a means of stimulating the male. However, these are also found in the tombs of women, though their function is much debated.

Royal Rameside women were given a gender fluidity to achieve the afterlife through being described in male terms.[147] Women of this period are given a red-brown skin colour usually reserved for men and images of kings are missing from the tombs of women, presumably to protect the woman's association with Osiris and Re. This role would otherwise be usurped by the superior position of the king, who would be more appropriately identified with these gods. Additionally, if king and queen were shown together, the queen would need to be shown in a secondary, feminine role and would not be able to take on identification with Osiris and Re.

Often coffins, shabtis and scarabs appear to use male and female pronouns on the same artefact. On several coffins of the Third Intermediate Period, which belong to women, the deceased is depicted in male dress. Some have said that this shows that such high quality items were mass produced and simply altered slightly to suit the gender of the deceased. However, it has been suggested[148] that, for women, this could actually be a deliberate act of gender ambiguity; women wished to show their connection with Osiris and Re to achieve the afterlife, but also keep their own gender once in the afterlife. During the transformation in the afterlife Hall of Truth, one woman is given a masculine pronoun, but elsewhere the feminine pronoun is used. In other funerary items, however, the division between male and female does not so easily divide between transformation to reach the afterlife and existence in the afterlife. Certainly, by the Third Intermediate Period, transformation scenes on coffins may show the deceased as a female, while at the same date, one coffin may show the deceased as alternately male and female. There is no clear pattern; at this period, the lids of coffins often show an androgynous Osirian form.

Some have suggested an increasingly gendered afterlife for women during the Graeco-Roman Period[149] citing a female mummy of the Period with both false nipples and a linen penis. It is possible that this shows an attempt to ensure a masculine form for Osirian transformation and femininity for afterlife existence. It may alternatively be a case of later rewrapping of the mummy by priests unsure of the gender of the deceased. Generally, from the fourth century BC on, there appears to be a change in outlook which meant that the deceased female came to be associated with the goddess Hathor. Thus, the reborn female is called 'The Hathor N'.[150] As stated above, it is during this period that the woman is credited with more of a role in forming the child, and at this time too, more burial equipment is made for women rather than being subsumed in male burials.

THE POWER OF THE EROTIC

Coded erotic scenes are common in the reanimating environment of temple and tomb. In various cultures, areas of the body which are considered erotic are hidden, possibly relating to the power thereof. Additionally, for the ancient Egyptians, that which was considered sacred and powerful, such as an image of a god, was hidden, and as stated above, this may explain hidden elite phalli. The power of female sexuality could be dangerous if not controlled.

This idea might in part explain the strange story of Hathor exposing herself before her father. In the *Contendings of Horus and Seth*,[151] written down in Rameside times, the sun-god Re-Horakhty presides over a contest between Horus and Seth. However, the god is weary and the contest founders. Hathor exposes her genitals before her father, and the sun-god laughs and is revived. One theory[152] as to why this act would have been found funny suggests that it could in part be due to the incongruity of a goddess exposing her genitals, that is, the shock of such a bawdy act elicits laughter. In this story, the revival of the male causes the continuation of proceedings, but Hathor acts as the stimulus.

There is also a later Egyptian practice of women exposing themselves before the Apis bull, and Graeco-Roman depictions of Isis exposing herself. The Greek historian, Herodotus, states that other festivals (he notes the festival of Bubastis) also include women acting in this manner. A steatite bowl dating to 525–500 BC shows a procession to a temple of Hathor, including animals to be sacrificed, several female musicians, and a woman apparently slapping her bottom in time to the music while displaying her genitals. This woman could be mirroring Hathor as 'Lady of the Dance', or 'Lady of the Vulva'.

This exposure of that normally hidden may also reflect the idea that female sexuality was a powerful tool, not normally flaunted, at least in 'polite society', but nevertheless utilized where creation and rebirth were desired. Sexuality could be a bawdy act, but was also a sacrament. Mirroring Hathor, the Egyptian woman may have played a supporting role, but without her, creation was impossible.

Queens and harems

QUEENSHIP

Although kingship, that is, the holding of supreme power, was essentially masculine, it is impossible to discuss Egyptian divine kingship without discussing
women. The king could not rule without a female counterpart, and so throughout Egyptian history, kings always had queens despite that, statistically speaking,
at least some kings must have been homosexual. As the female counterpart of
kingship, necessary for the fecundity of Egypt, queens took part in royal rituals
of revival and rebirth. They were therefore among a small number who could
enter sacred spaces with the king.

Androgyny in kingship was discussed in the last chapter, but the prevailing
idea of kingship is masculine, hence decorum demanded that queens who ruled
in the same way as kings sported beards and engaged in the violence of warfare,
as this was what kingship meant. The king suppressed chaos and was central to
creation; only the male rulers were said to have carried out the act of *iri ḫt* (doing
things), which may be interpreted as meaning carrying out acts which maintain
cosmic order.[1] Kings are given the title *nb irt-ḫt* ('Lord of Doing Things') and the
feminine form of this phrase is only ever used of two women, Sobekneferu and
Hatshepsut. Hatshepsut uses the title only when she acts as a king, and as will be
shown below, there is evidence that Sobekneferu was also a king. Very few women
wielded authority as kings. Of over 500 known rulers, only four were women.
This very occasional acceptance of female kings was arguably made acceptable
by the Egyptian acceptance of gender fluidity, rather than through acceptance
of essentially female individuals performing the role of supreme leader. 'Queens'
were royal women, adjuncts to kings, not women who held real power in the way
kings did. There was no Egyptian word for 'queen', but rather, what we would call
'queens' were identified by their relationship with the king. They were 'King's
Mother' or 'King's Principal Wife'. Queens were protectors, nurturers and agents
of sexual arousal.

While the royal family must have included large numbers of women, only the principal wives and the king's mothers are usually mentioned, and thus known to us. It is very often difficult to distinguish between royal women, except from their titles, and it was not until the Twelfth Dynasty that the title 'King's Principal Wife' (*ḥmt-nswt wrt*) is first attested. Other wives were simply known as 'King's Wife'. Principal wives could be daughters of foreign kings, Egyptian commoners, or even sisters or daughters of the king. Some who bore the title 'King's Principal Wife' also had the title 'King's Mother'. For much of Egyptian history, the latter was more important than the Principal Wife. A King's Mother only assumed her status on the accession of her sons, and at times this meant that a previously non-royal lady could be elevated to first lady position. The high status of the King's Mother may in part be due to the status of mothers in general, but also undoubtedly rested on mythic counterparts.

For the Egyptians, male and female compliment one another, as shown by paired gendered elements such as night and day, earth and heaven, cyclical time and eternity. These pairs represent two aspects of the same phenomenon.[2] Thus, the feminine was essential to masculine kingship and followed the mythic prototypes of the actions of the gods. When living, the king was the god Horus, when dead, he was the god Osiris. The queen took on aspects of goddess' consort. Queens, like goddesses, could be portrayed as both motherly and aggressively protective. Kings are often shown with female relatives – their daughters, wives and mothers – but not with sons. This is because depicting a king and his male heir together would be mythologically confusing. The king is Horus, and the son of Osiris. Horus can only claim the throne from the dead king, his father.

For most of Egyptian history, Hathor was the archetypal mother goddess, the wife and mother of Horus. The early association of Hathor and Horus is shown by Hathor's name (*ḥwt-ḥrw* 'House of Horus'). As Hathor is both mother and consort of the god, both queen and king's mother are Hathor. This model of queenship could undergo transformation, as Hathor became identified with other goddesses such as Maat, Mut or Isis. However, the personalities of these goddesses were very much transformations of an archetypal goddess, rather than distinct individuals; indeed, one could argue that Hathor was a type of deity, rather than a single entity. In the Graeco-Roman Period, the queen is identified with the goddess Isis, who had taken over many of the aspects of Hathor.

The personality of these various goddesses, mothers and consorts was one of protection and of nurturing. It was also one of sexuality and aggression. This was mirrored in the portrayals of the queen, at once the protective and at times the aggressive Eye of Re, the daughter of the sun-god, personified both as a cobra or a lioness, and as the passive, beautiful, motherly goddess. The former could be the fearsome leonine Sekhmet, the latter the gentle cow-like Hathor.

SYMBOLS OF QUEENSHIP

Before the Fifth Dynasty, clothing worn by queens does not differ from that worn by other women. However, from the Fifth Dynasty onward, royal insignia relate to goddesses. Often these insignia take the form of headdresses and crowns and highlight the dual nature of queens as both protective and motherly.

The earliest symbols of queenship relate to the Two Ladies, the vulture and the cobra, Nekhbet and Wadjet, goddesses of Upper and Lower Egypt. The importance of these goddesses to kingship is underlined, from the end of the First Dynasty, by the king taking a name relating to the Two Ladies. The Two Ladies are mothers of the king and the creative and aggressive Eyes of Re. From the Fifth Dynasty on, queens also wore the vulture headdress (taking the appearance of a bird draped over the head with wings drooping down each side of the face). The vulture was considered a protective, motherly creature, and the bird was used as the hieroglyph for 'mother'. During the Sixth Dynasty, the cobra appears as a sign of queenship, displayed on the crown of a queen.[3] The cobra, or uraeus, is not only the mother, but refers to the queen as the daughter, and fearsome protectoress, of the king. The uraeus is the fire-spitting Eye of Re. She is also Wadjet, the goddess of Lower Egypt. Cobra and vulture may be worn together.

Several other insignia associated with queenship refer to a duality, mother and daughter, the Eyes of Re, or the vulture and the cobra. From the Eighteenth Dynasty on, a double uraeus, which probably also symbolized the goddesses Nekhbet and Wadjet, was worn by queens. While Nekhbet could be symbolized as a vulture, she could also take the form of a snake. From the Thirteenth Dynasty on, but more commonly in the New Kingdom, queens wear a headdress of double straight feathers on a circular support. In the *Book of the Dead*, the double feathers are identified with the double uraeus, and a New Kingdom sun-hymn identifies them with the Eyes of Re.[4]

Kings are often associated with lions, but many of the goddesses who are the Eye of Re may be depicted as fearsome lionesses, or as cats (sometimes it is difficult to know which is meant). There is speculation that the Middle Kingdom increase in feline links with royal women may have been due to the domestication of cats in the First Intermediate Period,[5] though royal women had been associated with the lion in the Old Kingdom. By the Middle Kingdom, queens are shown in sphinx form, as lions with human heads,[6] and during the same period, cat and lion-like qualities of royal women were also emphasized by their wearing of cat or lion claw amulets. By the New Kingdom, the lion is associated with the queens, Tiy and Hatshepsut; however, Hatshepsut is often portrayed in lion form as a sphinx when she ruled as a king. Giant granite statues of her as a sphinx have been found at Deir el-Bahri, complete with kingly *nemes*-headdress. Of course, one might argue that the feline association of royal women was not simply due to their association with the Eye of Re. In our own culture, women tend to be associated with cats and it is popularly said that women prefer cats and are cat-like. It is possible that women in ancient Egypt were more generally associated with cats. Several canopic jars belonging to the women of Amenhotep III's harem were purchased in 1904 by George Legrain.[7] Besides their titles, the jars display their nicknames, such as 'the much sought after one', 'the cat-like one', or 'she hot-tempered like a leopard'.

The epithets of queens can mirror their fierce nature. During the reign of Amenhotep III, for example, a statue of a queen, probably Tiy, bears the title 'Great of Terror',[8] a title also borne by the sistrum and *menit*-necklace.[9] The sistrum, *menit* and uraeus, like the queen, are apotropaic, as well as the symbols of a soothing and reviving Hathor. In this guise, the queen may take the role of the dangerous side of Hathor, not only a protective mother, but a rampaging lioness.

THE QUEEN AS HATHOR

It has been suggested that the triads of Hathor, King Menkaure and nome deities, found in the Old Kingdom Menkaure pyramid complex, show that this king identified himself as Horus and his wife as Hathor.[10] Several Old Kingdom titles of royal women concentrate on their link with the divine Horus, such as 'Follower of Horus', 'She who sees Horus and Seth' and 'Companion of Horus'. These titles suggest that the queen is divine consort to Horus. However, it is not really until the Middle Kingdom that queens are clearly shown mirroring Hathor herself, as opposed to other mother goddesses. As will be demonstrated below, Mentuhotep II of the Middle Kingdom even used marriage to the priest-esses of Hathor to legitimize his reign, though whether the marriages were cultic or actually consummated is debatable, and by the reign of Amenemhat II, hathoric jewellery, such as headdresses, and toilet articles, with Hathor ears, were being made for royal women.[11] In this period, the wearing of Hathor plaits is popularized,[12] and the names of royal princesses, such as Sat-Hathor (daughter of Hathor) and, Sat-Hathor-Iunet (daughter of Hathor of Dendera), also attest to identification with the goddess. Finally, the Middle Kingdom *Tale of Sinuhe* describes how the hero is welcomed back by the royal daughters shaking sistra and paralleling the actions of Hathor.[13]

By the New Kingdom, the king's legitimacy and creative power were very reliant on his union with Hathor.[14] It has been suggested that the depiction of the *sed* (jubilee)-festival in the tomb of Kheruef, showing the king seated next to Hathor with queen Tiy behind him, may represent a sacred marriage between the goddess and the king.[15] From the late Eighteenth Dynasty on, the sun disk and horns of Hathor were worn by the queen.

DIVINE BIRTH

The divine nature of kingship and the relationship between king and gods is shown iconographically. Divine conception is first implied in a small chapel for the cult of King Nebhepetre Mentuhotep (Mentuhotep II) of the Eleventh Dynasty. Here Hathor, on the right, shakes a sistrum before the king, who is seated on a bed. On the left, Hathor carries the infant king.[16] However, in the New Kingdom the association between mortal and god is explicitly demonstrated through the scenes of divine conception and birth in the temple of Hatshepsut at Deir el-Bahri, and the temple of Amenhotep III at Luxor, where Amun-Re is depicted symbolically impregnating the queens who bore Hatshepsut and Amenhotep III, respectively.[17] Sexual intercourse is never explicit, as this would reduce the dignity of queen and god; a bed is present but separated from the couple, god and queen face one another and legs overlap, but do not intertwine. Amun-Re holds the ankh to the queen's nose, giving her life, or, as at Deir el-Bahri, Amun-Re passes the hieroglyphs for life and dominion to the queen at waist level.

INCEST AND THE HEIRESS THEORY

The extent to which kings practised incest is not clear, largely because of difficulties in understanding ancient Egyptian kinship terms. In love songs, the beloved is called 'sister', thus the term was not limited to siblings. Even the title 'King's Principal Wife' may at times have been a merely honorary or cultic title. The term *s3* (sa meaning 'son') or *s3t* (sat meaning 'daughter') may have meant exactly what we mean by these terms, or it could have referred to grandchildren or spouse's children.[18] In the case of the king, the 'Father of his People', one might expect more distantly related younger members of the household to be called 'son' or 'daughter'.

Most Egyptologists now believe it possible that, occasionally, kings married actual daughters or sisters, especially in the New Kingdom. Two of the first four kings of the Eighteenth Dynasty both took a sister or half sister as their principal wife.[19] The case of a child born to Bintanath, 'daughter' and 'wife' of Rameses II, is often cited as proof that such marriages were consummated.

Father-daughter marriages, whether consummated or ritual, allowed the daughter to take on the ritual role previously provided by an aging mother. These marriages would also have given daughters more status in a society where only the king's wife and mother were considered important. Marriage to daughters would help ensure that a consort already trained in royal roles was procured. It would also put the king apart from his monogamous subjects and place him in the realm of divinity. Kings were not mere mortals and thus could take more than one wife.

In the past, Egyptologists tried to explain away such incestuous couplings by the theory of matrilineal descent, the idea that the right to the throne passed through the female line, or the heiress theory. However, as others[20] have pointed out, not all kings actually married royal women.[21] This is especially clear in the second half of the Eighteenth Dynasty, perhaps to stop women gaining power as Hatshepsut had.[22] Queen Tiy, for example, the principal wife of Amenhotep III, was a commoner. Furthermore, the scenes of divine birth make it absolutely clear that a king was king because of his divine father, not his earthly mother. Finally, if the heiress was so important, why was she not always clearly distinguished from other wives before the new king ascends the throne? Royal women were only ever depicted as important after the accession of their male royal relative. Thus the matrilineal descent theory is now debunked.

ROYAL POLYGAMY

Polygamy is unlikely to have occurred outside the royal family. But it is likely that kings had several wives. Again, the possibility that titles such as 'King's Wife' could well have been cultic, rather than implying any actual sexual relationship, obscures understanding of relationships between royal couples. Secondly, there is a dearth of surrounding evidence, other than that concerning the family of the 'King's Principal Wife' and the 'King's Mother'. Firm evidence for kings having several sexual partners is available in the New Kingdom, but it is much less clear for earlier periods.

During the New Kingdom, officials associated with the *ipt-nsw* (an institution of royal women, see below) multiplied, suggesting expansion of the royal female household.[23] While these institutions, as we shall see, were important for both business and entertainment, this does not rule out an increase in multiple marriages. The huge number of children borne to kings of the New Kingdom bears witness to polygamy. Rameses II, for example, fathered around 100 children, approximately 50 sons and 50 daughters.[24]

The period before the New Kingdom is much more difficult to understand. A number of subsidiary burials belonging to women appear around the burials of the First Dynasty Kings at Abydos. While some Egyptologists have labelled these ladies 'concubines', they may well have been court ladies serving the queen.[25] Perhaps the most well known of possible royal harems is that of the Middle Kingdom king, Mentuhotep II.

THE 'HAREM' OF MENTUHOTEP II

On the west bank of the Nile at Thebes, Mentuhotep II (Mentuhotep Nebhepetre) built an impressive temple tomb and incorporated within it tombs and chapels for at least eight women. These were the women introduced in Chapter 6, some of whom were tattooed. These women are often said to be wives of the king, that is, his harem. The reality, yet again, is a little more complicated. What is clear is that a number of these women were priestesses of Hathor and that the king had some special relationship with them.

Egyptologists have discussed these ladies and their titles. One argues[26] that Mentuhotep does appear to have had more than one wife at the same time, perhaps three or four. Another[27] points out that evidence for these women as consorts comes not only from their titles, but also from iconography from the chapels where the king embraces the women. That the king embraces the women Ashayt and Sadeh is particularly unusual, with these cases being among the very few.[28] However this intimacy is not unique; a Fifth Dynasty fragment from the mortuary temple of King Sahure shows the king embracing his wife.[29] Embracing can also show power relations but in such cases embracing is carried out by the lesser partner.

One scholar,[30] however, makes a convincing case that the only actual wife was Neferu, while Tem was the mother of the king. The title ḥmt-nsw ('King's Wife') is held by six of the women, but importantly this title only occurs in their chapels and temple relief scenes, not in their funerary structures. Furthermore, the depictions of the king embracing them do not occur in their funerary structures. It seems that these women were king's wives only for the purpose of cult, as shown in chapels and temple scenes. They were all priestesses of Hathor and their chapels were designed to show the king's special relationship with the goddess. A special relationship between this king, the founder of a united Middle Kingdom, and Hathor is also attested by inscriptions at Thebes and elsewhere,[31] where, for example, the king chose to identify himself with Harsomtus, the son of Hathor, and the goddess is shown suckling the king. It is possible that he used his connection with Hathor to legitimize his claim to the throne.

We need not assume that *ḥmt-nsw* means wife in the sense of secular sexual relations. The title *ḥmt-Mnw* (Min's Wife) applied to priestesses of the god Min, is, for example, attested from the Old Kingdom.[32] Mentuhotep, in at least one inscription, calls himself 'The Living God' and thus would be assumed to have had wives/priestesses, in the same way that other gods had.

Interestingly, there is no documentary evidence that any of these women were associated with the two institutions usually associated with 'harems', that of the *ipt-nsw* (ipet-nesw), or *pr-ḫnr* (per-khener), which are discussed next.

INSTITUTIONS OF WOMEN IN THE NEW KINGDOM: IPET-NESW AND PER-KHENER

While there were certainly institutions of women in ancient Egypt, we should not assume that they were harems in the usual meaning of the word, that is, they were probably not places where the king kept a selection of women purely for sexual services. Rather these were institutions of women and children connected with the king. Most clear evidence for these comes from the New Kingdom, the time from which we know that kings would have taken numerous wives. While the Second Intermediate Period Kahun Papyrus discusses provision for royal women housed in a collective,[33] the structure and workings of such collectives are hard to unravel; indeed, we cannot even be sure of the ancient Egyptian name for them.

Two terms are often suggested as meaning royal institutions of women – *ipt-nsw* (ipet-nesw) and *pr-ḫnr* (per-khener). The term *ipt-nsw* first appears in the Old Kingdom and may refer to an institution of queens, royal children, and favoured non-royal children.[34] Others[35] see the term as more likely to mean 'accounting office', with the word *ip* deriving from the word 'to count'.[36] A third interpretation is possible; for others, the word *ipt* is derived from the word meaning to 'muster', or 'assemble people', but it can mean 'private office'.[37] These are places associated with women.[38] The Old Kingdom text of Weni says, 'When there was a secret charge in the *ipt-nsw* against the King's Wife . . .' and here it does not make sense to read *ipt-nsw* as counting house. Why should the queen have been involved in the royal counting house?[39] Perhaps the queen was involved in embezzlement.[40] Additionally, the same text suggests a female dance official was involved in this counting house, which seems unlikely given that the dance official's titles all concern entertainment.[41] Finally, in Dynasties 1–12 the determinative sign used for the word *ipt* is a domed building. However, some Early Dynastic and Twelfth Dynasty texts have a sign similar to a carrying chair used by queens. This reinforces the link between royal women and the *ipt-nsw*.

The term per-khener also appears to be used of institutions housing women, although some see it as some kind of institution engaged in business. As is discussed in Chapter 5, *khener* referred to a group of musicians. The *khener* could be in the service of the king, and the per-khener of Medinet-Gurub is known to have housed royal women. By the New Kingdom, Papyrus Rollin reveals a plot against the king involving both the *ipt-nsw* and the per-khener (see below).

Thus, the term *ipt* is most likely to correspond to the households of royal women, with which the per-khener was sometimes associated. The function of both institutions is likely to have changed through time.

Large households, which are particularly prevalent in the New Kingdom, attest to the might of the king, as well as being important in securing the loyalty of the elite. Women in such institutions did not spend their days in idleness, but rather produced textiles, a valuable source of income, and of course, in the case of the *khener*, provided musical entertainment. As early as the First Dynasty, a cylinder seal from the tomb of King Semerkhet mentions the 'cellar of the weaving workshops of the ipt'.[42] In the Nineteenth Dynasty, we have a letter from an overseer at Gurob revealing that she supervised weaving at Medinet-Gurob, known to be an institution of royal women. Women and children, as stated above, are also employed in a ritual role, frequently in processions. The daughters of the foreign chiefs can be seen depicted in the tomb of the courtier Kheruef attending the king's *sed*-festival and making libations to the king.

Young adult women are shown in the Eastern High Gate (sometimes termed a *migdol*) at Medinet Habu, the Temple of Rameses III.[43] These seem to be post-pubescent adolescents. Some are labelled as *msw nsw* ('king's children'). They are shown entertaining the king with board games and music. They wear jewellery including broad collars and transparent dresses. The king is shown stroking a girl under the chin, and has his arm around another. The accompanying hieroglyphs show that the girls refer to the king by a nickname, Sesi. The erotic nature of this scene may seem shocking in the light of their labelling as 'king's children'. It is possible that the scenes represent a purely cultic representation, with the princesses mirroring the role of Hathor. Additionally, the title 'children of the king' might not necessarily have had the same meaning as it does today. It may have implied children of the royal household, in other words, it could have

included the children of retainers. The purpose of this room is far from clear. It
has been suggested that it is here that the king enjoyed the sensual company of
his women, while at least some plotted his murder. This is probably, however, a
somewhat romantic interpretation. Similar scenes occur on faience vessels from
Serebit el-Khadem.[44]

The royal harem probably included not only the women of the king, but also
'children of the nursery'. The tomb of a Rameside prince, Ramessu-nebweben,
who died in his early twenties, was found near Medinet-Gurob, suggesting
that royal children also resided here.[45] Royal children from the Old Kingdom
are referred to as *ḥrd n kȝp*, 'children of the nursery', and were educated by *ipt*
personnel.[46] During the Eighteenth Dynasty, numerous officials of the king's
court were also been educated at the *ipt*.[47]

The harem was administered by male officials such as tax collectors and scribes
whose titles are attested. The highest administrative official was the 'Overseer of
the Royal Harem' (*imy rȝ ipt-nsw*), a title known as early as the Fourth Dynasty.[48]
The institution had doorkeepers, but this need not imply any special seclusion
of the women; doorkeepers appear to have been common personnel in elite
Egyptian households. There is no evidence for eunuchs in such institutions, and
indeed little evidence for such individuals in Egypt generally.

MEDINET-GUROB (MI-WER)

Various sites have been suggested as harems. However, identifying the living
quarters of elite women is not easy and it is possible that very often they were not
housed separately from other courtiers. Of possible sites, that of New Kingdom
Medinet-Gurob or Mi-Wer, situated at the entrance to the Fayum, is the most
clearly a harem. It seems to have been founded as an institution of women under
Thutmose III (1479–1425 BC).

Various building complexes have been suggested as dedicated to the housing of
court ladies. At Malqata, a total of eight suites, each consisting of an antechamber
with two columns and a columned hall with three inner rooms, are identified
as harem quarters.[49] However, there is very little to actually suggest that these
housed only women of the court. Similarly, several sites at Amarna have been
suggested as harems. Certainly, inscriptions suggest that the North Palace at
Amarna was originally built for Nefertiti or Kiya, but later taken by Meritaten.
The walled building complex is notable for its naturalistic paintings of animals,
particularly birds, and plants, and for its gardens and ponds. Its axial arrangement and the existence of what appears to be a 'Window of Appearances' (a

window from which the king could view rituals and distribute rewards) might suggest it is more likely to be a ceremonial palace than a house of women.[50] It is possible that it was both a ceremonial palace celebrating the life-giving Aten (hence the naturalistic paintings) and an institution of royal women, who would anyway have had cultic significance. However, it is also possible that royal women were housed elsewhere at Amarna.

A scene in the Amarna tomb of Ay shows a building which has been interpreted as a harem. Doorkeepers stand outside the doors. Each section contains a larger room with columns and two smaller rooms off the main room. In the smaller rooms, musical instruments are hung, while the larger rooms show women playing instruments. In one room, a woman eats while another is arranging the hair of a third. Whether these are the rooms of royal women, or other women of the palace, is not clear. The concentration of musical instruments suggests that this may be the residence of the *khener*, which, as stated above, was closely associated with the *ipt-nsw*. Some of these women, it is claimed, have foreign hairstyles, suggesting that they are not Egyptian.

The town of Medinet-Gurob (Mi-wer) is more clearly a site housing members of the royal harem, but also large numbers of the household and support staff including male employees. Inscriptions from the site record titles of officials connected with the per-khener of Mi-wer. We also know, from the existence of a papyrus found at Gurob (Petrie Museum Papyrus 32795), that the Hittite queen of Rameses II, Maathorneferura, lived here.

The name per-khener might suggest that some women from Medinet-Gurob were involved in music making. While this may have been the case, archaeological evidence suggests that the town was linked to textile manufacture, at least in part carried out by foreign women – perhaps the diplomatic brides mentioned in texts. A small wooden statue found in excavations has the title of Lady Tiy, Chief of Weavers. The papyrus Gurob III.1 is from a lady overseer to the king in the Nineteenth Dynasty. She states that foreign people had been sent to her to learn how to weave.[51] Indeed, foreign spindle whorls are recorded in graves from Gurob, and wool woven in Egypt may suggest the presence of foreigners, since the Egyptians, it is traditionally assumed, wove linen.[52] It is perhaps more difficult to attribute the quantities of high-status, imported pottery found at the site to the presence of foreigners, since elite pottery may have been the result of trade. However, the large number of ethnic names supports the idea that the town employed foreign women,[53] though it seems the majority of the town's inhabitants were Egyptian.

The archaeology of the site may be outlined thus: two large rectangular complexes are laid parallel to one another,[54] each one is divided into two parts by a corridor, and the north part has column bases and doors partially cased in stone. The town site lay within a walled enclosure (like other Egyptian towns) and was divided into three areas: southern, main and northern. The individual buildings at Medinet-Gurob have not been completely recorded. Petrie believed the houses were relatively poor with no coloured dados, or stairs leading to the roof. But this could have been due to the state of preservation of the site. Animals, goats, sheep and oxen were kept; metal tools, carpentry tools, hunting and fishing equipment, pottery and glass manufacture all attest to a complex settlement site. Artefacts such as jewellery, cosmetic items, children's toys, and of course, weaving equipment, were found. Tombs of men and women were found nearby. Not only harem workers, but presumably also those supporting the temple, lived here. The residence of the women cannot be identified with any certainty.

ROYAL CHILDREN

As we have seen, royal children were probably brought up in the harem. There is little sign of kings having large numbers of children until the reign of Rameses II, though one would expect them to have done so if they had several wives. In fact we know very little of the lives of royal children. What we do know is that daughters of pharaohs were not in a wholly enviable position. Although, at times they might take the role of king's principal wife, many more had a much more lowly status, and after the New Kingdom may even have been discouraged from marrying, perhaps to prevent claims to the throne through marriage to a royal daughter.

In the New Kingdom, at least, princes spent their formative years with a male tutor and were brought up in the *ipt-nsw*. One would assume that royal daughters would have done the same. Certainly Neferure, Hatshepsut's daughter, had a tutor. Princesses played a ritual role; in the Twelfth Dynasty *Tale of Sinuhe*, they are said to welcome the hero with their sistra. In the Eighteenth Dynasty tomb of Kheruef (TT192), unnamed royal children in the third *sed*-festival of Amenhotep III carry sistra, and in the temple of Soleb, 3 daughters of Amenhotep III are shown carrying sistra in the first *sed*-festival. The named daughters of Rameses II are shown in the Great Temple of Abu Simbel shaking sistra.[55] Women in the migdol (a gatehouse similar to those found in contemporary Asiatic fortresses) at Medinet Habu are called 'king's children'. As described above, these are shown in an erotic attitude, caressing the king. Others at Medinet Habu are shown in processions, carrying sistra and *menit*.[56] Their headdress, in both instances, consists of a modius (flat-topped headdress) adorned with the double feathers. Princes are also shown in processions at Medinet Habu, but unlike the females, the princes are named (though it may be that the inscriptions for the princesses were unfinished).

DIPLOMATIC MARRIAGES

In the New Kingdom, large numbers of women were sent to the kings of Egypt by foreign kings as diplomatic brides. Generally, we do not know if more than a handful of these ladies had sexual relations with the king, whether generally they resided in separate institutions or were resident at court, whether they were ill-used or treated with honour. They appear to have had little or no say in their lot. Women acted as valuable assets in diplomacy. The Amarna letters contain a number of documents about arranged royal marriages formed to make alliances between the kings of the Near East. Negotiations were lengthy and the bride would be sent with a sizable dowry, displaying the wealth of her native kingdom, while the groom would present a large bride-price. Egyptian kings saw marriages to foreign brides as a way of showing their own superiority, while foreign kings saw themselves as gaining the upper hand as the father-in-law of the bride.[57]

It was not only royal women who were sent to Egypt. When Amenhotep III married Gilukhepa, daughter of Shutturna II of Mitanni, she arrived with 317 attendants. On another occasion, Abdikheba of Jerusalem gave 21 women, and another ruler, '50 cattle and 20 maidens'.[58] It would seem unlikely that all these women actually resided at the court of the king, and unlikely that all were given the title 'King's Wife'. It seems more likely that some were sent to the institutions of women such as Mi-wer. There is also the possibility that foreign children were given as gifts, an idea possibly reflected in the biblical story of Moses.

Among the important diplomatic brides was the daughter of a Hittite king; when Rameses II married the first Hittite princess, she was given an Egyptian name, Maathorneferure, and became the 'King's Principal Wife'. No other foreign princess achieved this rank. She was specifically stated to be 'caused to reside in the palace of the king's house',[59] which may suggest that she was not hidden away in a house of women, but rather was at the court of the king. However, we also know that for a time she resided at Mi-wer, an institution for women, though one visited by the king.

Some lesser royal women were given honourable Egyptian burials. In 1916, a tomb on the west bank at Thebes belonging to three women, each with the title 'King's Wife', was robbed by villagers.[60] Many of the stolen funerary objects were eventually tracked down and now reside in the Metropolitan Museum of Art in New York. These funerary objects suggest that the royal women were wives, at least in the ritual sense, of Thutmose III, and were buried around 1450 BC. Their names, Manuwai, Manhata and Maruta, are not Egyptian, but appear to be West Semitic. All three had similar sets of funerary equipment, including spectacular gold jewellery, headdresses and sandals, apparently made three at a time. This suggests that these women may have died within a short period of one another, perhaps during an epidemic. None of them had the headdresses or titles suggesting that they had been a 'King's Principal Wife', but evidently these women were not without standing. While they were given elite Egyptian funerals, suggesting that these women were cared for, we know nothing of their lives.

Sadly, the treatment of foreign wives by the king of Egypt did not always meet the expectations of their kinsfolk. While foreign kings sending women to Egypt expected their women to be treated as queens, the Egyptian king, at times, merely added them to his household.[61] In one of the Amarna letters from King Kadashman-Enlil of Babylon, he complains that Amenhotep III had asked for his daughter's hand even though 'my sister, whom my father gave to you, has been there with you and no one has seen her to know if she is alive or dead'. It seems Amenhotep singled out one of a number of his women before the Babylonian messengers saying, 'Behold your mistress who stands before you'. But, the woman was not allowed to speak with the messengers, so Kadashman-Enlil replies, 'Perhaps she is the daughter of a beggar, she whom my messengers have seen. Who is to tell them, "Yes, it is indeed she," for she did not open her mouth nor say anything to them'.[62] We do not know what became of this lady.

Unlike other nations in the Near East, Egyptians did not consider their own royal women expendable, at least during the New Kingdom. Amenhotep III explained to a Babylonia king that Egyptian kings did not give away their women to foreigners. However, while instances of the giving of Egyptian royal women did not occur when Egypt was powerful,[63] during the Twenty-first Dynasty, when Egypt was no longer a powerful nation, a daughter of a king was given in marriage to King Solomon of Israel. It has been suggested[64] that since royal daughters were important in legitimization, kings were reluctant to send them off, lest it allowed foreign rulers to take control of Egypt. Thus a letter, probably from Ankhesenamun, wife of Tutankhamun, to a Hittite king reads: 'My husband died. I do not have a son . . . If you would give me one of your sons, he would become my husband . . . We are seeking a son of our Lord for the kingship in Egypt'. Naturally, the Hittite king was surprised at such as request but sent a son, who subsequently seems to have been murdered on his way to Egypt. There is another possible reason why Egyptian kings would not give away their womenfolk. Plausibly, the Egyptians considered women from foreign lands as tribute.

'HAREM PLOTS'

It is perhaps not surprising that at times royal women plotted to overthrow the king. Not only might one argue that their restricted lives made such plots inevitable, but the consequences of having one's own son succeed would have been highly desirable. Such mothers of kings were considered semi-divine and their elevation raised the status of their families. Pepi's non-royal father-in-law was allowed to call himself 'Father of the God'.[65] Power struggles may have been fermented as much by individuals related to the queen as by the queen herself, which might explain an apparent prohibition against mentioning that one was related to the queen.

Such plots by royal women are hinted at rather than explicitly described, perhaps because to admit to them would admit to absence of order, and Egyptian kings desired to portray themselves as masters of order. It could well be that in reality there were more plots than those recorded. In the Old Kingdom, an autobiography of Weni includes the information that an official had presided over the trial of a wife of Pepi I, Queen Weret-imtes, though the nature of her crimes is not stated.[66]

The Middle Kingdom *Instruction of King Amenemhat I* recounts the dismay of a king apparently attacked by his own servants, including women:

> It was after supper, night had come. I was taking an hour of rest, lying on my bed for I was weary. As my heart began to follow sleep, weapons for my protection were turned against me, while I was like a snake in the desert. I awoke at the fighting, {alert}, and found it was a combat of the guard . . .
>
> Had women ever marshalled troops?
> Are rebels nurtured in the palace?[67]

The most famous 'harem plot' however, is that of Rameses III.

THE HAREM PLOT OF RAMESES III

The Judicial Papyrus of Turin, a court transcript over 3,000 years old, gives an unusual insight into fermenting villainy within a New Kingdom harem. Supporting evidence relating to the event is given in Papyrus Rollin and Papyrus Lee. Susan Redford has published a book outlining the events.[68] It seems that Tiy, a wife of Rameses III (1184–1153 BC), plotted with other women and officials to kill the aged king and put her son, Pentewere, in his place. This would have made Tiy 'King's Mother' and eminently powerful. Papyrus Rollin suggests that the plot included magic: 'It happened because writings were made for the enchanting, for banishing and confusing. Because some gods and some men were made of wax ...'[69] The plot failed in that the conspirators were unmasked, though it is possible Rameses was killed. He died aged 65, though his mummy 'lives on' in Cairo Museum. It shows no obvious wounds and it remains unclear as to how he died, though Haslauer[70] suggests the probable cause of death as being arteriosclerosis.

A number of conspirators were forced to commit suicide and others had ears and nose chopped off. For several, the records state that the examining officials 'caused his punishment to overtake him', and it is assumed that these were killed. It is not known what happened to Tiy. Those who were executed would have suffered a lingering death by impaling, or the terror of being burnt alive. Both the *khener* and the *ipt-nsw* were involved, suggesting a close connection between the two at this date.

FEMALE KINGS

As stated above, queens were vital to kingship in the cultic sense. We know that queens mirrored the role of goddesses and that at times a king might have several wives, some of whom may have been close relatives. Here we examine a selection of particularly notable women who were more than wives or mothers of kings, including those who actually ruled as king of Egypt, and one who is famous through her bust as an icon of both Egypt and, of all places, Berlin.[71]

At certain times in Egyptian history, the King's Mother was particularly elevated; this was especially so in the Old Kingdom, though continued through to the New Kingdom. Other royal women, however, were given high status in this period. From the First Dynasty, the giant mastaba at Naqada, once called the tomb of Menes, is now considered to be that of the wife of Horus Aha, Queen Neithhotep. Her name has also been found elsewhere. A later queen, Merneith, may have reigned some years after her husband, Horus Djet, and before the succession of their son, Den. This lady was buried in Abydos tomb Y, and also built the funerary enclosure at North Abydos.

Queens of the Fourth Dynasty, the wives and mother of Khufu, had pyramid tombs, texts and funerary boats, unlike other commoners. Later in that dynasty, royal women's mastaba tombs were intermingled with those of their brothers. In the Sixth Dynasty, the queens of Pepi II and Teti were given expensive burials and allowed pyramids with texts, again something other commoners were not allowed at this time.

Occasionally, royal women of the late Middle Kingdom were given exceptional privileges. At Lahun, the king's daughter, Sat-Hathor-Iunet, was buried in the complex of King Senusret II. In the 1950s, a small pyramid about two kilometers from Amenemhat III's pyramid at Hawara was excavated; it proved to be that of Neferuptah, his daughter. Within the tomb, her name was written in a royal cartouche, despite the fact that she did not, as far as we know, hold the title 'King's Wife'; this is the first instance of a royal woman having her name in a cartouche.

Shortly after this date, around 1800 BC, Queen Sobekneferu ('The Beauty of Sobek') becomes the first female ruler whom we can be certain ruled in her own right. Africanus, a Roman historian, states she was the sister of Amenemhat IV.[72] Sobekneferu was perhaps the younger sister of princess Neferuptah and it has been suggested that Neferuptah was intended as the heir but died.[73] Such grooming of women for kingship appears extremely strange. Sobekneferu apparently legitimized her rule as rightful heir – on a red granite column, the Horus name of Amenemhat III offers life to the Horus name of Sobekneferu, suggesting the deceased king approved of her rule.[74] She carried the full king's titulary, the first woman to do so: 'The Horus, She Who Is Beloved of Re, She of the Two Ladies, Powerful Daughter, Mistress of the Two Lands, the Golden Falcon, Enduring of Appearances, King of Upper and Lower Egypt'. On a statue in the Louvre, she uses the *nemes*-headdress, a symbol of kingship, and wears a woman's dress with king's kilt over it.[75] She was only one of two female kings to use the epithet *nb irt-ḫt* ('Lord of doing things'), the other being Hatshepsut.[76] Sobekneferu was included in the king lists at Saqqara and Turin, as well as by Manetho (an Egyptian historian writing in the third century BC), showing that, at times, the Egyptians would accept the legitimacy of a female king. In the Turin king list, she is accorded a reign of around four years (c.1799–1795 BC). Unfortunately, since she seems mainly to have built in Memphis and the Fayum, her monuments have not survived, as stone was quarried for more recent building.

Ahhotep I, the mother of Ahmose, the founder of the Eighteenth Dynasty, quite clearly played a part in driving out the Hyksos, or so is credited by her son Ahmose: 'She has looked after Egypt's soldiers, she has guarded Egypt, she has brought back her fugitives and gathered her deserters, and she has pacified Upper Egypt and expelled her rebels'.[77] Evidently, the queen regent was not passive. She also held the title 'Mistress of the Two Lands',[78] comparable with the title given to kings. Against this background of kingly roles for women, the queens of the New Kingdom appear to further assert authority, for it is in this period that we encounter women such as Ahmes Nefertari, Hatshepsut and Nefertiti.

AHMES NEFERTARI (AHMES/AHMOSE NEFERTARI)
(c.1570–1506 BC)

This lady was the daughter of King Taa II (Seqenenre) and probably of his wife Ahhotep (not Ahhotep II just described).[79] She was mother of Amenhotep I, and wife and sister of Ahmose, founder of the Eighteenth Dynasty. Her titles include: 'King's Daughter', 'King's Sister', 'King's Principal Wife', 'God's Wife of Amun' and 'Mistress of Upper and Lower Egypt'. In later inscriptions (after Year 22), she is also called 'King's Mother'.

As shown by a stela at Karnak dated to around Year 18 of the reigning king, it seems her probable mother, Ahhotep, had stewardship.[80] Shortly after this, she apparently ceded pride of place to her daughter, Ahmes Nefertari.

Ahmes Nefertari used the title 'God's Wife' more than any other, possibly as her husband had given unprecedented power to this post. The power given to the 'God's Wife' by Ahmose is recorded on the Donation Stela at Karnak; the stela also records her title 'Divine Adoratrice', which accorded her even more wealth and power. Such wealth allowed her to undertake numerous works. She was strongly involved in the cult of Amun, but also in more secular works. Her name is recorded in Memphite limestone quarries and Asyut alabaster quarries with her husband. One stela even records that her husband consulted with her before erecting a cenotaph for Tetisheri at Abydos.

She had at least four sons and five daughters, five of whom died in infancy. After the death of Ahmose, she acted as regent for her son Amenhotep I for around seven years. After his wife Meritamun, she also acted as Amenhotep's consort. It is sometimes claimed that she overshadowed Meritamun, who is usually presumed to be the sister-wife of the king, though it is not certain that Meritamun was actually his wife.[81] It is possible that Ahmes Nefertari even played some part in the succession of Thutmose I, especially since he was not related to Amenhotep I. Amenhotep erected a mortuary temple for her, which unfortunately is now destroyed. When Amenhotep died, she continued to be honoured by his successor, Thutmose I, who erected a statue to her at Karnak.

It is not known exactly where she was buried, though it is said to be at Dra Abu el-Naga. Her body was found at Deir el-Bahri, in a cache of royal mummies which had been moved from their original burial places sometime in antiquity. The mummy shows that she died in her seventies, certainly a good age for an ancient Egyptian woman.

After her death, she was deified. Her cult was particularly popular among tomb workers of the pharaohs. This is not surprising, as the workers' village of the Theban necropolis was built under her and her son, Amenhotep I. She appears in various tomb paintings, often with her son. However, no certain contemporary depictions of her are known, except perhaps a bust in the Metropolitan Museum of Art.[82] She was known as 'Mistress of the Sky' and 'Lady of the West' and in this context is often shown with black skin. Contra to some views, the black skin does not mean that she was of southern African descent, but rather the colour is symbolic of the annual regeneration of the Nile, as befits a goddess of resurrection. The god Osiris, too, is frequently shown with black skin, and on some coffins mortal individuals may be shown alternately with both pale and black skin.

The power formerly concentrated in the post of this God's Wife now came to rest in the hands of another remarkable woman, Hatshepsut.

HATSHEPSUT (c.1470–1458 BC)

Hatshepsut's reputation has often followed popular opinion surrounding the roles of women in contemporary society, so that she has been considered variously as the archetypal wicked stepmother, or a heroic Joan of Arc figure, saviour of a dynastic line. These imaginative reconstructions of her life are in part due to the fact that so little is actually known of her, though it must be admitted that we know more about her than many other queens, or indeed, male kings.

Her name, Hatshepsut, means 'Foremost of Noble Women'. She was married to Thutmose II, her half-brother, when he was probably aged 14 or 15,[83] and bore him no sons, but one daughter, Neferure. Like Ahmes Nefertari, Hatshepsut used 'God's Wife of Amun' as her preferred title during the reign of her half-brother. When he died, the crown passed to Thutmose III, a young son of another wife of Thutmose II, called Isis, while Hatshepsut became regent. Hatshepsut's age at Thutmose's accession has been put anywhere between 15 and 25 years old.[84] Thutmose III seemed to have been proud of his mother Isis and promoted her posthumously to 'King's Principal Wife' and 'God's Wife of Amun'.

The death of Thutmose II and what transpired are described by the architect Ineni:

> [Thutmose II] ascended to heaven and united with the gods, while his son stood in his place as king of the two lands, having assumed rulership upon the throne of the one who begat him, and while his sister, the god's wife Hatshepsut, was conducting the affairs of the country, the two lands being in her care.[85]

There is no early indication that this was to be anything unusual. Women had held the reins of power previously on behalf of young kings. Although it is sometimes assumed that from the start Hatshepsut set out to take kingly power for herself, early depictions of her are of a woman without kingly titles. A stela in Berlin shows her in typical female pose standing behind her stepson and Ahmose. In Year 2 of Thutmose's reign, she is depicted in the Semna temple in Nubia as a minor figure, while Thutmose III is depicted as sole king. Her tomb was begun at Wadi Sikkat Taka el-Zeidi rather than the kingly burial grounds, the Valley of the Kings, and her quartzite sarcophagus survives with its prayer to Nut:

> The King's Daughter, God's Wife, King's Great Wife, Lady of the Two Lands, Hatshepsut, says: 'O my mother Nut, stretch over me so that you may place me amongst the undying stars that are in you, and that I may not die.'[86]

After several years of acting as regent for Thutmose III, she became king alongside him. It is not known exactly when she was crowned; she counted her reign from her co-regency with Thutmose III, and it is clear that she was not a king in Year 2 of Thutmose's reign, but was crowned before his Year 7. The tomb of Ramose and Hatnofer, parents of Senenmut, contained several amphora dating to Year 7. Two were stamped with the seal of 'The Good Goddess Maatkare' (Maatkare, 'Truth is the soul of Re' being the throne name of Hatshepsut). On her coronation, she had taken the kingly five-fold titulary: 'Horus, Powerful of Kas; Two Ladies, Flourishing of Years; Female Horus of Fine Gold, Divine-of-Diadems; King of Upper and Lower Egypt, Maatkare; Daughter of Re, Khenmet-Amun Hatshepsut (the One who is joined to Amun, the Foremost of Women)'. The traditional royal names were sprinkled with female endings. As has been pointed out,[87] at this period, Hatshepsut's father, husband and stepson are also sometimes given feminine epithets and pronouns. It is suggested that this appears too often to be accidental. It could be that this was a means of paving the way for future 'female kings', particularly Hatshepsut's daughter, Neferure, or that Hatshepsut sought to establish a more androgynous model of kingship.

She also used the title, *nbt t3wy* ('Mistress of the Two Lands)'. Sobekneferu had earlier used it as king, and it was first used in the New Kingdom by Ahhotep I, daughter of Taa I, and then by Ahmes Nefertari. Meritamun I, daughter of Ahmes Nefertari, used the closely related term *ḥnwt t3wy* ('Lady of the Two Lands'), which has an earlier pedigree.[88]

As king, Hatshepsut is shown wearing the kilt and insignia of a king, including the false beard, striding forward and reaching out, instead of in the passive pose of woman with feet close together and arms at her sides. In the temple at Deir el-Bahri, where her birth is shown, she is presented as a male child. In the form of a sphinx, an image previously used by royal women, she presents a more masculine image, enhanced by wearing the *nemes*-headdress of the king rather than a woman's wig. Much is made of the fact that Hatshepsut was shown dressed as a king, despite the fact the previous important female rulers, such as Khentkawes I and Sobekneferu,[89] did the same. It would be ridiculous to see Hatshepsut as a transvestite. Egyptian reliefs, such as hieroglyphs, were intended to show ideas and ideals. Thutmose III was also shown as an adult, active king even when a child. Additionally, although much is made of Hatshepsut taking on masculine symbols to assert her kingship, it is also evident that she emphasized her femininity. She does not, for example, take the title 'The Strong Bull' and she describes herself as a beautiful woman.

Why she should change from regent to co-regent is unclear. It seems she initially intended to rule in the name of Thutmose III, although could not officially do so as she was not his mother. If Hatshepsut had intended to take the role of king from the start, surely she would have taken it sooner? It is possible that without Hatshepsut, Thutmose would have been ousted, especially when a young king, and on campaigns outside Egypt.[90] The death of the mother of Thutmose III, Isis, may have necessitated Hatshepsut taking over as king, or alternatively, the death of her own mother Ahmes (Ahmose) may have been the catalyst.[91] Ahmes would have had some authority, due to her own ties with the royal family. For whatever reason, Thutmose III agreed to a joint sharing of power at this stage. There is no evidence for rivalry, or of attempts to depose him. In monuments and inscriptions, Hatshepsut did not portray him as any less a king than herself.[92] It was during this period that the necessity of writing the names of both kings led to the shortening of them as *per-aa*, (pharaoh, meaning 'Great House').

That Hatshepsut did not step down when Thutmose became king has been seen as proof of ambition. However, once crowned she could not abdicate. While some claim that her taking on the reins of power cannot have been gradual, others[93] suggest a more gradual metamorphosis.

Hatshepsut legitimized her title as king through her claim to be the intended heir of Thutmose I (Thutmose II was a less impressive ancestor) and the daughter of Amun. Her divine nature was declared on the walls of her mortuary temple at Deir el-Bahri through a description of her divine conception and birth. She was the first ruler to include the divine birth scene in her temple construction,[94] though of course not the first to claim rule by right of being divinely conceived. It is possible that she instituted this scene because her claim to rule was not routine. In the temple at Deir el-Bahri, Amun is shown visiting Hatshepsut's mother, Ahmes, whom she recognized by his divine odour. She is made pregnant by the god and gives birth to Hatshepsut. The inscription describes her mother's impregnation by the god Amun:

She awoke because of the savour of the god, and she laughed in the presence of his majesty. He was ardent for her. He gave his heart unto her. He let her see him in his form of a god, after he came before her. She rejoiced at beholding his beauty, his love it went through her body. The palace was flooded with the savour of the god, all his odours were as (those of) Punt. Then his majesty of this god did all he desired with her. She let him rejoice over her. She kissed him . . .[95]

The oracle of Amun reinforced Hatshepsut's legitimacy to rule. We do not know how the oracle of Amun actually spoke to Hatshepsut. Other Egyptian oracles answered questions by moving in response to questions, that is, the statue of the god would move, presumably with the aid of priests, in particular ways which were interpreted by priests. The Red Chapel at Karnak describes the oracle of Amun as proclaiming Hatshepsut as the rightful heir. Amun declares: 'Welcome my sweet daughter, my favourite, the King of Upper and Lower Egypt, Maatkare, Hatshepsut. You are the Pharaoh, taking possession of the two lands'.

As a king needed a queen, Neferure, Hatshepsut's daughter, rose to prominence and the title 'God's Wife' was passed to the daughter at the time of her mother's coronation. It has been suggested that Neferure was being groomed as heir apparent, but it could be simply that Hatshepsut needed a female partner for ritual. Little is known of the daughter. It is possible that Neferure is the unnamed God's Wife on the Red Chapel at Karnak. She possibly predeceased her mother[96] as she is not mentioned in Hatshepsut's later years.

Studies of Hatshepsut invariably consider the role of her most powerful courtier, Senenmut, tutor to Neferure, 'Steward of the Estates of Amun' and 'Overseer of all Royal Works', a man of relatively humble, though not lowly, birth. Modern commentators appear particularly interested in the relationship between the king and this courtier and are frequently fascinated by the question of whether or not the two were sexually involved.[97] Senenmut carved his name into Hatshepsut's mortuary temple and second tomb near Deir el-Bahri, suggesting a close relationship.

A graffito from an unfinished Middle Kingdom tomb at Deir el-Bahri, showing an unnamed woman being sexually penetrated from behind by an unnamed male is often claimed to be evidence of a sexual relationship between Hatshepsut and Senenmut.[98] In support, it is also said that he remained unmarried. However, the identification of the woman as Hatshepsut and the man as Senenmut, first put forward by Romer,[99] is based on very flimsy evidence; as neither figure is named, we cannot assume the identity of either. The cap worn by the female figure is said to look like a royal headdress without a uraeus, but this can equally be interpreted as a wig common to women of the Eighteenth Dynasty. Even if the figure was intended to be Hatshepsut, this does not prove a sexual relationship with Senenmut, only that workmen wondered about her sex life, just as today the sex lives of important women hold a fascination for the media. It is also possible that Senenmut was married; we should not make too much of the absence of a wife in Senenmut's tomb, as this was normal for men who served women. However, in support of his being a bachelor, it was Senenmut's brother, rather than a son, who carried out his funerary rites,[100] suggesting lack of an heir and, possibly therefore, lack of a wife.

Hatshepsut's reign was marked by many achievements: the extension of the cult of Amun, extensive trading, building projects and perhaps even a certain amount of warfare. It has been suggested that the most important contribution Hatshepsut made as king was the extension of the cult of Amun.[101] It was Hatshepsut who established the link between kingship and Amun in the Opet festival of Luxor, and through the Beautiful Feast of the Valley, brought Amun to the west bank.

Given that women are often considered gentle and passive, some might expect that Hatshepsut abstained from warfare. Certainly, with some exceptions, she rarely presented herself as a great warrior. However, her reign with Thutmose III saw at least two southern campaigns,[102] with at least one being led by Hatshepsut herself. An inscription at Sehel by a man called Tyt, the 'Overseer of the Seal', bears witness to the role of Hatshepsut in defeating Nubia[103]: 'I followed the good god, the King of Upper and Lower Egypt Maatkare, may she live! I saw him [i.e. Hatshepsut] overthrowing the Nubian nomads, their chiefs being brought to him as prisoners. I saw him destroying the land of Nubia while I was in the following of His Majesty . . .'[104] Additionally, from the stela of Djehuty comes a testimony that Hatshepsut herself was on the battlefield. The inscription at Speos Artemidos is discussed below, and while it is probably an exaggeration, it shows that the queen was certainly not averse to presenting an aggressive side.

However, it is Hatshepsut the trader, rather than Hatshepsut the warrior, who is the better known. Her missions to exotic Punt, the birthplace of the gods, are commemorated on her mortuary temple at Deir el-Bahri by depictions of strange flora and fauna, and scenes of tribute such as ivory, apes, ostrich feathers, eggs, ebony and incense; these are all things associated with revitalization and the essence of life. The queen of Punt is shown, in contrast to Egyptian women, as a grotesquely obese figure. This is perhaps to emphasize her foreign otherness, to display the fecundity of the land of Punt, or maybe because Puntite elite women were obese. It is not known exactly where Punt was, though it is generally believed to be in the area of Ethiopia, a journey which would have involved carrying a boat across the desert, and then travelling south from the Red Sea Port of Quseir.

Such a venture would have displayed the divine power of the queen; her role in the revitalization of Egypt and the arrival of rare and exotic goods from the land of the gods would have shown her to be a true king.

Hatshepsut also carried out major building projects in Nubia, Kom Ombo, Hierakonpolis, Elkab, Armant, Elephantine and elsewhere. Two temples were built at Elephantine. However, most of her work seems to have been around Thebes. A central part of the Karnak complex was largely due to Hatshepsut and Thutmose III, and Hatshepsut's Red Chapel provided a resting place for the processional boat of Amun. At Karnak, Hatshepsut built extensively for the god Amun and also added to the temple of Mut, Amun's consort.

In Middle Egypt, the rock-cut temple of Speos Artemidos dedicated to Pakhet is today little known by tourists, but is well worth a visit. Unlike some of the more popular tourist destinations, this temple retains an air of mystery. Pakhet, 'She who Scratches' was said to roam the wadis sharpening her claws of stone on the rocks (the marks left by the torrents of water are visible in the dry desert earth and one can imagine these as her claw marks). Pakhet was a lioness goddess associated with Sekhmet, the more aggressive side of Hathor. The temple, like other temples to Hathor, emerges from the natural rock, at the entrance to a ravine, a link between the underworld and this world, a liminal place. An inscription here bears Hatshepsut's testament:

> I have never slumbered as one forgetful, but have made strong what was decayed. I have raised up what was dismembered, even from the first time when the Asiatics were in Avaris of the North Land, with roving hordes in the midst of them overthrowing what had been made; they ruled without Re . . . I have banished the abominations of the gods, and the earth has removed their footprints.[105]

There is no evidence that Hatshepsut rid Egypt of the Hyksos, the Asiatics, as their rule had ended years before her birth. She did, however, restore Egypt's monuments.

Deir el-Bahri, another of Hatshepsut's rock-cut temples, is much more famous. Known to the ancients as *Djeser-Djeser*, 'Holiest of the Holy', this temple was built in a spot sacred to the goddess Hathor, close by Mentuhotep II's mortuary temple in western Thebes. It is one of the most well-known and impressive temples standing in Egypt today. The whole area of Thebes west is replete with imagery of gods, or more usually goddesses, emerging from the living rock,[106] and the natural rock formations above the Deir el-Bahri have been said to show the sacred uraeus, the hooded cobra, the daughter and Eye of Re and protector of kings. It is possible that the female king felt an especial affinity with Hathor and other goddesses.[107] In this temple, Hatshepsut is shown being suckled by the goddess Hathor herself, in her form as a cow.

While the west bank bears a concentration of female gods, the main sanctuary at Deir el-Bahri is dedicated to Hatshepsut's divine father, Amun. There are also other chapels, including one devoted to Thutmose I and one to Hatshepsut herself, another to Anubis (who is here ranked almost with Osiris), and one to Hathor. The temple is decorated with a series of colossal statues of Hatshepsut in the form of the mummified Osiris. The architect of the temple is assumed to have been Senenmut.

A stela at Armant suggests that Hatshepsut died around 1458 BC after having reigned for 22 years. We have her sarcophagus and canopic chest, but the tomb associated with her, KV20, contained no body. KV60, the tomb of the Royal Nurse, Sitre, was discovered by Carter in 1903 and found to contain two female mummies. Carter was not interested in the tomb and resealed it. Edward Ayrton reopened the tomb in 1906 and removed Lady Sitre to the Cairo museum; the other body was left in the tomb. In 1989, Donald P. Ryan rediscovered the tomb and in June 2007, the mummy from KV60 was identified as Hatshepsut on the grounds of a DNA comparison with her great-grandmother Ahmes Nefertari and a molar tooth. The tooth had been found inside a small wooden box inscribed with Hatshepsut's name. Zahi Hawass declared that the tooth fitted exactly a missing tooth from the KV60 mummy. The mummy was that of an obese woman aged around 50 who was suffering from cancer.

Towards the end of Thutmose III's reign, he tried to obliterate Hatshepsut's name by chiselling her cartouches and images from monuments. This erasure, however, was not fully carried out and seems to have been somewhat half-hearted. It is also noticeable that Thutmose did not do this immediately on becoming sole ruler, but rather some twenty years after Hatshepsut's death. There are various ideas as to Thutmose motives and the timing of his actions. It is suggested[108] that her name may have been erased to stop other powerful females asserting authority, while others[109] argue that Hatshepsut's name was obliterated because she overstepped the boundaries of acceptable behaviour in her manifestation of a female king. Caution is required in this respect, as the Egyptians held a fluid idea of sexuality.[110] Additionally, Thutmose did not erase all her inscriptions; it is possible that at this important stage in his military career, he saw it as the continuation of his power to claim that he, not Hatshepsut, had ruled. Alternatively, it could be suggested that as a powerful man, sycophantic advisors had told him that it was indeed he who should have ruled in Hatshepsut's place. He was thus perhaps less willing to give any credence to Hatshepsut's achievements, as he had in the early years of his 'reign'. He may not have obliterated Hatshepsut's name until he had made the decision to make his son, Amenhotep II, co-regent.[111] Amenhotep II's name replaced that of Hatshepsut on the eighth pylon at Karnak, suggesting that Thutmose wanted a clear patrilinear lineage for his son. He did not usually replace her image with his own, but generally with that of his father or grandfather, Thutmose I or II.[112] Whatever the reason for erasing her name, it appears unlikely that Thutmose hated her as a person, as her names and figures were left intact. As a general of her army, he could have destroyed her earlier, had he wished to. It is likely that we will never know the true reasons, but we cannot assume that Hatshepsut had been the grasping, wicked stepmother.

Thus, Hatshepsut's achievements were certainly impressive. As far as her contribution to women's roles, it was during the reign of Thutmose III that the role of non-royal women changed and it was during this period that the title 'Chantress of Amun' became established.

NEFERTITI (c.1390–1340 BC)

While Hatshepsut extended the cult of Amun, our next royal lady, Nefertiti, is famous through her marriage to Akhenaten, the heretic pharaoh who abandoned Amun in favour of the Aten. Nefertiti is certainly one of the most well-known Egyptian women; copies of her elegant bust are displayed on jewellery and tee shirts, and she is proclaimed in popular literature as the most beautiful woman in the world. Her famous bust now resides in the Berlin Museum, and is not only an icon of Egypt, but of Berlin itself! There have been numerous television programmes and books, both popular and academic, dealing with this enigmatic, though undoubtedly powerful, lady. Her life was certainly remarkable. She was one of the most significant women in Egyptian history, she lived in unusual, one might say revolutionary, times, but what she actually looked like, and the mystery of her fate on the death of her husband, remain unclear.

Nefertiti was born around 1380 BC. Her name means 'A Beautiful One Has Come'. She does not seem to have been a member of the immediate royal family and may have been the daughter of Ay, one of Akhenaten's officials who later succeeded Tutankhamun. Ay was granted a tomb in the Amarna cliffs, in which he is shown receiving golden necklaces from the royal couple. He also had the title 'God's Father', which, it has been suggested, means 'King's Father-in-law'. His wife Tiy appears to have been Nefertiti's wet nurse.

Nefertiti was 'King's Principal Wife' to Akhenaten. Within five years of his succession, Akhenaten altered Egypt's religion, changing the emphasis from the worship of Amun at Karnak to that of the rays of the sun's disk, the Aten. He is sometimes credited with being the first monotheistic pharaoh, though this is unlikely. On moving to Amarna, Nefertiti's name is changed to Neferneferuaten-Nefertiti, meaning 'Beautiful are the Beauties of the Aten. A Beautiful One has Come'.

Nefertiti is shown in early depictions, such as on the tomb of Ramose (TT55), wearing a uraeus and a Nubian-style, short, bobbed wig, which from then on was associated with royal women. At other times, she wears a variety of crowns, sometimes the Hathor sun disk between horns, the single or double uraeus, the double feathers or a combination of Hathor's crown and the feathers. She also develops her own unique headdress – a blue, straight-edged, flat-topped helmet shape, reminiscent of the blue war-crown of kings. This headdress is depicted in the famous and much copied Berlin bust. She does not wear the vulture headdress of Mut, perhaps as Mut was the consort of Amun, the god whom Akhenaten largely usurped in favour of the Aten.

After his fifth year, or thereabouts, Akhenaten is shown in statuary as a semi-feminine form, with wide hips, slight breasts, narrow waist, protruding stomach and an elongated head. Although speculation has arisen that he was suffering from disease, it is perhaps more likely that this was an ideological depiction of the king in which he possibly wished to show himself as the mother and father of his people. At the same time, Nefertiti and other members of the court are depicted in similar form to the king. Both Nefertiti and Queen Tiy are shown, unusually for Egyptian elite women, nude or semi-nude and with flabby stomachs, possibly to emphasize their fertility. The similarity between depictions of Nefertiti and Akhenaten at this time sometimes makes it hard to distinguish between the two, especially as the conventions of portraying women with pale skin and men with dark skin were not followed. Instead, a red-brown skin hue was used for both.

Her six daughters are given unusual prominence in the temple and palace reliefs at Amarna. No male heirs are ever mentioned or depicted, though princes are rarely depicted in pre-Nineteenth Dynasty Egyptian art anyway. The princesses are shown with the royal couple in scenes of intimacy which were extraordinary until this period.

Nefertiti was not the only wife of Akhenaten. He was also married to Mitannian and Babylonian princesses, about whom little is known. Kiya, another woman who also appears on monuments as 'King's Wife', but never 'King's Principal Wife', is sometimes considered to be a Mitannian princess. It is not known what happened to her, but her monuments appear to have been usurped by the daughters of Nefertiti. Her coffin and canopic jars were found in KV55, but had been reused for another burial.

To celebrate his jubilee, Akhenaten built temples at Karnak including the Gem Pa Aten ('The Sun Disk is Found') and the Hwt Benben ('Mansion of the

Benben Stone'). The bulk of these temples was destroyed in antiquity, though blocks from them remain, reused for other building works. The larger of the two temples at Karnak, the Gem Pa Aten, had rows of piers showing Nefertiti and her eldest daughter, Meritaten, sacrificing to the sun disk. When the king and queen are shown together, Nefertiti is in the subsidiary role behind him; where Akhenaten is not shown, Meritaten assumes the role of queen to Nefertiti. The Hwt Benben at Karnak is wholly given over to depictions of the queen, possibly suggesting that it was a mortuary structure.[113] At this date, funerary monuments of royal women did not show their husbands.

Although queens are often considered passive, talatat blocks (stone blocks of standard size employed in the Amarna Period) from Amarna show Nefertiti smiting the female enemies of Egypt. This follows from the tradition of showing Queen Tiy as a female sphinx trampling the enemies of Egypt (see above for the feline associations of royal women). The Amarna Period does not appear to have been particularly passive or egalitarian; the royal couple processed through Amarna accompanied by soldiers; and common people are shown in the royal tomb bowing and scraping before their might. Nor should we assume that this was a new monotheistic religion; Nefertiti and Akhenaten assume the roles of the gods of Shu and Tefnut, and together are depicted as the only persons to receive the life rays of the Aten. The common people appear to have prayed before the royal couple.

Nefertiti evidently had an important religious role, but did she have any political power? It is sometimes suggested that Nefertiti ruled as co-regent, though there is no actual evidence for this. She is not included in the royal archives, the Amarna letters, unlike Queen Tiy. One of her titles *nbt t3wy* ('Mistress of the Two Lands') was not novel in itself, having been used by Hatshepsut before she assumed power. Nefertiti, however, uses it in front of her cartouche (like the king she uses the double cartouche). In the tomb of Panehsy, Nefertiti and Akhenaten are shown wearing the *atef* crown, an elaborate headdress usually associated with the cult of Osiris. The only other female ruler known to have worn the *atef* was Hatshepsut.[114]

How Nefertiti achieved her unusually prominent role will never be known. It is possible that to some extent, she was able to build upon the achievements of her predecessors, such as Ahmes Nefertari and Queen Tiy. Queen Tiy, wife of Amenhotep III, mother of Akhenaten, and thus matriarch of the Amarna royal family, also seems to have had a prominent role.

By the king's fourteenth year, it is assumed that Nefertiti had died, though the only evidence of her death is a single broken shabti (a funerary figurine). At the same time, four of her daughters disappear from the record, suggesting that they too died at this time. An infectious disease has been suggested, possibly plague. An alternative theory is that Nefertiti assumed the role of co-regent in order to succeed her husband, and took the name Smenkhare (whose second name, Neferneferuaten, she shared). Against this theory, a body of a young man was found in tomb KV55 in the Valley of the Kings, which has been tentatively identified as Smenkhare. The Queen was probably buried in the royal tomb at Amarna, with her husband, though no trace of a mummy survives. One of Nefertiti's daughters, Ankhesenamun, married Tutankhamun.

Nefertiti remains well known; her image is recognized largely through copies of the famous limestone bust from the workshop of the sculptor Thutmose at Amarna, found by the German excavator, Ludwig Borchardt. When Thutmose left Amarna, he left behind over fifty unfinished busts, or artists' teaching aids, among them that of Nefertiti in her blue crown, her kohl-rimmed eyes gazing serenely over the millennia. The fact that the bust has only one eye may suggest either that it was unfinished, or that a second eye was not needed as the bust was a teaching aid. The bust is now considered an archetype of female beauty. Of course, we cannot know that Nefertiti actually looked like this. As with all Egyptian art, representations were idealized and stylized.

The bust now resides in the museum at Berlin, an object of controversy as Egypt declares it was illegally taken from the country. She has been adopted as an icon for several diverse groups. Her depiction as a serene, mature and elegant woman is today partly a symbol of Berlin, but also a symbol of modern Egyptian femininity.

It is often said that during the Amarna Period, the role of women was particularly marked[115] and there are many more representations of women in tombs. The role of royal women, in particular, appears to have expanded during the Eighteenth Dynasty.

CLEOPATRA VII (c.69–31 BC)

We now move forward over a thousand years to a time when Egypt was very different. It was no longer the centre of its own Empire, but a part of the Graeco-Roman world, with Greek as the official language. However, the Egyptian religion continued, though with some changes. Indeed, most of the major temples which we see standing in Egypt today are largely a product of the Graeco-Roman Period. Cleopatra was the name given to several Ptolemaic queens of Egypt, of which Cleopatra VII is the most well-known. Greek women did not enjoy the same freedom as Egyptian women, although Ptolemaic queens were remarkably privileged among their sex. Although this book is largely about Pharaonic Egypt prior to the Graeco-Roman Period, Cleopatra VII is included as she is arguably the most famous of female Egyptian rulers, popularized by Shakespeare and Elizabeth Taylor.

At a time when Rome had troops stationed in Egypt, Cleopatra VII first shared a co-regency with her father, Ptolemy XII, and then with her brother, Ptolemy XIII. Her brother ousted her from power and threatened her life. She fled east and then returned to Egypt in 48 BC with an army. The same year, the 15-year-old Ptolemy XIII agreed to the murder of Pompey, a rival of Julius Caesar. But, Caesar was angered by this agreement and on being confronted with Pompey's pickled head, attempted to restore Cleopatra as co-regent. However, the people of Alexandria had another queen in mind, Cleopatra's sister, Arsinoe IV, and Cleopatra and Caesar were besieged in the palace at Alexandria. When Roman reinforcements arrived in March 47 BC, Ptolemy XIII fled and drowned in the Nile while Arsinoe was captured and taken to Rome. Cleopatra took as her husband her 11-year-old brother Ptolemy XIV, but approximately a year later bore a son whom she claimed was fathered by Caesar. He was named Ptolemy Caesar (known as Caesarion).

In 46 BC, she visited Rome with Ptolemy XIV, stayed for over a year on Caesar's private estate, but left when he was assassinated. Some commentators believe that she did not stay for a year but took several shorter trips to Rome during the course of the year. A statue representing her was erected next to an image of Venus in Rome.[116] On returning to Egypt, Ptolemy XIV died, possibly also assassinated, and Cleopatra replaced him with her son Caesarion. She then killed her sister Arsinoe, now freed by the Romans. When Mark Anthony, with Octavian and Marcus Lepidus, arrived in Egypt as part a group intending to revenge Caesar's death, she met with Anthony and offered an alliance. In 40 BC, she gave birth to twins, Cleopatra Selene and Alexander Helios, Anthony's children. She then officially married him even though he already had a Roman wife, Octavia, and a male lover, Messala. A further son by Mark Anthony was named Ptolemy Philadelphos.

In 34 BC, Mark Anthony gave parts of the Eastern Roman Empire to Cleopatra and her children, justifying this by claiming Cleopatra and her sons as client rulers for Rome. In 32 BC, Anthony divorced Octavia. Both actions caused dissent in Rome and Cleopatra became the victim of a propaganda campaign which further turned Rome against her. In 31 BC, Octavian attacked and defeated Mark Anthony at Actium, partly as Cleopatra's fleet unexpectedly withdrew. Anthony committed suicide, closely followed by Cleopatra. Whether she died from the bite of a snake or by some other means is not known. Octavian then had Caesarion killed and proclaimed himself king of Egypt. The other children were taken to Rome and displayed in a public triumph. They were later raised by Octavia, Anthony's Roman wife. Cleopatra's tomb has never been found.

Unlike Hatshepsut, Cleopatra did not portray herself in masculine attire, but rather played on her femininity as a mother and the personification of the mother goddess, Isis.

However, she does seem to have associated herself with her father Ptolemy XII. Not only did she resemble him on coins, but she called herself 'New Isis', in parallel to Ptolemy XII's title 'New Dionysus'. Another title, 'Daughter of Geb', had been used earlier by Arsinoe II. Cleopatra was regarded as a goddess; her personal cult lasted almost 350 years after her death.[117]

Cleopatra is often seen as a black African. While she was descended from Macedonian Greeks, her family had lived in Egypt for 272 years and we do not know her mother's identity.[118] However, in her own country, she presented herself as an Egyptian,[119] not a Greek, and as Egypt is in Africa she should surely remain an African icon, though her skin colour is unknowable. Ethnic identity is not only about genetics, but also about choice.

Sadly perhaps, for today's women, one of the greatest preoccupations with Cleopatra seems to surround her looks; was she beautiful or ugly? One can hardly imagine such a question being asked about a male Egyptian king. The answer is, of course, that we do not know. The coinage of Cleopatra does not, to our eyes, portray a beauty, but such images were more idealized than actual. She was portrayed as suited the occasion – on Egyptian monuments as the slender goddess Isis, and on Greek-style portraits with the harsh features of her father. Later Arab writers talk of her intelligence, rather than her beauty, and this aspect of her person is hard to deny. We know she was well educated, speaking several languages, and reputedly the only Ptolemaic ruler to have learnt to read hieroglyphs.

EGYPTIAN ATTITUDES TO WOMEN IN POWER

While it is very clear that the Egyptian king was ideally male, and that Egypt was essentially patriarchal, this does not mean that it was not possible for royal women to hold positions of authority. We should not assume that the ancient Egyptians were completely unable to accept the idea of a woman as ruler. While gender was a duality, androgyny was possible in the realm of the mythic, and both male and female could, in theory, be incorporated in one. For mortals, the idea of gender fluidity was made necessary for women to attain the afterlife. Not only is there ample evidence for powerful queens as 'King's Mother', with several acting as regents, but female kings, such as Sobekneferu, are even included in king lists. The assumption that the eradication of the name of queens who ruled in their own right was carried out because of the Egyptian dislike of female rulers, is misplaced. Women who ruled as kings were usually the last of each dynasty, and were thus succeeded by kings of less legitimacy, who strengthened their own right to rule by obliterating the names of their predecessors.[120]

Goddesses

Contrary to popular opinion, the Egyptians did not worship animals, but rather the characters of deities were symbolized in animal forms. Cows and vultures were among those animals considered motherly. Many female goddesses had the characteristics of the perfect wife and mother – kind, gentle and nurturing – and were thus depicted in cow or vulture form. However, there were also aggressive, fiery goddesses, who killed and maimed, and here the lioness was a more suitable metaphor. Strangely, to us, goddesses could change form.

The ancient Egyptians did not consider deities as individuals, like people. Their specific names were not as important as their characters. Thus, deities could be merged, or in the case of the myth of the 'Return of the Distant One', could even transform from one to another. In some instances, a deity apparently represented as one individual could be given two names, or names could be combined. On a Twenty-first Dynasty coffin in the Egypt Centre, Swansea, a tree-goddess is called both Nut and Maat.

While there are parallels between the way gods are described and the way women were understood in ancient Egypt, we need to be wary of assuming that goddesses acted as role models for female human society. Goddesses are often shown in ways in which a female human would never be: goddesses are shown suckling, elite women are not; goddesses are shown holding knives, women are not. Here, a selection of deities will be explored with the aim of revealing the essential nature of some of the most important ones.

The Eye of Re, or Horus, is a vital element of the male god Re. However, this is a female entity, the daughter of Re, sometimes associated with Hathor, and at other times with Mut, Sekhmet, and Tefnut. It appears as the protective uraeus on the forehead of the king. It always relates to the illuminating, active, creative or seeing aspect of Re,[1] so goddesses are described as the Eye when creative, or active roles are ascribed to them.

NUT

Nut was considered the daughter of Shu, the sister and wife of Geb, and the mother of Isis, Seth, Osiris and Nephthys and sometimes of Re. She was never a goddess of everyday life, but instead is connected to temple and tomb.[2] She is the protector of the deceased and the concealed uterine space from which the deceased may be reborn.

In the *Pyramid Texts*, Nut is a protector of the king, allowing him to be reborn. As such, she is later identified with the lids of coffins and the interiors of some examples are decorated with depictions of the goddess. On Twenty-first Dynasty coffins, in particular, Nut is portrayed as the tree-goddess providing sustenance and protection for the deceased. She is shown either in front of the sycamore fig, or as an integral part of the tree, pouring refreshment for the deceased.

The scene of a Nut stretching over the heavens and above a reclining Geb develops from the New Kingdom, becoming particularly popular at Thebes in the tenth and eleventh centuries BC. Here Nut is the sky-goddess. In New Kingdom iconography, Nut is frequently depicted as naked. This may correspond with the idea of a sexual union between Geb and Nut, which is described in the *Pyramid Texts*, or may be to show that Nut is giving birth, as ancient Egyptian women may have given birth naked.[3]

Most cultures consider the earth female; in ancient Egypt, however, the sky-goddess, Nut, is depicted as arching over the male earth god, Geb. A convincing explanation has been proposed for why this should be so: in most cultures the sky is the active entity bringing forth rain to fertilize the passive earth. In Egypt, the earth was fertilized by the annual inundation of the Nile, which came from the earth and not the sky. The female sky, however, acted to stimulate the earth into procreation.[4]

As a sky-goddess, the sun passed through Nut's mouth and body each night and was reborn again each morning. One myth describes how Geb quarrelled with Nut because she kept swallowing their children, the stars. The idea of Nut receiving her children by swallowing and giving birth to them, and of the quarrel between Geb and Nut, is recorded for the first time in the Osirian text in the cenotaph of Seti I at Abydos.[5]

Nut could also be portrayed as a cow arching over the sky, although Nut as a cow is never a common motif. The Hathor horns with sun disk are, however, not infrequently used to adorn her head from the New Kingdom onward. Occasionally too, Nut may take other maternal forms such as a vulture or hippopotamus.

NEITH

Neith is possibly the earliest of the commonly worshipped female deities to which we can attribute a name. She is attested as early as the Predynastic Period, or at least her sign of crossed arrows appears on Naqada III pottery and on Predynastic rock art.[6] A wooden label of King Aha, the first ruler of a united Egypt, from Abydos (c.3100 BC), shows him visiting her sanctuary. Two of the most important First Dynasty royal women, Neithhotep (meaning 'Neith is content') and Merneith (meaning 'Beloved of Neith') had names which incorporated that of the goddess. That her standard appears above the names of these women, in the same way that Horus appears above the name of early kings, might suggest that Early Dynastic women had similar roles to that of the king.[7]

Although early evidence for Neith comes from Abydos in Upper Egypt, she was usually shown wearing the red crown of Lower Egypt and as such personified the kingship of Lower Egypt. The king was known as 'He of the Sedge and the Bee' and Neith's temple at Saïs, Lower Egypt, was sometimes known as the 'House of the Bee'. In Roman times, inscriptions at the temple of Khnum in Esna claim she was an Upper Egyptian goddess who only later settled in Lower Egypt. The importance of Neith in Early Dynastic Egypt may reflect the importance of the Delta and Saïs, in particular, during the period of state formation.[8] In the Early Dynastic Period, Neith was associated with both male and female royalty. As shown in the *Pyramid Texts*, she is a protector of the king in the afterlife, though the fact that she is mentioned less frequently than Isis and Nut may suggest she was more a goddess of the living at this date. By this date, Neith had become known as the consort of Seth and the mother of Sobek.

From early times, Neith appears to have been associated with the sign of the crossed arrows, sometimes overlaid on a shield. Some have suggested that another sign, that of the elatarid (the coleoptera beetle or click beetle) placed head to head was earlier and then reinterpreted as a shield with two crossed arrows.[9] Which emblem came first is open to debate. The sign of the arrows suggests her warrior or huntress nature, but why she should be associated with the beetles is unclear. Click beetles are often found near water, and Neith was associated with both Mehet-Weret, the goddess whose name means 'The Great Flood', and with the waters of origins.[10] Additionally, some of these beetles are luminous, perhaps relating to Neith's Old Kingdom epithet 'Opener of the Way', in which role she can be seen as a double of Wepwawet, the male jackal god of Upper Egypt, whose name also means 'Opener of the Way'. The title perhaps referred to her role as opening up the afterlife ways for the deceased, or perhaps her role as opening the path for the daily journey of the sun across the sky and its cycle of rebirth.

The importance of Neith in the Old Kingdom is clearly shown in the fact that of personal names containing those of deities, 40 per cent are of Neith. After the Fourth Dynasty, her importance appears to have given way to that of Hathor.

However, she is never an insignificant goddess. In the *Coffin Texts* of the Middle Kingdom, for example, the deceased is associated with her. In the *Coffin Text* 846 (CT 846), she is described as a cow sky-goddess whose horns are 'adorned with two stars' recalling the enigmatic Predynastic-Early Dynastic bovine deity discussed in Chapter 2. As a sky and mother goddess she was also associated with the 'Great Cow' and with Nut and Hathor. As one of the goddesses of weaving, she was linked with mummy bandages. She also continued her role as a protector of kings and the deceased.

At times, she is considered sexless and associated with the primeval waters of the Nun. She is said to be the first born of the gods. In the New Kingdom, she is sometimes referred to as 'The Mother and Father of All Things'. It is notable that other primeval deities are also considered androgynous, one example being Atum who is said to have masturbated to create himself. Such gods are usually primeval, alone in the beginning and without consorts. Although certain gods are said to be androgynous, they are usually largely one sex or another. Thus Neith is largely female, but with some male characteristics.

Neith's androgynous, or at least partly masculine, character is said to be shown by her symbol of the crossed arrows,[11] warfare and hunting being male pursuits. Her masculinity is emphasized in the Eighteenth Dynasty; in the Eleventh Hour of the Amduat, her name is written with the phallus determinative.[12] At Esna, she is described as 'the male who acts the role of the female, the female who acts the role of the male'.[13]

In the Twenty-sixth Dynasty (664–525 BC), with the rise of Saïs as the capital of Egypt, the importance of Neith also increased. Indeed, she continued to be referred to as a mother, sky-goddess and primeval goddess until at least the Ptolemaic Period. The arrows of Neith were able to shoot the enemies of the sun-god Re[14] and she became associated with the Greek warrior goddess Athena.

ISIS AND NEPHTHYS

The two sisters Isis and Nephthys were essential in the revival of Osiris, king of the deceased, and thus are pivotal in rebirth rites. Isis and Nephthys first appear in the *Pyramid Texts* of Unas c.2400BC. They continue in importance until the Graeco-Roman Period. Isis in particular assumes huge popularity in this period, her fame spreading throughout the Roman Empire.

From the *Pyramid Texts* and later documents, we see Isis and Nephthys as a pair, sisters who together mourn the death of Osiris and are instrumental in bringing him to life. They are sometimes referred to as the two 'mooring posts', 'to be moored' being a phrase used to denote death. The pair are shown standing together behind the throne of Osiris, or at the head and foot of the deceased. Isis and Nephthys could be depicted as two birds, kites, their plaintive and shrill cries mourning the death of Osiris. In the Graeco-Roman Period, the laments of Isis and Nephthys for the death of Osiris, and their search for his body, would be acted out by two women during the Osirian festivals, and at funerals of mortals, professional mourners would re-enact their story. Isis cries:

> While I can see I call to you
> Weeping to the height of heaven!
> But you do not hear my voice,
> Though I am your sister whom you loved on earth,
> You loved none but me, the sister the sister![15]

The two could also be depicted individually, though Isis is the best known of the sisters. She is the sister and wife to Osiris and mother of Horus. There are many hundreds of Late Period bronzes showing Isis with baby Horus on her lap. Some have seen this image as being paralleled in later Christianity in representations of Mary and the baby Jesus. Isis is a protector of the young and has magical powers. She cures bites of poisonous animals; she is sent by Re to deliver his sons. In her role as a goddess reviving the deceased, she is shown as a kite hovering above Osiris to bring him to life. Isis also has a devious side. She tricks the sun god Re into telling her his secret name by making a snake mixed from Re's saliva and mud, which bites him. Isis offers to cure the god of his terrible pain if he tells her his secret name. In the *Contendings of Horus and Seth*, her cunning enables her son Horus to gain the throne of his father.

In the Old Kingdom, to some extent she shared in Hathor's glory at Qusae in Middle Egypt; and during the Middle and New Kingdoms, she was worshipped along with Osiris at Abydos, and Min at Coptos. From the New Kingdom onward, she is often associated with Hathor and, like Hathor, wears the sun disk between cow horns. However, until later periods, Hathor had a great many more temples than Isis.

In the fourth century BC, Isis rises to prominence and temples to her alone were founded for the first time, of which the temple of Isis at Philae is perhaps the best known. Nineteenth century visitors called this temple 'The Jewel of the Nile'. The Romans adopted the cult of Isis throughout the Empire, so that temples to Isis were set up in Rome and as far away as London. Even after most Egyptian temples had been desecrated by Christians, the worship of Isis was continued by Egyptian nomadic desert peoples until the sixth century AD.

Nephthys was never as famous as Isis and had no temple or cult centre. Her name, *Nebet-hwt*, means 'Mistress of the Mansion'. She was the wife of Seth and sister of Osiris. In the *Pyramid Texts*, she is the helper of the deceased. Like Isis, she had magical powers. She was one of the goddesses of weaving, and mummy bandages were sometimes referred to as the tresses of Nephthys. Plutarch, a Greek writer of the First and Second Centuries AD speaks of Nephthys sleeping with Osiris through trickery and then giving birth to Anubis. Plutarch describes Nephthys as representing the barren desert, and therefore as a goddess of death, while Isis was associated with life. Plutarch was, however, reporting a Romanized version of stories concerning the goddess.

HATHOR

There were more temples to Hathor than any other goddess. She personified love, beauty and rebirth, but was also a goddess of minerals and the Eastern Desert. Her name means 'Mansion of Horus'. Generally, Hathor is a nurturing goddess and is associated with many other goddesses.

From early times, Hathor was linked with Giza, Memphis and Dendera, as well as other sites and, as outlined in Chapter 2, the cult of Hathor followed the ruling elite of the Old Kingdom. In the Middle Kingdom, Mentuhotep Nebhepetre used Hathor's cult to legitimize his rule. At Dendera, she is shown offering her sistrum and *menit*-necklace to the king for the first time, and suckling him.[16] Her link with royal women from the Middle Kingdom, and especially the New Kingdom, is discussed in an earlier chapter. The king celebrated his regenerative potency through union with Hathor as wife and mother.[17]

In many ways, Hathor is a link to other worlds. Jan Assmann,[18] who seeks to deny the ecstatic experience in Egyptian religion in general, admits that the cult of Hathor was an exception. The other worlds of distant mines, the other worlds of ecstatic experience and the other world of death and rebirth are all Hathorian.

Cross culturally, women have a proclivity to embrace ecstatic religion, possibly due to their subordinate status.[19] Ecstatic religion, if it existed to any great extent in Egypt, may be difficult to identify, especially if largely associated with women. This is due to the fact that state religion, writing, and so forth were largely in the hands of men.[20] To some extent, the association of ecstatic religion with Hathor and women can only be supposition, but the female prominence in music and dance together with Hathor's otherworld connections support this.

Hathor as a mortuary goddess is described in the *Pyramid Texts* and in the *Coffin Texts*.[21] The dying desired to be 'in the following of Hathor'. She is depicted stepping out of the other world to greet the deceased. However, not only the deceased, but also the living, could commune with her; two stelae record joyous epiphanies of men meeting Hathor.[22] She was also associated with the desert and foreign lands, mines and mining, and thus with mountains (mines were linked with mountains in the Egyptian mind). She was 'The Lady of Byblos' and was also associated with the sky. The Seven Hathors were goddesses of prophecy, seeing across time.

Some[23] do not see Hathor as a mother goddess, but rather a goddess of childbirth and related to this, sexuality. The goddess Nebethetep, the personification of *djeret*, the hand of the creator god, became known as the 'Lady of the Vulva'. By the Eighteenth Dynasty, this aspect had become associated with Hathor. It has been suggested that the dancers in Papyrus Westcar, who act as midwives, were Hathor dancers as they hold out sistra and *menit*-necklaces to the woman's husband.[24] As we have seen, Hathor even revives the aged Re by displaying her genitals. While childbirth and pregnancy are not normally associated with ecstatic status, the sexual act is; Hathor is associated with the entangled ideas of intoxication, love, erotic beauty and euphoric dancing.

At Dendera, Hathor is 'mistress of the dance, queen of happiness'.[25] Music, dance and intoxication are not only Hathorian, but occur in many religions in association with breaking down barriers between our world and that of the gods and the deceased. Ecstatic emotion is one means of transcending this world. The association of Hathor, and hence of Hathorian dancers, with breaking down barriers between one world and another appears in a text which describes the movements performed by Hathorian musicians in night-time dances for the goddess[26]: 'Singers, vital and beautiful, are intoxicated by speedily moving their legs out before them'. Perhaps this was a kind of *zikr* designed to bring on an altered state of consciousness during the ritual.

One might wonder if at times the goddess Hathor was a means by which it was possible to see into 'other worlds'. The mirrors associated with the goddess, as well as being linked to her solar and beauty aspects, might be linked with scrything (a means of seeing into other worlds through reflective surfaces), and music (hand clappers and sistra) is also associated with inducing trance-like states. Mirror dances, like other dances, took place for Hathor;[27] mirrors were used in religious rituals, not simply for personal grooming, and were often owned by priestesses.[28] The words 'for your *ka*' are associated both with offering alcohol and with offering mirrors.[29] The phrase 'for your *ka*' might be taken literally, with the mirror being the depository of the soul. Each person has his *ka* – a part of his soul – and he goes to it when he dies.

DRUNKENNESS

While intoxication by alcohol was not normally approved of, 'holy intoxication' was encouraged, possibly as a link to the world of the gods, an alternative state of being. It is difficult to prove, but one may postulate that such intoxication also included erotic euphoria. The link between drunkenness and erotic euphoria is also apparent in today's western cultures, where it is a cliché that men and women tend to become intimate after heavy drinking. Hathor was not only a goddess of love, but also of drunkenness.

That drunkenness had the possibilities of mystical communion is suggested by the Middle Kingdom *Dispute Between a Man and his Ba*. The nearness and desirability of death is suggested:

> 'Death is before me today
> Like the fragrance of a lotus
> Like sitting on the shores of drunkenness'[30]

This might explain tomb scenes of banquets in which no food is eaten, but at which guests imbibe alcohol. The tomb of Paheri at Elkab has a banqueting scene in which a female cousin of Paheri declares, 'Give me eighteen cups of wine; I want to drink to drunkenness; my throat is as dry as straw'.[31] It is noticeable that while women and drunkenness are particularly disapproved of in the west, there was not this apparent gender-linked disapproval of drunken women in ancient Egypt. There is even one scene of a woman vomiting from overindulgence.

'The Festival of Drunkenness', associated with Hathor, is known in the Middle Kingdom, but is more usually associated with the Graeco-Roman Period. The twentieth day of the first month was marked by the 'Festival of Drunkenness'. *Menou*-jugs were filled with wine and offered to Hathor, 'Lady of Drunkenness in the Place of Drunkenness'. At the temple of Hathor at Philae, scenes on columns show Bes dancing at the return of the 'Lady of favours, mistress of the dance, great of attraction ... Lady of drunkenness with many festivals'.[32]

In the last few years, the American Egyptologist, Betsy Bryan, has been excavating at the Temple of Mut at Karnak (1470 BC) and has uncovered evidence that the Festival of Drunkenness was celebrated in the New Kingdom. Mut was a goddess closely linked with Hathor. Bryan has discovered a 'Porch of Drunkenness' associated with Hatshepsut. It seems that in the Hall of Drunkenness, worshippers got drunk, slept and then were woken by drummers to commune with the goddess, Mut. Some scenes linked drunkenness with 'travelling through the marshes', a possible euphemism for sexual activity. The festival re-enacted that of Sekhmet after the inundation (this is a version of the myth of the 'Return of the Distant One'). Bryan believes that the Festival of Drunkenness fell out of favour after the reign of Hatshepsut, but was later resumed.

THE RETURN OF THE DISTANT ONE

The story of the quarrel between the solar Eye and her father, and her later return, is sometimes called the 'Return of the Distant One'. The Eye was considered the female active force, the daughter of Re. In myths, this goddess goes to Libya or Nubia, though reasons for her departure are not always given. The goddess is then brought back to Egypt, usually by a male god who is Shu, Thoth, or Onuris. Sometimes the goddess is named as Mut, Bastet, Hathor, Wadjet, Tefnut or Sekhmet. The celebration of the return of the goddess usually coincided with the annual inundation of the Nile, the source of the Nile being in Nubia. One version of the story in which the goddess goes to Nubia was particularly poignant in the Late Period, when the kings from the South had conquered Egypt and renewed many of Egypt's earlier traditions.

An early version of this myth is extant in the *Book of the Heavenly Cow*, which first appears, though in incomplete form, on the outermost of the four gilded shrines of Tutankhamun. The story, called 'The Destruction of Humanity', goes that, in times past, a golden age existed when humans and gods existed under Re, and night and death did not exist. Humanity plots against Re and the god sends his daughter, the Eye in the form of Hathor, to kill them all. 'Hathor, the Eye of the Sun, went into the desert transformed into the raging lioness Sekhmet, the powerful one. There she began slaying humanity for the evil they had done'. She goes on the rampage wading in their blood. Re changes his mind, but no one knows how to stop the furious goddess, so he orders 7,000 jars of beer to be made and coloured with ochre. Thinking that this is blood, the goddess drinks, and then in a drunken stupor, becomes happy and pacified, with all thought of killing forgotten. Once again, she is the beautiful and gentle Hathor. Her return to Egypt is celebrated by song and dance and drinking. Re returns to the sky on the back of the heavenly cow and institutes the netherworld as a dwelling for the dead.

There are several variations to this myth: in one version Hathor becomes cross with Re and that is why she storms off to Nubia. Thoth has to coax her back by telling her stories. She bathes in the Nile, which becomes red with her anger, and then she becomes peaceful and happy. In other variations, it is Tefnut who goes to Nubia and Shu who brings her back.

All versions demonstrate that the Egyptians saw a double nature to the feminine, which encompassed both extreme passions of fury and love. This aspect of the female is reflected in texts describing mortal Egyptian women, as we have seen.

Conclusion

The fragmentary evidence of ancient Egypt allows us only tantalizing glimpses of a sophisticated and complex society. As always, any detailed study of the past reveals contradictions and anomalies. On one level, women in ancient Egypt enjoyed rights and freedoms, which to other societies appeared shocking,[1] while on another they were sexually exploited tools of an elite male society. Additionally, contradictions in the data suggest that the dominant ideal was frequently contested. Throughout Egyptian history, gender is inextricably linked with economics and religion. Just how much relevance does this have for women of today?

In many ways, the understanding of the roles of men and women in the ancient past was very different from that of today. Sexuality, for example, does not seem to have been separated out from other areas of life. The place of the male in procreation may be considered unusual in today's societies. So, we might argue, it makes little sense to compare the present with the past, but there are also similarities.

The lives of women continue to be heavily influenced by religion and economics. The restriction of women to certain roles is a facet of several religions. Many Christians will not tolerate women priests, for example; some see a woman's place as in the home and women as the source of sexual temptation. As for economics, what we call the 'glass ceiling' still exists and women are paid less than men. Today too, the lives of women vary considerably and yet, generally, they are still more restricted than those of men.

It is clear that in ancient Egypt women were not overtly considered of any less status than men. The fact that certain functions were assumed by men and not women seems to be more a result of accepted custom rather than a deliberate policy of oppression. The few letters from women that we have do not suggest a cowed group, and they do not seem to have felt themselves repressed (or at least did not express this view). At times, women did become kings or otherwise involve themselves in the affairs of state, but few chose, or were able, to do so.

Egyptian women did have unequal property rights compared with men, but their restriction to home was not necessarily of male making.

All views of the past are influenced by the present[2] and we have looked at two specific examples earlier in this book.

The first example was that, like gods, some kings also practiced incest, and at times they married their daughters. Father-daughter marriages would have allowed the daughter to take on the ritual role previously provided by an aging mother. They would also have given daughters more status is a society where only the 'King's Principal Wife' and 'King's Mother' were considered important. In the past, Egyptologists tried to explain away such incestuous couplings by the theory of matrilineal descent, the idea that the right to the throne passed through the female line, the so-called heiress theory. However, as two eminent writers on ancient Egypt, Barbara Mertz[3] and Gay Robins[4] have pointed out, not all kings actually married royal women, a seemingly obvious failing, and thus the theory has now been debunked. The heiress theory appears to have been an attempt to explain away what we would see as an abhorrent practise.

The second example was that it is sometimes said that in ancient Egypt prostitution was connected with female musicians and dancers. The connection perhaps says more about Egyptologists than the ancient Egyptians. This is not to deny an association between music and sexuality,[5] but simply that there is no evidence for musicians as prostitutes.

Understanding the past in the light of the present is something we all do. It is impossible to understand ancient Egyptian women other than in the light of the present, and impossible to ignore similarities between us and them.

Glossary

Amun. Originally a Theban god who rose to prominence throughout Egypt. His name probably means 'the hidden one'.

Anthropoid coffin. Coffin in the shape of a person.

Apotropaic wand. A ritual implement, usually made from hippopotamus tusk with images of various protective deities inscribed thereon. Such implements are associated with childbirth.

Atef crown. An elaborate headdress commonly associated with Osiris.

Ba. A part of the soul which became manifest after the person died. The *ba* could eat, drink, speak and move.

Bat. A nome deity represented by a cow's head with curling horns.

Beautiful Festival (Feast) of the Valley. An annual festival involving a procession from Karnak to the temples on the west bank at Thebes.

Bes. The name given to a type of deity usually taking the form of a bandy-legged dwarf with a leonine head.

Canopic jar. Jars used for containing the internal organs removed during mummification.

Cartouche. Name of a king written in an oval symbolizing eternity.

Chantress. Title given to a singer or chanter who worked in a temple on a part-time basis.

Coffin Texts. These are later versions of the *Pyramid Texts* which date from the First Intermediate Period. Some were written on coffins and others on papyri or tomb walls.

Deben. A weight of copper referring to a monetary value.

Determinative. A hieroglyphic symbol placed after another hieroglyphic symbol or group of symbols denoting a word in order to clarify the meaning of the previous word.

Emmer. A hulled wheat eaten in Pharaonic Egypt.

Eye of Re. The creative element of Re, personified as his daughters. These could include female deities such as Isis and Hathor.

Faience. A ceramic usually glazed blue or green.

Fish-tailed knife. A flint knife in the shape of a fish tail.

Hathor. A goddess who was regarded as the divine mother of each reigning king. She was often shown in the form of a cow.

Herodotus. A Greek historian who travelled in Egypt around 450 BC and wrote an account of Egyptian life and history.

Horus. A falcon god who embodied divine kingship.

Isis. The goddess who was sister and wife to Osiris and mother of Horus.

Ka. This can be roughly translated as part of the soul equivalent to the life-force of the individual.

Khener. A musical troupe.

Lit-clos. A brick, elevated structure – often with enclosed sides – found in some houses.

Lotus. A water lily which symbolized Upper Egypt.

Maat. Goddess of truth, justice and cosmic order.

Menit-necklace. A heavy necklace consisting of strings of small beads and with a counterpoise attached to the rear. The item could be used as a musical instrument, in the form of a rattle. It was closely associated with Hathor.

Meretseger. Theban cobra goddess whose name means 'she who loves silence'. She was associated with the mountain area overlooking the Valley of the Kings.

Min. Ithyphallic god who symbolized male power and was associated with mining and the Eastern Desert.

Modius. A cylindrical headdress worn by deities and queens.

Mut. A vulture goddess whose name means 'mother'.

Natron. Naturally occurring mix of sodium carbonate and sodium bicarbonate. This was used in mummification, in cleaning and in the manufacture of faience.

Neith. A creator goddess whose cult centre was in Saïs.

Nemes-headdress. A head-cloth worn by kings which consisted of a piece of striped cloth.

Nome. A province of Egypt. For most of the Dynastic period, there were twenty-two Upper Egyptian nomes and twenty Lower Egyptian nomes.

Opet festival. An annual festival in which gods in statue form were carried from Karnak to Luxor. The purpose of the festival was to celebrate the sexual intercourse between Amun and the mother of the king so that she could give birth to the eternal royal *ka*. The physical form of the king could then combine with the royal and divine *ka*, making the king also divine.

Osiris. The primary Egyptian god of death and resurrection.

Ostracon (plural ostraca). Sherd of pottery or flake of stone with text or drawing thereon.

Palette. A flat piece of stone, sometimes decorated, which was used to grind pigments. In the Predynastic and Early Dynastic Periods, oversize ceremonial palettes were also made.

Phyle. A workgang. Priests were organized into phyles, or groups, and each group worked one month in turn.

Pylon. A ceremonial gateway consisting of two towers linked by a bridge.

Pyramid Texts. A corpus of funerary texts found in Old Kingdom and First Intermediate Period pyramids. These consist of around 800 spells designed to ensure a successful afterlife. The earliest extant examples date from the Fifth Dynasty pyramid of Unas (2375–2345 BC), though these may be based on an earlier tradition.

Re. A sun god often shown as a hawk-headed deity.

Sed-festival. A festival of royal renewal. Ideally, this would be celebrated after a king had ruled for thirty years.

Sekhmet. An aggressive female god often shown in lioness form.

Seth. A god of chaos and confusion.

Sistrum (plural sistra). A type of rattle usually played by women, or by the king. It is an instrument associated with Hathor and seems to have a reviving and apotropaic role.

Sphinx. A mythical beast with the body of a lion and the head of a human.

Stela (plural stelae). A slab of stone or wood with inscriptions of a religious nature.

Taweret. A goddess taking the form of a hippopotamus, often with the back and tail of a crocodile. She is associated with the protection of women in childbirth.

Titulary. The five names and titles given to the king.

Uraeus. A rearing cobra often shown as a head ornament. The uraeus functioned to protect the wearer and is shown as if it were about to strike. Various deities take the form of the uraeus, particularly those who represent the Eye of Re. The uraeus is also used as a symbol of queenship.

Vizier. The chief minister in Egyptian administration.

Votive. A gift to a deity given in the hope of gain, or as a gift in thanks for a gain.

Wochenlaube. A birth or post-birth arbour. Representations of these show mothers with a young baby, often on a bed with convolvulus.

Notes

Chapter 1: Rich women, poor women

1 Peet 1977, 172.
2 The calculation is based on Janssen's (1975, 534) estimation of a workman of the Nineteenth Dynasty earning 11 deben per month, and a passage from the court document (Peet 1977, 172) saying the stolen piece had a value of 90 deben.
3 Schultz and Seidel 2005, 372.
4 Meskell 1999, 209–11.

Chapter 2: Changing worlds

1 Ward (1986, 59), for example, claims that the status of women varied little throughout Pharaonic history.
2 See Goodison and Morris 1998 for an introduction, with references, to the 'goddess movement'.
3 For example, Lesko 1999, 16.
4 Baumgartel 1947, 31, 36; 1960, 73–4, 144–47.
5 Hassan 1992, 1998.
6 Lesko 1999.
7 For an outline of the importance of cattle in the religion of Predynastic and Early Dynastic Egypt, see Wengrow 2001 and Hendrickx 2002, with references.
8 Fischer 1962; 1975, 630–32.
9 Reisner 1931, 123–4, pl. 38–46.
10 The interpretations of the Hierakonpolis bowl and seal impression are

difficult. The Hierakonpolis bowl shows the bovine head with human eyes and mouth. On both the bowl and the seal impression, the bovine head is shown together with a bird. On the Hierakonpolis bowl, this is identified as the Saddle Bill or Jaribu stork, which Fischer (1962, 11) points out has the same phonetic value as that of the Bat deity, that is, the name of the Saddle Bill in ancient Egypt was *ba*, and thus, claims Fischer, implies that the bovine head is Bat. However, there is doubt surrounding the claim that the bovine is this deity. Fischer also states that the Bat fetish is rarely shown with the stork. Additionally, there is a possibility that the fragments come from separate bowls and have been incorrectly assumed to be one. Finally, as regards the Hierakonpolis bowl, the mouth of the Bat head has been totally reconstructed. Its features may have been less recognizably human in the original, and therefore less like the later known Bat deity. Burgess and Arkell 1958; Adams 1974, 5.

11   Hartung 1998, pl. 37, 120.

12   For example, Hassan 1998, 110, fig. 48; Wilkinson 1999, 282.

13   Smith 1992, 241–244.

14   *Pyramid Texts* 729, 2003.

15   *Pyramid Texts* 1285a, 1303c.

16   *Pyramid Texts* 332, 397, etc.

17   Petrie et al. (1913, 21–2, pl. II). See also Petrie and Griffith (1901, 24, pl. 6.22) for a similar bovine with curled horns identified as a bull.

18   See Fischer 1962, 8 for the stela and Chapter 8 in this volume for information on khener.

19   See Fischer 1962, 12; Gillam 1995, 215; and Wilkinson 1999, 283 for Fourth Dynasty references to Hathor. Hassan (1998, 106) cites identifications of Hathor in the Early Dynastic though these are based on over-interpretive translations. While the temple at Gebelein was dedicated in later times to Hathor, and the temple itself dates back to the Second Dynasty, we do not know if it was dedicated to Hathor in the Second Dynasty (Wilkinson 1999, 312).

20   The figurines are discussed in Ucko 1968, 188. Hendrickx (2002, 283–84) makes the interesting observation that a flint object from Naqada which is usually interpreted as a bull's head could also be viewed as a woman with raised arms, though the ears of the head are difficult to understand as part of a female body. Hendrickx sees these as breasts, but if so, this is an unusual rendering for Early Dynastic Egypt.

21   Hassan 1998, 106, 107 fig. 46.

22   Baumgartel 1960, 144–47.

23   Zuener 1963, 226.

24   Ucko 1968, 188.

25   Kinney 2008, 43–4, 64–72.

26   Williams 1988; 47–51, 93, fig. 35, 36; Hendrickx 2002, 283.

27   Podzorski (1993) has suggested that in graves men tend to be associated with maces (although since only two maceheads were found in this study, the correlation may be insignificant) and Hassan and Smith's (2002, 52) study of 426 graves from five cemeteries suggested that maces were as likely to be associated with women's as with men's graves.

28   Fuchs 1989, 139, 145, 151, fig. 19, 28; Berger 1992, 116, fig. 9; Morrow and Morrow 2002.

29   Lankester 2007, 99.

30   For example, Morrow and Morrow 2002, 133, 159.

31   For example, Redford and Redford 1989, fig. 34; Morrow and Morrow 2002, 65.

32   Ellis 1992; Savage 2000; Hassan and Smith 2002.

33   Baumgartel 1960, 60–1.

34   Ellis 1992.

35   Savage 2000.

36   Podzorski 1993.

37   Hassan and Smith 2002.

38   The idea that these palettes are used for grinding eye make-up, as opposed to say general body paints, rests upon projecting ideas of the Dynastic Period back onto the Predynastic. However, to be sure of these results we really need to compare Predynastic mortuary evidence with later mortuary evidence, or we are not comparing like with like. Unfortunately, such studies have not yet been published. Richards (2005) has considered Middle Kingdom mortuary data and Meskell (1999, 2002) material from New Kingdom Deir el-Medina. However, Richards does not specifically analyse gender as information on this was only available less than 50 per cent of the time and the sexing of skeletons in the past was insecure (2005, 106). It would also be interesting to consider evidence of equality and gendered roles from physical anthropology, or the human remains themselves. Sexual division of labour and differential access to food resources leave their mark on skeletal remains. One would wonder if this changes through time.

39   Hasan and Smith 2002.

40   For example, a figure from Qau- published by Adams (1992); and another from Naqada published in Petrie and Quibell (1896, pl. 59) cited in Hassan

(1992, 313, fig. 2) possibly has grain but more clearly shows animals and water.

41 Lesko 1999, 11, 29.
42 Roth 2000.
43 Hassan and Smith 2002, 63.
44 Nelson 1998, 319–20, 330–31, with references.
45 Nelson 1998.
46 Hassan 1992; Hassan and Smith 2002, 64.
47 Hassan 1998.
48 Wengrow 2006.
49 Ibid., 33–4.
50 Sherratt 1981, 1983; Ehrenberg 1989, 99–107.
51 Wengrow 2006, 144–45.
52 Crabtree 2006, 584–85; Peterson 2006, 550.
53 Vogelsang-Eastwood 2000, 270.
54 Fischer 2000, 45–6.
55 Galvin 1981.
56 Gillam 1995.
57 Hassan 1992, 312.
58 Roth 2005, 11, 14, footnote 15.
59 Fischer 1989, 8; 2000, 5.
60 Fischer 1989, 10.
61 Roth 2005, 11.
62 Roth 1999b, 364.
63 Roth 2005, 11, 14, footnote 19.
64 Willems 1983.
65 Pflüger 1947, 128.
66 Fischer 2000, 59–60, footnote 50.
67 Fischer 1989; Bryan 1996.
68 Ward 1986, 2–21, 34–5.
69 Gillam 1995, 214.
70 Ibid., 222.
71 Galvin 1981, 16–19; Ward 1986, 28; Küllmer 2007, 158–63.
72 Fischer 2000, 41 pl. 1.
73 Galvin 1981, 203.
74 Ibid., 202.
75 Galvin 1981, 235–36, 240; Gillam 1995, 212–13.
76 Gillam 1995, 225.
77 Blackman 1914 I, 23, pl. 2; Galvin 1981, 210.

78 Galvin 1981, 235–39, 286.

79 Fischer 1989, 16; Fischer 2000, 19–20.

80 Gillam 1995, 213–14; Küllmer 2007, 85–8.

81 Blackman 1921, 29; Doxey 2001, 3, 71.

82 Routledge 2001, 2008.

83 Galvin 1981, 1984; Gillam 1995; Fischer 2000, 24–5.

84 Gillam 1995.

85 Ibid., 211.

86 Sethe 1933, 24–7; Gillam 1995, 212–13.

87 Blackman 1921, 24; Doxey 2001, 69.

88 Doxey 2001, 3, 71.

89 Blackman 1921, 29.

90 Roth 1991, 74–5.

91 Quirke 2007, 255–56.

92 Gillam 1995, 212, footnote 13.

93 Junker 1941, 55–6; Küllmer 2007, 143–44.

94 Fischer 2000, 20–1.

95 Ibid., 20–1.

96 Junker 1941, 52–4.

97 Küllmer 2007.

98 Wente 1990, 82; Quirke 2007, 255–56.

99 Robins 1993, 103.

100 Quirke 2007, 251.

101 Küllmer 2007, 15–21.

102 Eyre 1998, 175, fig. 1.

103 Ibid., 175.

104 Fischer 1989, 21–2; Fischer 2000, 38.

105 Lorenze 2009, 102.

106 Eyre 1998.

107 Fischer 2000, 4.

108 Fischer 1989, 22; 2000, 39–40.

109 Russmann 2005, 26.

110 Whale 1989, 275.

111 Janssen 1975, 226.

112 Van Walsem 1997, 374–75.

Chapter 3: Reversing the ordinary practices of mankind

1 Callender 2006, 121.
2 Robins 1999, 57.
3 Troy 1984.
4 Fisher 2000, 3–4.
5 Lichtheim 1973, 69.
6 Schneider 2007.
7 Troy 1984, 78.
8 Quirke 2007, 257.
9 Lichtheim 1976, 137.
10 Lichtheim 1976, 203–11.
11 Ibid., 211–14.
12 Troy 1984, 78.
13 Lichtheim 1980, 127–38.
14 Fischer 1989, 6–7; Fischer 2000, 3–4.
15 Whale 1989; Robins 1994.
16 Fischer 2000, 13.
17 Fischer 2000, 41–3.
18 Vogelsang-Eastwood 1993, 97–8.
19 Troy 1984, 79.
20 Routledge 2008.
21 Campbell 1994.
22 Lichtheim 1973, 137.
23 Fischer 1989, 43–4, fig. 33.
24 Shown in Quibell and Hayter 1927, Cairo, frontispiece.
25 Kanawati 2001, but see also Küllmer 2007, 32 for other examples of female guards.
26 Roth 1999b, 362.
27 Roth 2005, 11.
28 Routledge 2001, 188–90, 202.
29 Routledge 2008, 164–65.
30 Filer 1992.
31 Baker 1997.
32 Baker 1997, 111.
33 Toivari-Viitala 2001, 216–19.
34 Ward 1995.
35 Wente 1990, 217.
36 Gaballa 1977, 22–7, 30.

37 Allam 1989, 130–31; Toivari-Viitala 2001, 102.
38 Janssen 2006, 7.
39 Allam 1989.
40 Meskell 2002, 110.
41 Katary 1999.
42 Meskell 1999, 158 ff.
43 Published in Griffith 1898, 31–2 and discussed in Johnson 1999.
44 Janssen 1988.
45 Lichtheim 1980, 166.
46 Toivari-Viitala 2001, 63–5.
47 Lichtheim 1976, 137.
48 Faulkner et al. 1973, 18.
49 Ibid., 1973, 92–107.
50 McDowell 1999, 33.
51 McDowell 1999, 42; Meskell 2002, 101.
52 Meskell 2002, 102.
53 Barker 1997.
54 Lorton 1977, 44.
55 Toivari-Viitala 2001, 133.
56 Onstine 2005, 34.
57 Eyre 1998.
58 Fischer 1963.
59 Robins 2008, 211.
60 Gilchrist 1999, 50–51.
61 Lichtheim 1976, 136.
62 Assmann 1997, 255, footnote 48.
63 Robins 1993, 160.
64 Donohue 1992, 874–75; Graves-Brown 2006.
65 Ritner 2008, 183.
66 Robins 1989, 108.
67 Though private stelae were set up in temples and votive cloths donated at Deir el-Bahri, it is debatable as to whether these could be considered domestic piety.
68 Lichtheim 1973, 69.
69 Goldberg 1998, 109.
70 For example, for Deir el-Medina see McDowell 1999, 51–2.
71 Lichtheim 1976, 143.
72 Lichtheim 1973, 184–92.
73 Mead 1950.

74 Roehrig 1996, 24.

75 Lichtheim 1976, 140.

76 For example, Allen 2000; 2008.

77 Whale 1989.

78 Robins 1993, 107.

79 For example, Kuper 1982.

80 Allen 2000; 2008.

81 Meskell 2002, 137.

82 Wente 1990, 36.

83 Wente 1990, 200.

84 Sweeney 2008.

Chapter 4: Birth, life and death

1 Toivara-Viitala 2001, 181.

2 Lovell and Whyte 1999.

3 Janssen and Janssen (1990) and Szpakowska (2008) both summarize the possibilities.

4 Janssen and Janssen 1990, fig. 25.

5 Janssen and Janssen 1990, 57.

6 Fischer 2000, 27.

7 Ward 1989, 35–6.

8 McDowell 1995, 123.

9 Toivari-Viitala 2001, 189.

10 Ibid., 52–3.

11 When the word is used of males in work details it is usually translated as 'recruits'. While *nfrw* is often translated as 'beautiful', it also has connotations of newness and youthfulness.

12 The Third Intermediate Period *Onomasticon of Amenemipet* contrasts an adult woman (*st*) with a young woman (*nfrt*) (Gardiner 1947).

13 Lilyquist 1979.

14 Robins 1999.

15 Vogelsang-Eastwood 1993, 114.

16 Rowlandson 1998, 99–100.

17 Montserrat 1996, 43.

18 Nunn 1996, 197.

19 McDowell 1999, 59–61; Wilfong 1999, 430–31; Toivara-Viitala 2001, 162.

20 Quirke 2007, 255–56.

21 But see Wente 1990, 82–3 for yet another reading suggesting instead that the lady was a *wab*-priestess.
22 Wilfong 1999; Toivari-Viitala 2001, 163.
23 Montserrat 1996, 48.
24 Toivari-Viitala 2001, 164–67.
25 Ibid., 52, footnote 52 and 53, footnote 287.
26 Lichtheim 1976, 136.
27 Toivari-Viitala 2001, 53, footnote 287.
28 Teeter 1999, 410–11; Johnson 2003, 155–58.
29 Toivari-Viitala 2001, 155.
30 Lichtheim 1980, 178.
31 Toivari-Viitala 2001, 61–7.
32 Lichtheim 1980, 128.
33 Gee 2001.
34 Callender 2002, 302–303.
35 Simpson 1974.
36 Ward 1986, 65–9.
37 Wente 1990, 60.
38 Whale 1989 passim.
39 Lichtheim 1976, 212.
40 Gardiner 1940, 23–9.
41 Johnson 2003, 155.
42 Whale 1989, 247–48, 272–73.
43 Nunn 1996, 196.
44 Ritner 1984, 209–21.
45 Toivari-Viitala 2001, 169; Meskell 2002, 141.
46 Pinch 1993.
47 See Pinch 1983, 1993 for a study of these.
48 Reilly 1997.
49 Borghouts 1971, 25.
50 Nunn 1996, 191.
51 Nunn 1996, 192.
52 Toivari-Viitala 2001, 171.
53 Masali 1973, 194–96.
54 Derry 1935 and 1942, 250.
55 Strouhal and Callender 1992, 67–73.
56 Steindorff 1946, 50.
57 Szpakowska 2008, 30.
58 Bourriau 1988, 115–16.

59   Quirke 2007, 250.
60   Toivari-Viitala 2001, 175.
61   Ritner 1984.
62   Wilkinson 1971, 81.
63   Keimer 1949, 138.
64   Ritner 2008, 174–75.
65   Lichtheim 1973, 220.
66   Pinch 1983, 409–10.
67   Toivari-Viitala 2001, 178.
68   Pinch 1983, 406–407.
69   Pinch's type 6c, Pinch 1983, 406, pl. 6; Pinch 1993, 209.
70   el-Sabbahy 1999.
71   Brunner-Traut 1955, 24.
72   Pinch 1993, 209.
73   Pinch 1983, 406.
74   Robins 1993, 83.
75   Wegner 2002.
76   Bolger 1992, 156–58.
77   Lichtheim 1973, 221.
78   Toivari-Viitala 2001, 179.
79   McDowell 1999, 35.
80   Kiple 1993; Scott 1999, 30–32.
81   Berlin 3027 C, 1/9–2/6; Ritner 1993, 207 and 231; Yamazaki 2003.
82   Lichtheim 1976, 138.
83   Nunn 1996, 194.
84   Examples include: Sixth Dynasty Elephantine (Raue et al. 2004, 5); First Intermediate Period to Middle Kingdom Lisht (Arnold 1996); Middle Kingdom Elephantine (Pilgrim 1996, 85–100, 174; New Kingdom Deir el-Medina (Meskell 1999, 158–59); and fourth century AD Qasr Ibrim (Meskell 1999, 159).
85   David 1986, 112.
86   Pinch 1994, 132.
87   Filer 1998.
88   Meskell 1999, 171.
89   Lichtheim 1980, 169.
90   Though see the Second Intermediate statuette of Princess Sobek-nakht suckling a prince, Brooklyn Museum 34.137, Romano 1996.
91   Roehrig 1990, 315.
92   Desroches-Noblecourt 1952; Brunner-Traut 1970.

93 Lilyquist 2005, 64.

94 Roehrig 2005.

95 Leclant 1961.

96 Green 1998.

97 Yamazaki 2003.

98 Ritner 2001, 332.

99 Lichtheim 1976, 141.

100 Toivari-Viitala 2001, 206–207.

101 Masali and Chiarelli 1972; Podzorski 1990; Bagnall and Frier 1994; Nunn 1996, 22.

102 Massali and Chiarelli 1972.

103 Bednarski 2000, contra Tyldesley 1994, 32.

104 Rose 2006.

105 Sweeney 2004.

106 Fischer 1959, 251.

107 Janssen and Janssen 1996, 23–24, fig. 10.

108 Sweeney 2004, 82–3.

109 Wildung 2001.

110 Arnold 1996, 30, 79.

111 Baines 1991, 144.

112 Janssen 2006.

113 Wente 1990, 36.

114 Janssen 2006, 7.

115 Sweeney 2006, 138–39.

116 Janssen 2006, 6.

117 It is possible that the term $ḫꜣrt$ refers to a disadvantaged widow rather than to the average woman whose husband had died.

118 The widow is presumably gleaning.

119 Lichtheim 1976, II, 151, 161.

120 Robins 1993, 138–39.

121 Meskell 1999, 158.

122 Toivari-Viitala 2001, 132–33.

123 Janssen 2006, 7.

124 Ibid.

125 Roth 2000, 194–95.

Chapter 5: Women's work

1   Robins 1993, 96.
2   Meskell 2002, 110–121.
3   Assmann and Lorton 2005, 223–24.
4   Fischer 1989, 17; Fischer 2000, 21–2.
5   Sweeney 2006, 148.
6   Lichtheim 1973, 170.
7   McDowell 1999, 51–2; Koltsida 2007, 12.
8   Robins 1993, 97.
9   Ward 1989, 36–7.
10 Quirke 2007, 252.
11 Ward 1989, 37.
12 Ibid., 6–7.
13 Fischer 1989, 14; 2000, 19.
14 Robins 1989, 112.
15 Bryan 1996, 40; Richards 2005, 29.
16 Eyre 1987, 19, 38.
17 Eyre 1998, 184; Meskell 2002, 110.
18 Eyre 1998, 182–83.
19 Fischer 1989, 17.
20 Sweeney 2006, 143.
21 Though Roehrig (1996, 21) argues for the continued existence of the ground loom along with the vertical loom.
22 Sweeney 2006, 140, 142.
23 Lorenze 2009, 100.
24 Vogelsang-Eastwood 2001, 491.
25 Bowen 2006.
26 Pinch 1993, 103–134, 123–24.
27 Illustrated in Lesko 1987, 15.
28 Eyre 1998, 176, fig. 2.
29 Ibid., 182.
30 Eyre 1998, 186; Sweeney 2006, 152.
31 Eyre 1998.
32 McDowell 1999, 79–80.
33 Janssen 1975, 526.
34 Janssen 1975.
35 Janssen 1975, 534.
36 Wente 1990, 58–9.

37 Eyre 1998, 178.
38 Robins 1993, 104.
39 Karl 2000.
40 Toivari-Viitala 2001, 228–31.
41 Karl 2000, 132.
42 Fox 1985, 72.
43 WB II, 140.
44 Toivari-Viitala 2005, 151.
45 Fox 1985, 69.
46 Lichtheim 1980, 178.
47 Ibid., 176.
48 Ibid., 134.
49 Troy 1986, 92–4.
50 Blackman 1953, pl. 45; Fischer 2002, 9, fig. 8.
51 Fischer 1989, 11–12; Fischer 2000, 11–12.
52 Blackman 1924, 31, pl. 9, 10; Fischer 2000, 9 fig. 9.
53 Toivari-Viitala 2001, 150–51.
54 Nunn 1996, 24–25, fig. 6.5.
55 Fischer 2000, 27, 69 note 157.
56 Nunn 1996, 132.
57 Roehrig 1996, 17.
58 Ward 1986, 8.
59 Ibid., 3.
60 Robins 1989, 107.
61 Ward 1986, 8; Janssen and Janssen 1990, 17; Robins 1993, 89, 118.
62 Whale 1989 passim.
63 Ibid., 170.
64 McDowell 1999, 36.
65 Strouhal and Forman 1992, 23–4.
66 Capel 1996, 96, footnote 14.
67 Ward 1984.
68 Bryan 1996, 39.
69 Lesko 1991, 5.
70 Troy 1986, 179.
71 McDowell 1999, 169–70.
72 Ibid., 44–5.
73 Blackman 1921, 8.
74 Fischer 1989, 24; Gillam 1995, 213.
75 Ward 1986, 20–1, 34–5.

76   Ibid., 34.
77   Blackman 1921, 24.
78   Sabbahy 1997, 165.
79   Fischer 1989, 24.
80   Fischer 1989, 24.
81   Blackman 1921, 9.
82   Ibid., 10.
83   For an authoritative discussion on these women, see Ayad 2009.
84   For information on the institution, see Graefe 1981.
85   Robins 1993, 156.
86   Fischer 1989, 19; Ayad 2003, 14.
87   For example, Bryan 1996, 43.
88   Though see Dodson 2002, footnotes 9, 21 and 46, who questions whether or not Amenerdis II was ever a God's Wife.
89   Teeter 1999.
90   Ayad 2003, 18.
91   Ibid., 14.
92   Ibid., 21.
93   Ayad 2003.
94   Dodson 2002 argues that it is possible that Amenerdis II never became a God's Wife.
95   See Ayad 2009.
96   Rikala 2008.
97   Ayad 2003, 25.
98   Ibid., 22–3.
99   Robins 1999, 67–8.
100 Onstine 2005, 11–12.
101 Fischer 1989, 12.
102 Fischer 1989, 18.
103 Onstine 2005, 12.
104 Lesko 1987, 38.
105 Onstine 2005, 76.
106 Davies and Gardiner 1948, 15, pl. 12 upper right corner.
107 Duquesne 2008.
108 Ibid., 2008.
109 Onstine 2005, 37; DuQuesne 2008.
110 Naguib 1990.
111 Onstine 2005, 14.
112 Onstine 2005, 19.

113 Onstine 2005, 4.

114 Teeter 1999, 406.

115 Ibid., 406–407.

116 Nord 1975; Nord, 1981; Ward 1983, 71; Onstine 2005, 7–8.

117 Blackman 1921, 10, 15, 16.

118 Callender 1994, 8.

119 Ward 1983, 71.

120 Onstine 2005, 4.

121 Nord 1981, 141.

122 Nord 1981, 141.

123 Ibid., 142.

124 Roth 1992, 140–44.

125 Lichtheim 1973, 220.

126 Wente 1969, 88.

127 Teeter and Johnson 2009, 42.

128 Kinney 2008, 162.

129 Blackman 1924, 31, pl. 9, 10; Fischer 2000, 9, fig. 9.

130 Fischer 1989, 19–20; Fischer 2000, 26.

131 Eyre 1987, 37.

132 Robins 1993, 164; Sweeney 2006, 140.

133 Haring 1997, 459; Lesko 2002.

134 Meskell 1999, 127–28.

135 Robins 1993, 164; Meskell 2002, 190; Sweeney 2001, 46.

136 Whale 1989, 185.

137 Sweeney 2001, 29–30.

138 Sweeney 2001.

139 Sweeney 2001, 36.

140 Ibid., 48.

141 Fischer 2000, 25.

142 Blackman 1921, 28.

143 Diamond 2008.

144 Fischer 1989, 19; Fischer 2000, 26.

145 Tosi and Roccati 1972, 88.

146 Whale 1989 passim.

147 Onstine 2005, 11.

148 Nord 1981, 141–42.

149 Pinch 1993, 213.

150 Ibid., 279–81.

151 Gillam 1995, 233.

152   Blackman 1921, 14.
153   Onstine 2005, 11–12.

Chapter 6: Sexuality, art and religion

1   Foucault 1978.
2   Montserrat 1996, 19.
3   Meskell 2000, 253.
4   Parkinson 2008.
5   Ford 1945, 36.
6   Roth 2000.
7   Meskell and Joyce 2003, 119.
8   Roth 2000.
9   Strouhal and Forman 1992, 11–12.
10   Lichtheim 1976, 206.
11   Wente 1990, 149; Toivari-Viitala 2001, 161–62, 170.
12   Roth 2000, 190.
13   Dorman 1999, 96.
14   Roth 2002, 190.
15   Cooney 2008, 4.
16   Roth 2000, 189.
17   For general information on creation by the potter's wheel, see Dorman 1999, 2002.
18   Sauneron 1962, 233–34; Dorman 1999, 96; Gillam 2005, 119–20.
19   Dorman 1999, 96.
20   Dorman 2002, 119.
21   Sethe 1926, 61; Jonckheere 1954; Kadish 1969.
22   Lichtheim 1976, 206.
23   For same sex relations in ancient Egypt, see Parkinson 1995, 2008; Montserrat 1996, 136–62; Toivari-Viitali 2001, 159–61; Wilfong 2002; Reeder 2008.
24   Recently discussed by Reeder 2008; Parkinson 2008; and Dowson 2008.
25   Lichtheim 1976, 214–23.
26   Parkinson 1995.
27   Toivari-Viitala 2001, 160.
28   Szpakowska 2007, 402.
29   Westendorf 1977; Hornung 1982, 171; Troy 1986, 15–17; Zandee 1992.
30   Faulkner 1969, 198.
31   Allen 1988, 28.

32   Pinch 1994, 24.
33   Pinch 1993, 243–45; Robins 1993, 153.
34   Troy 1986, 188.
35   Troy 1986, 21.
36   Tobin 1986, 11–12.
37   Troy (2002, 3) sees kingship as largely androgynous, while others, including myself, see it as largely masculine.
38   Quirke 2007, 257.
39   Montserrat 2000, 48.
40   Hornung 1999, 55.
41   Kozloff and Bryan 1992, 213–14, 217.
42   Roth 2000, 194.
43   Troy 1986; Darnell 1997.
44   Parkinson 2008.
45   Westendorf 1977, 134, fig. 2; Andrews and Faulkner 1989, 163, pl. 12; Bryan 1996, 35, fig.12.
46   Davies 1953, pl. 2, III.
47   For Mut as an androgynous creator, see Troy 1997.
48   Sauneron 1982, 36–7.
49   Baines 2001.
50   Ward 1972.
51   Bösse-Griffiths 1977; Ritner 2006, 206–7, fig. 3.
52   Roth 2007, 229.
53   Manniche 1987, 44.
54   Toivari-Viitala 2001, 146.
55   Ibid., 144–45.
56   Janák and Navrátilová 2008.
57   For example, see Derchain 1976.
58   For a warning against assuming encoded messages, see Eaton-Krauss and Graefe 1985, Chapter 3.
59   Simpson 1977 cited in Roth 2007, 229.
60   Parkinson 1999, 170.
61   Hare 1999, 137.
62   Vogelsang-Eastwood 1993.
63   For women's hairstyles, see Robins 1999.
64   Meskell 2002, 158.
65   Meskell 2002, 159.
66   Derchain 1975.
67   Lichtheim 1976, 203–11; Graefe 1979; Manniche 1999, 129–30.

68 Aldred 1971, fig. 33, 35 and 48.
69 While some have seen the sistrum as erotic, Ayad (2009) sees this aspect as overplayed.
70 Mace and Winlock 1916, 18–19, 68–71.
71 Van Walsem 1997, 112.
72 Manniche 1999, 101.
73 Lilyquist 1979, 97.
74 Lilyquist 1979.
75 For further references, see Meskell 2002, 115, fig. 4.7 and Toivari Viitala 2001, 176, footnote 300.
76 Romano 1989.
77 For example, Keimer 1948, 101–5.
78 Vandier d'Abbadie 1938, 31.
79 For example, Strouhal and Forman 1992, 89; Tyldesley 1994, 160.
80 Mifflin 1997.
81 Montserrat 1996, 76, 77.
82 Montserrat 1996, 76.
83 Strouhal and Forman 1992, 89.
84 Daressy 1893, 166.
85 Poon and Quickenden 2006, 124, fig. 2.
86 Ward 1983, 74; 1986, 111.
87 For photos, see Keimer 1948, pls. 6–9; Ikram and Dodson 1998, 115.
88 Winlock 1923, 26, 28, fig. 20.
89 Meskell 2002, 161; 2003, 58.
90 Naville 1907, 50, 55; 1913, 9, pl. 2.
91 Pinch 1993, 213.
92 Bianchi 2004, 64.
93 Derry 1935.
94 Pinch 1993, 198–99, 211; Keimer 1948, pls. 12–13, 17–19.
95 Pinch 1993, 199.
96 Ibid., 212–13.
97 Keimer 1948, pls. 15–17.
98 Keimer 1948, 31.
99 Keimer 1948, pl. 26.
100 Strouhal and Forman 1992, 89; Poon and Quickenden 2006, 127–28.
101 Firth 1927, 50; Keimer 1948, 16.
102 Poon and Quickenden 2006, 128.
103 Bianchi 2004.
104 Poon and Quickended 2006, 128.

105 Keimer 1948, figs. 1–5.
106 Petrie 1901, 24.
107 Rice 1958.
108 Montserrat 1996, 75.
109 Poon and Quickenden 2006, 128, fig. 3.
110 Robins 1993, fig. 83.
111 Meskell 2002, 116.
112 Meskell 1999, 102–3; 2002, 115.
113 Bruyère 1934–35, 62.
114 Meskell 2002, 114.
115 Kemp 1979, 53.
116 See Koltsida (2006; 2007, 23–4) for the variety of views.
117 Toivari-Viitala 2001, 155.
118 Teeter et al. 2009, 43.
119 Papyrus Berlin 3033; Lichtheim 1975, 215–17.
120 Derchain 1975, 74.
121 See Parkinson 2008.
122 Parkinson 1995, 63.
123 Foster 1974, 56; Fox 1985, 74.
124 Fox 1985, 234–36; Foster 1995, 162.
125 Manniche 1991, 98; Simpson, 1972, 297.
126 Fox 1985, 305–6.
127 Ibid., 306.
128 Foster 1974, 20.
129 Ibid., 25.
130 Mathieu 1996, 152.
131 McCarthy 2008, 91.
132 Roth 2000.
133 Roth 1999a, 38.
134 Ibid., 39.
135 Roth 1999.
136 As suggested by Bryan 1996; McCarthy 2002; Robins 1988 and 1989; Roth 1999.
137 As suggested by Desroches-Noblecourt 1953 and Westendorf 1967.
138 Roth 1992, 2000, 198.
139 Roth 1992, 1993.
140 For arguments against this claim, see Quack 2006.
141 Ritner 2006, 212.
142 Roth and Roehrig 2002.

143 Faulkner and Goelet 1994, 104.
144 Cooney 2008.
145 Roth 2000, 199.
146 Cooney 2008, 6–7.
147 Bryan 1996, 35.
148 McCarthy 2008, 91–2.
149 Cooney 2008, 11–120.
150 Cooney 2008, 16.
151 Riggs 2005, 41–94.
152 Papyrus Chester Beatty I, Recto; Lichtheim 1976, 214–23.
153 Morris 2007.

Chapter 7: Queens and harems

1   Routledge 2008.
2   Troy 2002, 203.
3   Troy 1986, 120.
4   Troy 1986, 126–29; Robins 1993, 24.
5   Roth 2005, 9, footnote 6.
6   Troy 1986, 64–5; Gillam 1995, 248.
7   Redford 2002, 59.
8   Bryan 2008.
9   Troy 1986, 65, 136, 166.
10 Hawass 1995, 232–37.
11 Gillam 1995, 211–14, 233–34.
12 Ibid., 217, 234.
13 Derchain 1969.
14 Troy 1986, 61ff.
15 Wente 1969, 90.
16 O'Connor 1999.
17 Described in Rikala 2008.
18 Robins 1993, 98–9.
19 Robins 2002, 27.
20 Mertz 1952.
21 Robin 1983.
22 Robins 2002, 28.
23 Callender 1994, 17.
24 Dodson and Hilton 2004, 166.

25 Ward 1989, 41–2.

26 Ward 1986, 102–14.

27 Gillam 1982, 232.

28 Naville 1910, pl. 18A and pl. 11, respectively.

29 Callender 1994, 14, fig. 2.

30 Sabbahy 1997.

31 Allam 1963, 92–3.

32 Sabbahy 1997, 165.

33 Callender 1994, 11.

34 Nord 1975.

35 Lorton 1974.

36 Ward 1983.

37 Callender 1994, 9.

38 Ward 1983, 69–70.

39 Callender 1994, 10.

40 Lorton 1974.

41 Callender 1994, 10.

42 Haslauer 2001, 77.

43 Callender 1994, 20–2, fig. 4.

44 Discussed in Lilyquist 2008.

45 Robins, 1993, 39.

46 Callender 1994, 11.

47 Haslauer 2001, 77.

48 Ibid., 78.

49 Badawy 1966, fig. 5.

50 Spence 1999.

51 Wente 1990, 36.

52 Barber 1991, 64–5, 351–52.

53 Thomas 1981, 6.

54 Kemp 1978.

55 Dodson and Hilton 2004, 164.

56 Xekalaki 2007.

57 Meier 2000.

58 Robins 1993, 35.

59 Ibid., 34.

60 The tomb and contents has most recently been described by Lilyquist 2003.

61 Meier 2000.

62 Redford 2002, 57–8.

63 Schulman 1979, 180, footnote 13.
64 Spence 2007, 301.
65 Gillam 1995, 225.
66 Robins 1993, 39.
67 Lichtheim 1973, 137.
68 Redford 2002.
69 For an alternative translation, see Goedicke 1963.
70 Haslauer 2001, 80.
71 It is arguable as to whether or not Nefertiti ruled as queen in her own right after the death of her husband.
72 Bryan 1996, 29.
73 Tyldesley 2006, 74.
74 Bryan 1996, 30.
75 Ibid., 30, pl. 7.
76 Routledge 2008, 164.
77 Tyldesly 2006, 84.
78 Bryan 1996, 31.
79 See Gitton 1975 for more information on her.
80 Bryan 2000, 228–29.
81 Ibid., 229.
82 Russmann 2005, 29–30
83 Bierbrier 1995.
84 O'Connor 2006, 23.
85 Dorman 2006, 41.
86 Tyldesley 2006, 94.
87 Roth 2005, 13, 10, footnotes 9 and 10.
88 For the titles of these women, see Troy 1986.
89 Bryan 1996, 29–30; Tyldesley 2006, 52, 75.
90 This idea was put forward by Naville in 1906 (Davis et al. 1906, 74.) and is suggested by Dorman (2006, 58).
91 Roth 2005, 13.
92 Davies 2004.
93 Dorman 2005, 88; 2006.
94 Rikala 2008.
95 Blackman 1921, 17.
96 Robins 1993, 50.
97 Dorman (1988), however, largely discounts any romantic relationship between Hatshepsut and Senenmut.
98 For example, Tydesley 2006, 190.

99 Romer 1982, 156–59.

100 Dorman 1988, 166.

101 Bryan 1996, 33.

102 Davies 2005, 52–3.

103 Habachi 1957, 99–104; Gasse and Rondot 2003, 41–43, fig. 3.

104 Translation by Habachi 1957, 99.

105 Tyldesly 2006, 100.

106 Donohue 1992; Graves-Brown 2006.

107 See also Roberts 1995, 42–7, 118–28 for the link between Hatshepsut and Hathor.

108 Dorman 2005b, 269.

109 Robins 1999.

110 Bryan 1996.

111 Bryan 1996, 34.

112 Laboury 2006.

113 Roth 1999.

114 Tyldesley 2006, 133.

115 Green 1998, 483.

116 Ashton 2008, 57.

117 Ashton 2008, 132.

118 Ashton 2008, 1.

119 Ashton 2008.

120 Roth 2005, 12.

Chapter 8: Goddesses

1 Quirke 1992, 26.

2 Billing 2002, 310.

3 Asher-Greve and Sweeney, 145

4 Roth 2000.

5 Frankfort et al.1933, I, 83.

6 For the latter, see Redford and Redford 1989, fig. 63.

7 Capel et al. 1996, 132.

8 Wilkinson 1999, 291.

9 Sayed 1982, 23–4; Lesko 1999, 46.

10 Troy 1986, 17.

11 Ibid., 18.

12 Hornung 1963, I Text, 188.

13 See also Sayed (1982, I, 16 and 58–60) for both hieroglyphic rendering and discussion of the bisexual nature of Neith as creator/creatoress.
14 Brunner Traut 1956.
15 Lichtheim 1980, 116–21.
16 Gillam 1995, 231.
17 Ibid., 216.
18 Assmann 2001, 155.
19 Lewis 1989.
20 The following Egyptologists have explored aspects of evidence for a mystic or ecstatic religion in Pharaonic Egypt, expressed and practised by men, as well as women: Federn 1960; Wente 1982; Roberts 1995 and 2000; Naydler 2005.
21 Gillam 1995, 226.
22 Szpakowska 2003, 135–41.
23 Bleeker 1973, 38–42.
24 Pinch 1993, 213.
25 Bleeker 1973, 54.
26 Daumas 1968, 15.
27 Kinney 2008, 164–67.
28 Lilyquist 1979.
29 Ibid., 99.
30 Lichtheim 1973, 168.
31 Tylor et al. 1895.
32 Roberts 1995, 13.

Conclusion

1 Herodotus is often quoted, as we have seen: 'The Egyptians in their manners and customs, seem to have reversed the ordinary practices of mankind.'
2 Graves-Brown 2008, xvi–xvii.
3 Mertz 1952.
4 Robins 1983.
5 Onstine 2005, 8.

Bibliography

Adams, B. (1974), *Ancient Hierakonpolis*. Warminster: Aris and Phillips.

—— (1992), 'Curator's choice: A predynastic female figurine'. *KMT: A Modern Journal of Ancient Egypt*, 3(1), 12–13.

Aldred, C. (1971), *Jewels of the Pharaohs*. London: Thames and Hudson.

Allam, S. (1963), *Beiträge zum Hathorkult (bis zum Ende des mittleren Reiches)*. Berlin: B. Hessling.

—— (1989), 'Women as owners of immovables in pharaonic Egypt', in Lesko, B. S. (ed.), *Women's Earliest Records From Ancient Egypt and Western Asia. Proceedings of the Conference on Women in the Ancient Near East. Brown University, Providence, Rhode Island, November 5–7, 1987*. Atlanta: Scholars Press, pp. 123–35.

Allen, J. P. (1988), *Genesis in Egypt: The Philosophy of Ancient Egyptian Creation Accounts*. New Haven: Yale Egyptological Seminar Department of Near Eastern Languages and Civilizations Graduate School, Yale University.

Allen, T. D. (2000), 'Problems in Egyptology: Ancient Egyptian kinship'. *Journal of Black Studies*, 31(2), 139–48.

—— (2008), *The Ancient Egyptian Family: Kinship and Social Structure*. New York: Routledge.

Andrews, C. and Faulkner, R. O. (1989), *The Ancient Egyptian Book of the Dead*. London: British Museum Publications for the Trustees of the British Museum.

Arnold, D. (ed.) (1996), *The Royal Women of Amarna. Images of Beauty from Ancient Egypt*. New York: The Metropolitan Museum of Art.

Arnold, F. (1996), 'Settlement remains at Lisht-North', in Bietak, M. (ed.), *Haus und Palast im Alten Ägypten. Internationales Symposium 8. bis 11. April 1992 in Kairo*. Vienna: Österreichische Akademie der Wissenschaften, pp. 13–44.

Asher-Greve, J. M. and Sweeney, D. (2006), 'On nakedness, nudity and gender in Egyptian and Mesopotamian art', in Schroer, S. (ed.), *Images and Gender.*

Contributions to the Hermeneutics of Reading Ancient Art. Fibourg: Academic
  Press, pp. 125–76.
Ashton, S. A. (2008), *Cleopatra and Egypt*. Oxford, Malden and Carlton:
  Blackwell.
Assmann, J. (1997), *Moses the Egyptian: The Memory of Egypt in Western
  Monotheism*. Cambridge, Mass. and London: Harvard University Press.
—— (2001), *The Search for God in Ancient Egypt*. Trans. D. Lorton. Ithica and
  London: Cornell University Press.
Assmann, J. and Lorton, D. (2005), *Death and Salvation in Ancient Egypt*.
  Ithaca: Cornell University Press.
Ayad, M. F. (2003), *The funerary texts of Amenirdis I: Analysis of their layout and
  purpose*. PhD thesis, Department of Egyptology, Brown University.
—— (2009), *God's Wife, God's Servant: The God's Wife of Amun (c. 740–
  525 BC)*. Abingdon and New York: Routledge.
Badawy, A. (1966), *Architecture in Ancient Egypt and the Near East*. Cambridge,
  Mass. and London: M.I.T. Press.
Bagnall, R. S. and Frier, B. W. (1994), *The Demography of Roman Egypt*.
  Cambridge: Cambridge University Press.
Baines, J. (1991), 'Society, Morality, and Religious Practice', in Schafer, B. E.
  (ed.), *Religion in Ancient Egypt: Gods, Myths and Personal Practice*. New York
  and London: Cornel Ithica, pp. 123–200.
—— (2001), *Fecundity Figurines*. Oxford: Griffith Institute.
Baines, J. and Malek, J. (1980), *Atlas of Ancient Egypt*. Oxford: Phaidon.
Baker, B. J. (1997), 'Contributions of biological anthropology to the
  understanding of ancient Egyptian and Nubian societies', in Lustig, J. (ed.),
  Anthropology and Egyptology: A Developing Dialogue. Sheffield: Sheffield
  Academic Press, pp. 106–16.
Barber, E. J. W. (1991), *Prehistoric Textiles: The Development of Cloth in the
  Neolithic and Bronze Ages with Special Reference to the Aegean*. Princeton:
  Princeton University Press.
Barker, D. C. (1997), 'The place of residence of the divorced wife in Roman
  Egypt', in Kramer, B., Luppe, W., Maehler, H. and Poethke, G. (eds), *Akten des
  21. Internationalen Papyrologenkongresses, Berlin, 13–19.8.1995*. Stuttgart and
  Leipzig: Teubner, pp. 59–66.
Baumgartel, E. J. (1947), *The Cultures of Prehistoric Egypt I*. Oxford: Oxford
  University Press.
—— (1960), *The Cultures of Prehistoric Egypt II*. Oxford: Oxford University
  Press.
Bednarski, A. (2000), 'Hysteria revisited: Women's public health in ancient

Egypt', in McDonald, A. and Riggs, C. (eds), *Current Research in Egyptology 2000.* Oxford: Archaeopress, pp. 11–17.

Berger, M. A. (1992), 'Predynastic animal-headed boats from Hierakonpolis and southern Egypt', in Friedman, R. and Adams, B. (eds), *The Followers of Horus: Studies Dedicated to Michael Allen Hoffman.* Oxford: Oxbow Books, pp. 107–20.

Bianchi, R. S. (2004), *Daily Life of the Nubians.* Westport: Greenwood Press.

Bierbrier, M. L. (1995), 'How old was Hatshepsut?'. *Göttinger Miszellen*, 144, 15–19.

Billing, N. (2002), *Nut: The Goddess of Life in Text and Iconography.* Uppsala: Uppsala University.

Blackman, A. M. (1914), *The Rock Tombs of Meir: The Tomb-Chapel of Ukhhotp's Son Senbi.* London: The Egypt Exploration Society.

—— (1921), 'On the position of women in the ancient Egyptian hierachy'. *Journal of Egyptian Archaeology*, 7, 8–30.

—— (1924), *The Rock Tombs of Meir: The Tomb-Chapel of Pepi'onkh the Middle Son of Sebekhotpe and Pekhernefert (D, No. 2).* London: The Egypt Exploration Society.

—— (1953), *Rock Tombs of Meir. Part 5. The Tomb-Chapels A, no.1 (That of Ni'ankh-pepi the Black), A, no.2 (That of Pepi'onkh with the "Good Name" of Heny the Black), A, no.4 (That of Hepi the Black), D, no.1 (That of Pepi), and E, nos.1–4 (Those of Meniu, Nenki, Pep).* London: The Egypt Exploration Society.

Bleeker, C. J. (1973), *Hathor and Thoth. Two Key Figures of the Ancient Egyptian Religion.* Leiden: Brill.

Bolger, D. L. (1992), 'The archaeology of fertility and birth: A ritual deposit from Chalcolithic Cyprus'. *Journal of Anthropological Research*, 48(2), 145–64.

Booth, C. (2000), 'Tattooing instruments in the Petrie Museum'. *Journal of Egyptian Archaeology*, 87, 172–75.

Borghouts, J. F. (1971), *The Magical Texts of Papyrus Leiden. Papyrus I.348. Rijksmuseum van Oudheden te Leiden.* Leiden: Brill.

Bösse-Griffiths, K. (1977), 'A beset amulet from the Amarna period'. *Journal of Egyptian Archaeology*, 63, 98–106.

Bourriau, J. (1988), *Pharaohs and Mortals: Egyptian Art in the Middle Kingdom.* (ed.), Cambridge: Cambridge University Press.

Bowen, G. E., Chandler, T., Hope, C. A. and Martin, D. (2006), 'Reconstructing ancient Kellis Part II'. *Buried History. The Journal of the Australian Institute of Archaeology*, 42, 17–24.

Brunner, H. (1954), 'Die theologische Bedeutung der Trunkenheit', *Zeitschrift für Ägyptische Sprache und Altertumskunde*, 79, 81–3.

Brunner-Traut, E. (1955), 'Die Wochenlaube', *Mitteilungen des Instituts für Orientforschung*, 3, 11–30.

—— (1956), 'Atum als Bogenschütze', *Mitteilungen des Deutschen Archäologischen Instituts, Abteilung Kairo*, 14, 20–8.

—— (1970), 'Das Muttermilchkrüglein: Ammen mit Stillumhang und Mondamulett'. *Die Welt des Orients*, 6, 4–6.

—— (1986), 'Wochenlaube', in Helck, W., Otto, E. and Westendorf, W. (eds), *Lexikon der Ägyptologie Vol VI*. Wiesbaden: Otto Harrassowitz, pp. 1281–86.

—— (1996), 'In women good and bad fortune are on earth', in Capel, A.K. and Markoe, G.E. (eds), *Mistress of the House, Mistress of Heaven. Women in Ancient Egypt*. New York: Hudson Hills Press, pp. 25–46.

Bryan, B. M. (2000), 'The Eighteenth Dynasty before the Amarna period', in Shaw, I. (ed.), *The Oxford History of Ancient Egypt*. Oxford: Oxford University Press, pp. 218–71.

—— (2005), 'The temple of Mut. New evidence on Hatshepsut's building activity', in Roehrig, C. H. (ed.), *Hatshepsut from Queen to Pharaoh*. New York: The Metropolitan Museum of Art, pp. 181–83.

—— (2006), 'Administration in the reign of Thutmose III', in Cline, E. H. and O'Connor, D. (eds), *Thutmose III. A New Biography*. Michigan: University of Michigan Press, pp. 69–122.

Buckley, T. and Gottlieb, A. (eds), (1988), *Blood Magic: The Anthropology of Menstruation*. Berkley: University of California Press.

Burgess, E. M. and Arkell, A. J. (1958), 'The reconstruction of the Hathor bowl'. *Journal of Egyptian Archaeology*, 44, 5–11.

Callender, V. G. (1994), 'The nature of the Egyptian "harim". Dynasties 1–20'. *Bulletin of the Australian Centre for Egyptology*, 5, 7–25.

—— (2002), 'A contribution to the burial of women in the Old Kingdom'. *Archiv Orientální*, 70, 301–308.

—— (2006), 'The iconography of the princess in the Old Kingdom', in Bárta, M. (ed.), *The Old Kingdom Art and Archaeology: Proceedings of the Conference Held in Prague, May 31st–June 4th, 2004*. Prague: Czech Institute of Egyptology, pp. 119–126.

Caminos, R. (1974), *Late Egyptian Miscellanies*. Oxford: Cumberledge.

Campbell, A. (1994), *Men, Women and Aggression*. New York: Basic Books.

Capel, A. K. (1996), 'Relief of women and child between trees (Tomb of Mentuemhat)', in Capel, A. K. and Markoe, G. E. (eds), *Mistress of the House, Mistress of Heaven: Women in Ancient Egypt*. New York: Hudson Hills Press, pp. 59–60.

—— (1996), 'Occupations', in Capel, A. K. and Markoe, G. E. (eds), *Mistress of the House, Mistress of Heaven: Women in Ancient Egypt.* New York: Hudson Hills Press, pp. 91–102.

Cherpion, N. (1995), 'Sentiment Conjugal et Figuration à l'Ancien Empire', in *Kunst des Alten Reiches, Symposium in Deutschen Archäologischen Institut Kairo am 29. und 30. Oktober 1991*, Mainz, 33–37.

Cooney, K. M. (2008), 'The problem of female rebirth in New Kingdom Egypt: The fragmentation of the female individual in her funerary equipment', in Graves-Brown, C. (ed.), *Sex and Gender in Ancient Egypt: 'Don Your Wig for a Joyful Hour'.* Swansea: Classical Press of Wales, pp. 1–25.

Crabtree, P. (2006), 'Women, gender and pastoralism', in Nelson, S. M. (ed.), *Handbook of Gender Archaeology.* Lanham: AltaMira Press, pp. 571–92.

Daressy, G. (1893), 'Notes et remarques'. *Recueil de Travaux Rélatifs à la Philologie a l'Archéologie Égyptiennes et Assyriennes,* 14, 165–85.

Darnell, J. C. (1997), 'The Apotropaic Goddess in the Eye'. *Studien zur Altägyptischen Kultur,* 24, 35–48.

Daumas, F. (1968), 'Les propylées du temple d'Hathor à Philae et le culte de la déesse'. *Zeitschrift für Ägyptische Sprache und Altertumskunde,* 95, 1–17.

David, R. (1986), *The Pyramid Builders of Ancient Egypt: A Modern Investigation of Pharaoh's Workforce.* London and New York: Routledge.

Davies, N. de G. and Gardiner, A. H. (1948), *Seven Private Tombs at Kurnah.* London: Egypt Exploration Society.

—— (1953), *The Temple of Hibis in El-Khargeh Oasis III: The Decoration.* New York: Metropolitan Museum of Art.

Davies, V. (2004), 'Hatshepsut's use of Tuthmosis III in her program of legitimation'. *Journal of the American Research Center in Egypt,* 41, 55–66.

Davies, W. V. (2005), 'Egypt and Nubia. Conflict with the Kingdom of Kush', in Roehrig, C. H. (ed.), *Hatshepsut from Queen to Pharaoh.* New York: The Metropolitan Museum of Art, pp. 49–59.

Davis, T. M., Naville, E. and Carter, H. (1906), *The Tomb of Hatshopsitu.* London: A. Constable.

De Buck, A. (1937), 'The Judicial Papyrus of Turin'. *Journal of Egyptian Archaeology,* 23, 152–64.

Derchain, P. (1969), 'Snéfrou et les rameuses'. *Revue d'Égyptologie,* 21, 19–25.

—— (1975), 'La perruque et le cristal'. *Studien zur Altägyptischen Kultur,* 2, 55–74.

—— (1976), 'Symbols and metaphors in literature and representations of private life'. *Royal Anthropological Institute Newsletter,* 15, 6–10.

Derry, D. E. (1935), 'Note on five pelves of women of the Eleventh Dynasty in
Egypt'. *International Journal of Obstetrics & Gynaecology (BJOG)*, 42, 490–95.
—— (1942), 'Methods practised at different periods – Middle Kingdom',
in Engelbach, R. and Derry D. E. 'Mummification'. *Annales du Service des
Antiquités de l'Egypte*, 41, 233–65.
Desroches-Noblecourt, C. (1952), 'Pots anthropomorphes et recettes magico–
médicales dans l'Egypte Ancienne'. *Revue d'Égyptologie*, 9, 51–67.
—— (1953), '"Concubines du mort" et mères de famille au Moyen Empire.
A propos d'une supplique pour une naissance'. *Bulletin de l'Institut Français
d'Archéologie Orientale*, 53, 15–33.
Diamond, K.A. (2008), 'dmD(y)t: The "bone collector"'. *Göttinger Miszellen*,
218, 17–32.
Dodson, A. (2002), 'The problem of Amenirdis II and heirs to the office of
God's Wife of Amun during the Twenty–Sixth Dynasty'. *Journal of Egyptian
Archaeology*, 88, 179–86.
Dodson, A. and Hilton, D. (2004), *The Complete Royal Families of Ancient
Egypt*. London: Thames and Hudson.
Donohue, V.A. (1992) 'The goddess of the Theban mountain'. *Antiquity*, 66,
871–75.
Dorman, P. F. (1988), *The Monuments of Senenmut: Problems in Historical
Methodology*. London and New York: Kegan Paul International.
—— (1999), 'Creation on the potter's wheel at the eastern horizon of heaven',
in Teeter, E. and Larson, J. A. (eds), *Gold of Praise. Studies on Ancient Egypt
in Honour of Edward F. Wente*. Chicago: University of Chicago Press,
pp. 83–99.
—— (2002), *Faces in Clay: Technique, Imagery, and Allusion in a Corpus of
Ceramic Sculpture from Ancient Egypt*. Mainz am Rhein: P. von Zabern.
—— (2005a), 'Princess to queen to co-ruler', in Roehrig, C. H. (ed.),
Hatshepsut from Queen to Pharaoh. New York: The Metropolitan Museum of
Art, pp. 87–100.
—— (2005b), 'The proscription of Hatshepsut', in Roehrig, C. H. (ed.),
Hatshepsut from Queen to Pharaoh. New York: The Metropolitan Museum of
Art, pp. 267–69.
—— (2006), 'The early reign of Thutmose III: An unorthodox mantel of
coregency', in Cline, E. H. and O'Connor, D. (eds), *Thutmose III. A New
Biography*. Michigan: University of Michigan Press, pp. 39–68.
Dowson, T. A. (2008), 'Queering sex and gender in ancient Egypt', in Graves-
Brown, C. (ed.), *Sex and Gender in Ancient Egypt: 'Don Your Wig for a Joyful
Hour'*. Swansea: Classical Press of Wales, pp. 27–46.

Doxey, D. (2001), 'Priesthood', in Redford, D. (ed.), *The Oxford Encyclopedia of Ancient Egypt*. Oxford: Oxford University Press.

Dreyer, G., Hartung, U., Hikade, T., Köhler, E. C., Müller, V. and Pumpenmeier, F. (1998), 'Umm-el-Qaab. Nachuntersuchungen im frühzeitlichen Königsfriedhof 9./10. Verbericht'. *Mitteilungen des Deutschen Archäologischen Instituts, Abteilung Kairo*, 54, 77–167.

Dunham, D. and Museum of Fine Arts Boston (1937), *Naga-ed-Dêr Stelae of the First Intermediate Period*. Boston: Museum of Fine Arts, Boston.

Duquesne, T. (2008), 'Power on their own: Gender and social roles in provincial New Kingdom Egypt', in Graves-Brown, C. (ed.), *Sex and Gender in Ancient Egypt: 'Don Your Wig for a Joyful Hour'*. Swansea: Classical Press of Wales, pp. 47–63.

Eaton-Krauss, M. and Graefe, E. (1985), *The Small Golden Shrine from the Tomb of Tutankhamun*. Oxford: Griffith Institute.

Eaverly, A. A. (1999), 'Color and gender in ancient painting: A pan-Mediterranean approach', in Wicker, N. L. and Arnold, B. (eds), *From the Ground Up: Beyond Gender Theory in Archaeology*. Oxford: Archaeopress.

Ebbell, B. (1936), *The Papyrus Ebers. The Greatest Egyptian Medical Document*. Copenhagen: Levin and Munksgaard.

Ehrenberg, M. (1989), *Women in Prehistory*. London: British Museum Press.

el-Sabbahy, A. F. (1999), 'A funerary bed from the tomb of Sennedjem'. *Discussions in Egyptology*, 43, 13–18.

Ellis, C. (1992), 'A statistical analysis of the protodynastic burials in the 'Valley' cemetery of Kafr Tarkhan', in van den Brink, E. C. M. (eds), *The Nile Delta in Transition: 4th–3rd Millennium B.C.* Jerusalem: Israel Exploration Society, pp. 241–58.

Engels, F. (1884), *The Origin of the Family, Private Property and the State*. New York: International Publishers.

Eyre, C. J. (1987), 'Work and the organisation of work in the Old Kingdom', in Powell, M. A. (ed.), *Labor in the Ancient Near East*. New Haven: American Oriental Society, pp. 5–47.

—— (1998), 'The market women of pharaonic Egypt', in Grimal, N. and Menu, P. (eds), *Le Commerce en Égypte Ancienne*. Cairo: Imprimerie de l'Institut Français d'Archéologie Orientale, pp. 173–92.

Faulkner, R. O. (1969), *The Ancient Egyptian Pyramid Texts*. Oxford: Oxford University Press.

Faulkner, R. O. and Goelet, O. (1994), *The Egyptian Book of the Dead: The Book of Going Forth by Day. The First Authentic Presentation of the Complete Papyrus of Ani*. San Francisco: Chronicle Books.

Faulkner, R. O., Simpson, W. K. and Wente, E. F. (1973), *The Literature of Ancient Egypt: An Anthology of Stories, Instructions, and Poetry*. New Haven; London: Yale University Press.

Federn, W. (1960), 'The "transformations" in the Coffin Texts: A new approach'. *Journal of Near Eastern Studies*, 19, 241–57.

Filer, J. M. (1992), 'Head injuries in Egypt and Nubia: A comparison of skulls from Giza and Kerma'. *Journal of Egyptian Archaeology*, 78, 281–85.

—— (1998), 'Mother and baby burials', in Eyre, C. J. (ed.), *Proceeedings of the Seventh International Congress of Egyptologists. Cambridge, 309 September 1995*. Leuven: Uitgeverij Peeters, pp. 391–400.

Firth, C. M. (1927), 'The Archaeological Survey of Nubia. Report for 1910–1911'. Cairo: Government Press.

Fischer, H. G. (1959), 'An example of memphite influence in a Theban stela of the Eleventh Dynasty'. *Artibus Asiae*, 22/3, 240–52.

—— (1962), 'The cult and nome of the goddess Bat'. *Journal of the American Research Center in Egypt*, 1, 7–23.

—— (1963), 'Yellow skinned representations of men in the Old Kingdom'. *Journal of the American Research Center in Egypt*, 2, 17–24.

—— (1975), 'Bat', in Helck, W. and Otto, E. (eds), *Lexikon der Ägyptologie*. I Weisbaden: Otto Harrassowitz, pp. 630–32.

—— (1989), 'Women in the Old Kingdom and Heracleopolitan Period', in Lesko, B. S. (ed.), *Women's Earliest Records From Ancient Egypt and Western Asia. Proceedings of the Conference on Women in the Ancient Near East. Brown University, Providence, Rhode Island, November 5–7, 1987*. Atlanta: Scholars Press, pp. 5–24.

—— (2000), *Egyptian Women of the Old Kingdom and of the Herakleopolitan Period*. New York: The Metropolitan Museum of Art.

Ford, C. S. (1945), *A Comparative Study of Human Reproduction*. New Haven: Human Relations Area Files Press.

Foster, J. L. (1974), *Love Songs From the New Kingdom*. Austin: University of Texas Press.

—— (1995), *Hymns, Prayers, and Songs: An Anthology of Ancient Egyptian Lyric Poetry*. Atlanta: Scholars Press.

Foucault, M. (1978), *The History of Sexuality. Volume I: An Introduction*. New York: Pantheon.

Fox, M. V. (1985), *The Song of Songs and the Ancient Egyptian Love Songs*. Madison: University of Wisconsin Press.

Frandsen, P. J. (2007), 'The menstrual 'taboo' in ancient Egypt'. *Journal of Near Eastern Studies*, 81–105.

Frankfort, H., Buck, A. d. and Gunn, B. G. (1933), *The Cenotaph of Seti I at Abydos*. London: Egypt Exploration Society.

Friedman, F. A. (1994), 'Aspects of domestic life and religion', in Lesko, L. H. (ed.), *Pharaoh's Workers. The Villagers of Deir el Medina*. New York: Cornell University Press.

Fuchs, G. (1989), 'Rock engravings in the Wadi el-Barramiya, Eastern Desert of Egypt'. *The African Archaeological Review*, 7, 127–153.

Gaballa, G. A. (1977), *The Memphite Tomb-Chapel of Mose*. Warminster, Eng. and Forest Grove, Ore: Aris & Phillips.

Galvin, M. (1981), *The Priestesses of Hathor in the Old Kingdom and the First Intermediate Period*, PhD thesis, Classical and Oriental Studies, Brandeis University, Michigan.

Gardiner, A. H. (1940), 'Adoption extraordinary', *Journal of Egyptian Archaeology*, 26, 23–9.

—— (1947), *Ancient Egyptian Onomastica*. London: Oxford University Press.

—— (1961), *Egypt of the Pharaohs: An Introduction*. Oxford: Clarenden Press.

Gasse, A. and Rondot, V. (2003), 'The Egyptian conquest and administration of Nubia during the New Kingdom: The testimony of the Sehel rock-inscriptions'. *Sudan and Nubia*, 7, 40–46.

Gee, J. (2001), 'Notes on Egyptian marriage. PBM 10416 reconsidered'. *Bulletin of the Egyptological Seminar*, 15, 17–25.

Gilchrist, R. (1999), *Gender and Archaeology: Contesting the Past*. London: Routledge.

Gillam, R. A. (1995), 'Priestesses of Hathor: Their function, decline and disappearance'. *Journal of the American Research Center in Egypt*, 32, 211–37.

—— (2005), *Performance and Drama in Ancient Egypt*. London: Duckworth.

Gilroy, T. (2002), 'Outlandish outlanders: Foreigners and caricature in Egyptian art'. *Göttinger Miszellen*, 191, 35–52.

Gitton, M. (1975), *L'Éspouse du Dieu, Ahmes Néfertary: Documents sur sa Vie et Son Culte Posthume*. Paris: Annales littéraires de l'Université de Besançon.

Goedicke, H. (1963), 'Was magic used in the harem conspiracy against Ramesses II? (P. Rollin and P. Lee)'. *Journal of Egyptian Archaeology*, 49, 71–92.

Goldberg, M. Y. (1998), 'Deceptive dichotomy: Two case studies', in Casey, M., Donlon, D., Hope, J. and Welfare, S. (eds), *Redefining Archaeology: Feminist Perspectives. Proceedings of the Australian Women in Archaeology Conference*. Canberra: ANH (Australian National University) Publications, pp. 107–13.

Goodison, L. and Morris, C. (1998), 'Introduction. Exploring female divinity:

From modern myths to ancient evidence', in Goodison, L. and Morris, C. (eds), *Ancient Goddesses*. London: British Museum Press, pp. 6–21.

Graefe, E. (1979), 'Wnh "Lösen"'. *Studien zur Altägyptischen Kultur*, 7, 52–63.

—— (1981), *Untersuchungen zur Verwaltung und Geschichte der Institution der Gottesgemahlin des Amun vom Beginn des neuen Reiches bis zur Spätzeit*. Wiesbaden: Harrassowitz.

Graves-Brown, C. (2006), 'Emergent flints', in Szpakowska, K. (ed.), *Through a Glass Darkly: Magic, Dreams and Prophecy in Ancient Egypt*. Swansea: Classical Press of Wales, pp. 47–62.

—— (2008), 'Gender, sex and loss of innocence', in Graves-Brown, C. (ed.), *Sex and Gender in Ancient Egypt: 'Don Your Wig for a Joyful Hour'*. Swansea: Classical Press of Wales, pp. i–xv.

Green, L. (1998), 'Evidence for the position of women at Amarna', in Eyre, C. J. (ed.), *Proceedings of the Seventh International Congress of Egyptologists, Cambridge, 3–9 September 1995*. Leuven: Uitgeverij Peeters, pp. 483–88.

Griffith, F. L. (1898), *The Petrie Papyri: Hieratic Papyri from Kahun and Gurob (Principally of the Middle Kingdom)*. London: Bernard Quaritch.

Grunert, S. (2002), 'Nicht nur sauber, sondern rein. Rituelle Reinigungsanweisungen aus dem Grab des Anchmahor in Saqqara'. *Studien zur Altägyptischen Kultur*, 30, 137–51.

Habachi, L. (1957), 'Two graffiti at Sehel from the reign of queen Hatshepsut'. *Journal of Near Eastern Studies*, 16, 88–104.

Hare, T. (1999), *Remembering Osiris: Number, Gender, and the Word in Ancient Egyptian Representational Systems*. Stanford, Calif.: Stanford University Press.

Haring, B. J. J. (1997), *Divine Households Administrative and Economic Aspects of the New Kingdom Royal Memorial Temples in Western Thebes*. Leiden: Nederlands Institut Voor Het Nabije Oosten.

Harrington, N. (2005), 'From the cradle to the grave: Anthropoid busts and ancestor cults at Deir el-Medina', in Piquette, K. and Love, S. (eds), *Current Research in Egyptology 2003. Proceedings of the Fourth Annual Symposium University College London 2003*. Oxford: Oxbow Books.

Hartung, U. (1998), 'Prädynastische Siegelabrollungen aus dem Friedhof U in Abydos. (Umm el-Qaab)'. *Mitteilungen des Deutschen Archäologischen Instituts, Abteilung Kairo*, 54, 187–217.

Haslauer, E. (2001), 'Harem', in Redford, D. (ed.), *The Oxford Encyclopedia of Ancient Egypt. Vol. 2*. Oxford: Oxford University Press, pp. 76–80.

Hassan, F. A. (1992), 'Primeval goddess to divine king: The mythogenesis of power in the early Egyptian state', in Friedman, R. and Adams, B. (eds), *The*

Followers of Horus: Studies Dedicated to Michael Allen Hoffman. Oxford: Oxbow Books, pp. 307–22.

—— (1998), 'The earliest goddeses of Egypt: Divine mothers and cosmic bodies', in Goodison, L. and Morris, C. (eds), *Ancient Goddesses*. London: British Museum Press, pp. 98–112.

Hassan, F. A. and Smith, S. J. (2002), 'Soul birds and heavenly cows: Transforming gender in Predynastic Egypt', in Nelson, S. M. and Rosen-Ayalon, M. (eds), *In Pursuit of Gender. Worldwide Archaeological Approaches*. Walnut Creek: AltaMira Press, pp. 43–65.

Hawass, Z. (1995), 'The programs of the royal funerary complexes of the Fourth Dynasty', in O'Connor, D. and Silverman, D. P. (eds), *Ancient Egyptian Kingship*. Leiden, New York and Köln: Brill, pp. 221–62.

Hayes, W. C. (1953), *The Sceptre of Egypt. A Background for the Study of Egyptian Antiquities in the Metropolitan Museum of Art. Volume I*. New York: Metropolitan Museum of Art.

Hendrickx, S. (2002), 'Bovines in Egyptian Predynastic and Early Dynastic iconography: Ecological change and food security in Africa's later Prehistory', in Hassan, F. A. (ed.), *Droughts, Food and Culture*. New York: Kluwer Academic/Plenum Publishers, pp. 275–318.

—— (2005), 'The earliest example of Pharaonic iconograph'. *Nekhen News*, 17, 14–15.

Hickman, H. (1956), 'La danse aux miroirs: Essai de reconstitution d'une danse pharaonique de l'ancien empire'. *Bulletin de l'Institut d'Égypte*, 37, 151–90.

Hornung, E. (1963), *Das Amduat. Die Schrift des Verborgenen Raumes*. Wiesbaden: Harrassowitz.

—— (1982), *Conceptions of God in Ancient Egypt: The One and the Many*. Ithaca: Cornell University Press.

—— (1999), *Akhenaten and the Religion of Light*. Trans. D. Lorton. Ithica and London: Cornell University Press.

Ikram, S. and Dodson, A. (1998), *The Mummy in Ancient Egypt: Equipping the Dead for Eternity*. London: Thames and Hudson.

Janák, J. and Navrátilová, H. (2008), 'People vs. P. Turin 5501', in Graves-Brown, C. (ed.), *Sex and Gender in Ancient Egypt: 'Don Your Wig for a Joyful Hour'*. Swansea: Classical Press of Wales, pp. 63–70.

Janssen, J. J. (1975), *Commodity Prices from the Ramessid Period: An Economic Study of the Village of Necropolis Workmen at Thebes*. Leiden: Brill.

—— (1980), 'Absence from work by the necropolis workmen of Thebes'. *Studien zur Altägyptischen Kultur*, 8, 127–52.

—— (1988), 'Marriage problems and public reactions', in Baines, J. (ed.), *Pyramid Studies and Other Essays Presented to I.E.S. Edwards*. London: Egypt Exploration Society, pp. 134–37.

Janssen, R. (2006), 'The old women of Deir el-Medina'. *Buried History. The Journal of the Australian Institute of Archaeology*, 42, 3–10.

Janssen, R. and Janssen, J. J. (1990), *Growing Up in Ancient Egypt*. London: Rubicon.

Johnson, J. H. (1999), 'Speculations on Middle Kingdom marriage', in Leahy, A. and Tait, J. (eds), *Studies in Honour of H.S. Smith*. London: Egypt Exploration Society, pp. 169–72.

—— (2003), 'Sex and marriage in ancient Egypt', in Grimal, N., Kamel, A. and May-Sheikholeslami, C. (eds), *Hommages à Fayza Haikal*. Cairo: Institut Français d'Archéologie Orientale, pp. 149–59.

Jonckheere, F. (1954), 'Eunuchs in Pharonic Egypt'. *Revue d'Histoire des Science*, 7(2), 139–55.

Junker, H. (1941), *Gîza 5. Die Mastaba des Snb (Seneb) und die Umliegenden Gräber*. Vienna and Leipzig: Hölder-Pichler Tempsky.

Kadish, G. E. (1969), 'Eunuchs in ancient Egypt?', in Kadish, G. E. (ed.), *Studies in Honor of J.A. Wilson*. Chicago: University of Chicago Press, pp. 55–62.

Kanawati, N. (2001), 'A female guard buried in the Teti cemetery'. *Bulletin of the Australian Centre for Egyptology*, 12, 65–70.

Karl, D. (2000), 'Funktion und Bedeutung einer 'weisen Frau' im alten Ägypten'. *Studien zur Altägyptische Kultur*, 28, 131–60.

Katary, S. L. D. (1999), 'Land tenure in the New Kingdom: The role of women, smallholders and the military', in Bowman, A. K. and Rogan, E. (eds), *Agriculture in Egypt: From Pharaonic to Modern Times*. Oxford: Oxford University Press, pp. 61–82.

Keimer, L. (1948), *Remarques Sur le Tatouage Dans l'Egypte Ancienne*. Cairo: Institut Français d'Archéologie Orientale.

—— (1949), *Quelques Détails Oubliés ou Inconnus Sur la Vie et les Publications de Certains Voyageurs Européens Venus en Égypte Pendant les Derniers Siècles*. Cairo: Institut Français d'Archéologie Orientale.

Kemp, B. J. (1978), 'The harim-palace at Medinet el-Ghurab'. *Zeitschrift für Ägyptische Sprache und Altertumskunde*, 105, 122–33.

—— (1979), 'Wall paintings from the Workmen's Village at el-'Amarna'. *Journal of Egyptian Archaeology*, 65, 47–53.

Kinney, L. (2008), *Dance, Dancers and the Performance Cohort in the Old Kingdom*. Oxford: Archaeopress.

Kiple, F. (1992), 'Infant mortality', in Kiple, F. (ed.), *The Cambridge World*

History of *Human Disease*. Cambridge: Cambridge University Press, pp. 224–330.

Koltsida, A. (2006), 'Birth-bed, sitting place, erotic corner or domestic altar? A study of the so-called "elevated bed" in Deir el-Medina houses'. *Studien zur Altägyptischen Kultur*, 35, 165–73.

—— (2007), *Social Aspects of Ancient Egyptian Domestic Architecture*. Oxford: Archaeopress.

Kozloff, A. P. and Bryan, B. (1982), *Egypt's Dazzling Sun. Amenhotep III and his World*. Cleveland: Cleveland Museum of Art.

Küllmer, H. (2007), *Marktfrauen, Priesterinnen und, Edle des Königs' Untersuchung über die Position von Frauen in der sozialen Hierarchie des Alten Ägypten bis zum Ende der 1. Zwischenzeit*. Unpublished PhD thesis, University of Hamburg.

Kuper, A. (1982), *Wives for Cattle. Bridewealth and Marriage in Southern Africa*. London, Boston, Melbourne and Henley: Routledge and Kegan Paul.

Laboury, D. (2006), 'Royal portrait and ideology: Evolution and significance of the statuary of Thutmose III', in Cline, E. H. and O'Connor, D. (eds), *Thutmose III. A New Biography*. Michigan: University of Michigan Press, pp. 260–91.

Landgráfová, R. (2008), 'Breaches of cooperative rules: Metaphors and parody in ancient Egyptian love songs', in Graves-Brown, C. (ed.), *Sex and Gender in Ancient Egypt: 'Don Your Wig for a Joyful Hour'*. Swansea: Classical Press of Wales, pp. 71–82.

Lankester, F. (2007), 'Rock art in Egypt's eastern desert', in Griffin, K. (ed.), *Current Research in Egyptology VIII. Proceedings of the Eighth Annual Synposium Swansea University*. Oxford: Oxbow Books, pp. 97–101.

Lansing, A. and Hayes, W. C. (1937), 'The Museums excavations at Thebes'. *Bulletin of the Metropolitan Museum of Art*, 32, 4–39.

Leclant, J. (1961), 'Sur un contrepoids de Menat au nom de Taharqa: Allaiment et 'apparition' royale'. *Institut Français d'Archéologie Orientale, Bibliothèque d'Étude*, 32, 251–84.

Lesko, B. S. (1987), *The Remarkable Women of Ancient Egypt*. Providence: BC Scribe Publications.

—— (1989), 'Comment at end of day 1', in Lesko, B. S. (ed.), *Women's Earliest Records From Ancient Egypt and Western Asia. Proceedings of the Conference on Women in the Ancient Near East. Brown University, Providence, Rhode Island, November 5–7, 1987*. Atlanta: Scholars Press, p. 98.

—— (1991), 'Women's monumental mark on ancient Egypt'. *The Biblical Archaeologist*, 54, 4–15.

—— (1999a), *The Great Goddesses of Egypt*. Norman: University of Oklahoma Press.

—— (1999b), '"Listening" to the ancient Egyptian woman: Letters, testimonials, and other expressions of self', in Teeter, E. and Larson, J. A. (eds), *Gold of Praise. Studies on Ancient Egypt in Honour of Edward F. Wente*. Chicago: University of Chicago Press, pp. 246–53.

—— (2002), *Women and Religion in Ancient Egypt*. Available at http://www. stoa.org. Accessed 2007.

Lewis, I. M. (1989), *Ecstatic Religion. A Study Of Shamanism and Spirit Possession*. London and New York: Routledge.

Lichtheim, M. (1973), *Ancient Egyptian Literature. Vol. 1*. Berkeley: University of California Press.

—— (1976), *Ancient Egyptian Literature. Vol. 2. The New Kingdom*. Berkeley: University of California Press.

—— (1980), *Ancient Egyptian Literature. Vol. 3*. Berkley: University of California Press.

Lilyquist, C. (1979), *Ancient Egyptian Mirrors from Earliest Times Through the Middle Kingdom*. Berlin: Münchner Ägyptologische Studien.

—— (2003), *The Tomb of the Three Foreign Wives of Tuthmosis III*. New York: The Metropolitan Museum of Art.

—— (2005), 'Egypt and the Near East. Evidence of contact in the material record', in Roehrig, C. H. (ed.), *Hatshepsut from Queen to Pharaoh*. New York: The Metropolitan Museum of Art, pp. 60–74.

—— (2008), 'Ramesside vessels from Sinai', in D'Auria, S. H. (ed.), *Servant of Mut. Studies in Honor of Richard A. Fazzini*. Leiden: Brill, pp. 155–65.

Lords, K. (2008), *The Importance of Gender Studies for Predynastic Egypt: A Case Study of Cemetery N7000 at Naga-ed-Deir*. Available at http:// repositories.cdlib.org. Accessed 2008.

Lorenze, M. (2009), 'Women and their employment', in Teeter, E. and Johnson, J. H. (eds), *The Life of Meresamun. A Temple Singer in Ancient Egypt*. Chicago: The Oriental Institute of the University of Chicago, pp. 98–104.

Lorton, D. (1974), 'Review of Elfrieda Reiser, Der königliche Harim im Alten Ägypten und seine Verwaltung'. *Journal of the American Research Centre in Egypt*, 11, 98–101.

—— (1977), 'The treatment of criminals in ancient Egypt'. *Journal of the Economic and Social History of the Orient*, 20(1), 2–64.

Lovell, N. C. and Whyte, I. (1999), 'Patterns of dental enamel defects at ancient Mendes, Egypt'. *American Journal of Physical Anthropology*, 110(1), 69–80.

Mace, A. C. and Winlock, H. E. (1916), *The Tomb of Senebtisi at Lisht*. New York: Metropolitan Museum of Art.

Manniche, L. (1987). *Sexual Life in Ancient Egypt*. London: Routledge.

—— (1991), *Music and Musicians in Ancient Egypt*. London: Opus Publishing Limited.

—— (1999), *Sacred Luxuries: Fragrance, Aromatherapy, and Cosmetics in Ancient Egypt*. New York: Cornell University Press.

Masali, M. (1973), 'Body size and proportions as revealed by bone measurements and their meaning in environmental adaptation', in Brothwell, D. R. and Chiarelli, B. A. (eds), *Population Biology of the Ancient Egyptians*. New York: Academic Press.

Masali, M. and Chiarelli, B. (1972), 'Demographic data on the remains of ancient Egyptians'. *Journal of Human Evolution*, 1, 164–69.

Mathieu, B. (1996), *La Poésie Amoureuse de l' Égypte Ancienne: Recherches Sur un Genre Litteraire au Nouvel Empire*. Cairo: Institut Français d'Archéologie Orientale.

McCarthy, H. L. (2002), 'The Osiris Nefertari: A case study of decorum, gender and regeneration'. *Journal of the American Research Center in Egypt*, 39, 173–95.

—— (2008), 'Rules of decorum and expressions of gender fluidity in Tawosret's tomb', in Graves-Brown, C. (ed.), *Sex and Gender in Ancient Egypt: 'Don Your Wig for a Joyful Hour'*. Swansea: Classical Press of Wales, pp. 83–113.

McDowell, A. G. (1992), 'Agricultural activity by the workmen of Deir el-Medina', *Journal of Egyptian Archaeology*, 78, 195–206.

—— (1995), 'Patterns of instruction in the New Kingdom', in Eyre, C. J. (ed.), *Seventh International Congress of Egyptologists. Cambridge, 3–9th September 1995. Abstracts of Papers*. Oxford: Oxbow Books for International Association of Egyptologists, pp. 123.

—— (1999), *Village Life in Ancient Egypt: Laundry Lists and Love Songs*. Oxford: Oxford University Press.

Mead, M. (1950), *Male and Female: A Study of the Sexes in a Changing World*. London: Gollancz.

Meier, S. A. (2000), 'Diplomacy and international marriages', in Cohen, R. and Westbrook, R. (eds), *Amarna Diplomacy. The Beginnings of International Relations*. Baltimore and London: The John Hopkins University, pp. 165–73.

Mertz, B. (1952), *Certain Titles of the Egyptian Queens and their Bearing on the Hereditary Right to the Throne*. Unpublished PhD thesis, Chicago: University of Chicago.

Meskell, L. (1999), *Archaeologies of Social Life*. Oxford: Blackwell.

—— (2000), 'Re-em(bed)ding sex: Domesticity, sexuality, and ritual in New Kingdom Egypt', in Schmidt, R.A. and Voss, B.L. (eds), *Archaeologies of Sexuality*. London and New York: Routledge.

—— (2002), *Private Life in New Kingdom Egypt*. Princeton: Princeton University Press.

Meskell, L. and Joyce, R. A. (2003), *Embodied Lives: Figuring Ancient Maya and Egyptian Experience*. London: Routledge.

Mifflin, M. (1997), *Bodies of Subversion: A Secret History of Women and Tattoo*. New York: Juno Books.

Montserrat, D. (1996), *Sex and Society in Graeco–Roman Egypt*. London: Kegan Paul.

—— (2000), *Akhenaten. History, Fantasy and Ancient Egypt*. London and New York: Routledge.

Morris, E. F. (2007), 'Sacred and obscene laughter in "The Contendings of Horus and Seth", in Egyptian inversions of everyday life, and in the context of cultic competition', in Schneider, T. and Szpakowska, K. (eds), *Egyptian Stories. A British Egyptological Tribute to Alan B. Lloyd on the Occasion of his Retirement*. Münster: Ugarit-Verlag, pp. 197–224.

Morrow, M. and Morrow, M. (2002), *Desert Rats. Rock Art Topographical Survey in Egypt's Eastern Desert*. London: Bloomsbury Summer School.

Moussa, A. M. and Altenmüller, H. (1971), *The Tomb of Nefer and Ka-hay*. Mainz am Rhein: Von Zabern.

Naguib, S.-A. (1990), *Le Clergé Féminin d'Amon Thébain à la 21e Dynastie*. Louvain: Peeters.

Naville, E. (1907), *The XIth Dynasty Temple at Deir El-Bahari I*. London: Egypt Exploration Fund.

—— (1910), *The XIth Dynasty Temple at Deir El-Bahari II*. London: Egypt Exploration Fund.

—— (1913), *The XIth Dynasty Temple at Deir El-Bahari III*. London: Egypt Exploration Fund.

Naydler, J. (2005), *Shamanic Wisdom in the Pyramid Texts. The Mystical Tradition of Ancient Egypt*. Rochester: Inner traditions.

Nelson, S. M. (1998), 'Gender hierarchy and the queens of Silla', in Hays-Gilpin, K. and Whitley, D. S. (eds), *Reader in Gender Archaeology*. London and New York: Routledge, pp. 319–35.

Niwinski, A. (1989), *Studies On The Illustrated Theban Funerary Papyri of the 11th and 10th Centuries B.C.* Fribourg: Biblical Institute of the University of Fribourg Switzerland.

Nord, D. (1975), 'Der königliche Harim im alten Ägypten und seine
   Verwaltung, by Elfreide Reisner'. *Journal of Near Eastern Studies*, 34, 142–45.
—— (1981), 'The term Xnr: "Harem" or "musical performers?"', in Simpson,
   W. K. and Davis, W. (eds), *Studies in Honor of Dows Dunham. Studies
   in Ancient Egypt and the Sudan*. Boston: Museum of Fine Art Boston,
   pp. 137–45.
Nunn, J. F. (1996), *Ancient Egyptian Medicine*. London: British Museum
   Press.
O'Connor, D. (1999), 'The Dendereh chapel of Nebhepetre Mentuhotep: A
   new perspective', in Leahy, A. and Tait, J. (eds), *Studies in Ancient Egypt in
   Honor of HS Smith*. London: Egypt Exploration Society, pp. 215–20.
—— (2006), 'Thutmose III: An enigmatic pharaoh', in Cline, E. H. and
   O'Connor, D. (eds), *Thutmose III. A New Biography*. Michigan: University of
   Michigan Press, pp. 1–38.
Omlin, J. A. (1973), *Der Papyrus 55001 und Seine Satirisch-Erotischen
   Zeichnungen und Inschriften*. Turin: Edizioni d'arte Fratelli Pozzo.
Onstine, S. L. (2005), *The Role of the Chantress (šmʿyt) in Ancient Egypt*.
   Oxford: Archaeopress.
Parkinson, R. B. (1995), '"Homosexual desire" desire in Middle Kingdom
   literature'. *Journal of Egyptian Archaeology*, 81, 57–76.
—— (1999), *Cracking Codes. The Rosetta Stone and Decipherment*. London:
   British Museum Press.
—— (2002), *Poetry and Culture in Middle Kingdom Egypt. A Dark Side to
   Perfection*. London and New York: Continuum.
—— (2008), '"Boasting about hardness": Constructions of Middle Kingdom
   masculinity', in Graves-Brown, C. (ed.), *Sex and Gender in Ancient Egypt:
   'Don Your Wig for a Joyful Hour'*. Swansea: Classical Press of Wales,
   pp. 115–42.
Peet, T. E. (1977), *The Great Tomb-Robberies of the Twentieth Egyptian Dynasty*.
   Hildesheim: Olms.
Pestman, P. W. (1961), *Marriage and Matrimonial Property in Ancient Egypt*.
   Leiden: Brill.
Peterson, J. D. (2006), 'Gender and early farming societies', in Nelson, S. M.
   (ed.), *Handbook of Gender in Archaeology*. Lanham: AltaMiraPress,
   pp. 537–70.
Petrie, W. M. F. (1953), *Ceremonial Slate Palettes and Corpus of Proto-Dynastic
   Pottery*. London: British School of Egyptian Archaeology.
Petrie, W. M. F., Griffith, F. L. and Newberry, P. E. (1890), *Kahun, Gurob and
   Hawara*. London: Kegan Paul, Trench, Trübner.

Petrie, W. M. F. and Quibell, J. E. (1896), *Naqada and Ballas: 1895*. London: B. Quaritch.

Petrie, W. M. F., Griffith, F. L. and Egypt Exploration Fund. (1901) *The Royal Tombs of the Earliest Dynasties*. London: Egypt Exploration Fund.

Petrie, W. M. F., Wainwright, G. A. and Gardiner, A. H. (1913), *Tarkhan I and Memphis V*. London: School of Archaeology in Egypt.

Pflüger, K. (1947), 'The private funerary stelae of the Middle Kingdom and their importance for the study of ancient Egyptian history'. *Journal of the American Oriental Society*, 67(2), 127–35.

Pilgrim, C. v. (1996), *Untersuchungen in der Stadt des Mittleren Reiches und der Zweiten Zwischenzeit*. Mainz am Rhein: P. von Zabern.

Pinch, G. (1983), 'Childbirth and female figurines at Deir el-Medina and el-Amarna'. *Orientalia*, 52, 404–14.

—— (1993), *Votive Offerings to Hathor*. Oxford: Griffith Institute.

—— (1994), *Magic in Ancient Egypt*. London: British Museum Press.

Podzorski, P. V. (1993), 'The correlation of skeletal remains and burial goods: an example from Naga-ed-dêr N7000', in Davies, W. V. and Walker, R. (eds), *Biological Anthropology and the Study of Ancient Egypt*. London: British Museum Press, pp. 119–129.

Poon, K. W. C. and Quickenden, T. I. (2006), 'A review of tattooing in ancient Egypt'. *The Bulletin of the Australian Centre for Egyptology*, 17, 123–36.

Pyburn, K. A. (2004), 'Rethinking complex society', in Pyburn, K. A. (ed.), *Ungendering Civilization*. New York: Routledge, pp. 1–46.

Quack, J. F. (2006), 'Fragmente des Mundöffnungsrituals aus Tebtynis', in Ryholt, K. (ed.), *The Carlsberg Papyri 7. Hieratic Texts from the Collection*. Copenhagen: CNI Publications, pp. 69–150.

Quibell, J. E. and Hayter, A. G. K. (1927), *Excavations at Saqqara: Teti Pyramid, North Side*. Cairo: Institut Français d'Archéologie Orientale.

Quirke, S. (1992), *Ancient Egyptian Religion*. London: British Museum Press.

—— Quirke, S. (2007), 'Women of Lahun (Egypt 1800 BC)', in Hamilton, S., Whitehouse, R. D. and Wright, K. I. (eds), *Archaeology and Women. Ancient and Modern Issues*. Walnut Creek: Left Coast Press, pp. 246–62.

Raue, D., Pilgrim, C. v., Bommas, M., Cortopassi, R., Driesch, A. v. d., Keller, D., Hikade, T., Kopp, P., Peters, Y., Pilgrim, B. v., Schaten, S., Schmidt-Schultze, T., Schultze, M. and Seidlmayer, S. J. (2004), *Report on the 33rd Season of Excavation and Restoration on the Island of Elephantine*. Available at http://www.dainst.org. Accessed 2009.

Redford, D. (1967), *History and Chronology of the Eighteenth Dynasty of Egypt: Seven Studies*. Toronto: University of Toronto Press.

Redford, S. (2002), *The Harem Conspiracy. The Murder of Ramesses III*. Illinois: Northern Illinois University Press.

Redford, S. and Redford, D. B. (1989), 'Graffiti and Petroglyphs Old and New from the Eastern Desert'. *Journal of the American Research Centre in Egypt*, 26, 3–49.

Reeder, G. (2008), 'Queer Egyptologies of Niankhkhnum and Khnumhotep', in Graves-Brown, C. (ed.), *Sex and Gender in Ancient Egypt: 'Don Your Wig for a Joyful Hour'*. Swansea: Classical Press of Wales, pp. 143–55.

Reilly, J. (1997), 'Naked and limbless. Learning about the feminine body in ancient Athens', in Koloski-Ostrow, A. O. and Lyons, C. L. (eds), *Women, Sexuality and Gender in Classical Art and Archaeology*. London and New York: Routledge, pp. 154–73.

Reiser, E. (1972), *Der Königliche Harim im Alten Ägypten und Seine Verwaltung*. Vienna: Verlag Notring.

Reisner, G. A. and Joint Egyptian Expedition of Harvard University and the Boston Museum of Fine Arts (1931), *Mycerinus: The Temples of the Third Pyramid at Giza*. Cambridge, Mass.: Harvard University Press.

Rice, D. S. (1958), 'A drawing of the Fatimid Period'. *Bulletin of the School of Oriental and African Studies, University of London*, 21, 31–9.

Richards, J. (2005), *Society and Death in Ancient Egypt. Mortuary Landscapes of the Middle Kingdom*. Cambridge: Cambridge University Press.

Riggs, C. (2005), *The Beautiful Burial in Roman Egypt: Art, Identity, and Funerary Religion*. Oxford: Oxford University Press.

Rikala, M. (2008), 'Sacred marriage in the New Kingdom of ancient Egypt: Circumstantial evidence for a ritual interpretation', in Nissinen, M. and Uro, R. (eds), *Sacred Marriages. The Divine-Human Sexual Metaphor from Sumer to Early Christianity*. Winona Lake: Eisenbrauns, pp. 115–44.

Ritner, R. K. (1984), 'A uterine amulet in the Oriental Institute'. *Journal of Near Eastern Studies*, 43, 209–21.

—— (1993), *The Mechanics of Ancient Egyptian Magical Practice*. Chicago: Oriental Institute of the University of Chicago.

—— (2001), 'Magic in everyday life', in Redford, D. (ed.), *The Oxford Encyclopedia of Ancient Egypt. Vol 2*. Oxford: Oxford University Press, pp. 329–333.

—— (2006), '"And each staff transformed into a snake": the serpent wand in ancient Egypt', in Szpakowska, K. (ed.), *Through a Glass Darkly: Magic, Dreams and Prophecy in Ancient Egypt*. Swansea: Classical Press of Wales, pp. 205–25.

—— (2008), 'Household religion in ancient Egypt', in Bodel, J. and Olyan,

S. M. (eds), *Household and Family Religion in Antiquity. The Ancient World: Comparative Histories*. Oxford: Blackwell Publishing, pp. 171–96.

Roberts, A. (1995), *Hathor Rising*. Totnes: NorthGate.

—— (2000), *My Heart, My Mother: Death and Rebirth in Ancient Egypt*. Rottingdean: NorthGate.

Robins, G. (1983), 'A critical examination of the theory of the right to the throne of ancient Egypt passed through the female line in the 18th Dynasty'. *Göttinger Miszellen*, 62, 67–77.

—— (1988), 'Ancient Egyptian sexuality'. *Discussions in Egyptology*, 11, 61–72.

—— (1989), 'Some images of women in New Kingdom art and literature', in Lesko, B. S. (ed.), *Women's Earliest Records From Ancient Egypt and Western Asia. Proceedings of the Conference on Women in the Ancient Near East. Brown university, providence, Rhode island, November 5–7, 1987*. Atlanta: Scholars Press, pp. 105–116.

—— (1993), *Women in Ancient Egypt*. London: British Museum Press.

—— (1994), 'Some principals of compositional dominance and gender hierarchy in Egyptian art'. *Journal of the American Research Centre in Egypt*, 31, 33–40.

—— (1996), 'Dress, undress, and the representation of fertility and potency in New Kingdom Egyptian art', in Kampen, N. B. (ed.), *Sexuality in Ancient Art. Near East, Egypt, Greece and Italy*. Cambridge: Cambridge University Press, pp. 27–40.

—— (1999), 'Hair and the construction of identity in ancient Egypt c.1480–1350 B.C.' *Journal of the American Research Center in Egypt*, 36, 55–69.

—— (2002), 'Problems concerning queens and queenship in Eighteenth Dynasty Egypt'. *NIN Journal of Gender Studies in Antiquity*, 3, 25–31.

—— (2008), 'Male bodies and the construction of masculinity in New Kingdom Egyptian art', in D'Auria, S. H. (ed.), *Servant of Mut. Studies in Honor of Richard A. Fazzini*. Leiden: Brill, pp. 208–15.

Roehrig, C. H. (1990), *The 18th Dynasty Titles Royal Nurse (mnʿt nswt), Royal Tutor (mnʿ nswt), and Foster Brother/Sister of the Lord of the Two Lands (sn/snt mnʿ nb t3wy)*, PhD thesis, University of California at Berkley.

—— (1996), 'Women's work: Some occupations of nonroyal women as depicted in ancient Egyptian art', in Capel, A. K. and Markoe, G. E. (eds), *Mistress of the House, Mistress of Heaven. Women in Ancient Egypt*. New York: Hudson Hills Press, pp. 13–24.

—— (2005a), 'The two tombs of Hatshepsut', in Roehrig, C. H. (ed.), *Hatshepsut from Queen to Pharaoh*. New York: The Metropolitan Museum of Art, pp. 184–89.

—— (2005b), 'Figure vases', in Roehrig, C. H. (ed.), *Hatshepsut from Queen to Pharaoh*. New York: The Metropolitan Museum of Art, pp. 233–41.

Romano, J. F. (1989), *The Bes-Image in Pharaonic Egypt*, PhD thesis, Michigan: Ann Arbor, pp. 2 v. in 3, (xiii, 879 leaves).

—— (1996), 'Statuette of princess Sobek-nakht nursing a prince', in Capel, A. K. and Markoe, G., E. (eds), *Mistress of the House, Mistress of Heaven. Women in Ancient Egypt*. New York: Hudson Hills Press, pp. 60–1.

Romer, J. (1982), *Romer's Egypt: A New Light on the Civilization of Ancient Egypt*. London: Michael Joseph Ltd.

Rose, J. C. (2006), 'Paleopathology of commoners at Tell Amarna, Egypt, Akhenaten's capital city'. *Memórias do Instituto Oswaldo Cruz*, 101 (Suppl. II), 73–76.

Roth, A. M. (1991), *Egyptian Phyles in the Old Kingdom: The Evolution of a System of Social Organization*. Chicago: Oriental Institute of the University of Chicago.

—— (1992), 'The PSŠ–KF and the "Opening of the Mouth" Ceremony: A ritual of birth and rebirth'. *Journal of Egyptian Archaeology*, 78, 113–47.

—— (1993), 'Fingers, stars, and the "Opening of the Mouth": The nature and function of the ntrwj–blades'. *Journal of Egyptian Archaeology*, 79, 57–79.

—— (1999a), 'The absent spouse: Patterns and taboos in Egyptian tomb decoration'. *Journal of the American Research Center in Egypt*, 36, 37–53.

—— (1999b), 'The Ahhotep coffins: The archaeology of an Egyptological reconstruction', in Teeter, E. and Larson, J. A. (eds), *Gold of Praise. Studies on Ancient Egypt in Honour of Edward F. Wente*. Chicago: University of Chicago Press, pp. 361–77.

—— (2000), 'Father earth, mother sky: Ancient Egyptian beliefs about conception and fertility', in Rautman, A. E. (ed.), *Reading the Body: Representations and Remains in the Archaeological Record*. Philadelphia: University of Pensylvania Press, pp. 187–201.

—— (2005), 'Models of authority. Hatshepsut's predecessors in power', in Roehrig, C. H. (ed.), *Hatshepsut from Queen to Pharaoh*. New York: The Metropolitan Museum of Art, pp. 9–22.

—— (2007a), 'Gender roles in ancient Egypt', in Snell, D. C. (ed.), *A Companion to the Ancient Near East*. Oxford: Blackwell, pp. 227–34.

—— (2007b), 'Royal women and the exercise of power in the ancient Near East', in Snell, D. C. (ed.), *A Companion to the Ancient Near East*. Oxford: Blackwell, pp. 235–44.

Roth, A. M. and Roehrig, C. (2002), 'Magical bricks and the bricks of birth'. *Journal of Egyptian Archaeology*, 88, 121–39.

Routledge, C. (2001), *Ancient Egyptian Ritual Practice: Ir-ḫt and nt-ʿ*. Unpublished PhD thesis, Department of Near and Middle Eastern Civilizations, University of Toronto.

—— (2008), 'Did women "do things" in ancient Egypt (c. 2600–1050 BCE)?', in Graves-Brown, C. (ed.), *Sex and Gender in Ancient Egypt: 'Don Your Wig for a Joyful Hour'*. Swansea: Classical Press of Wales, pp. 157–77.

Rowlandson, J. (ed.) (1998), *Women and Society in Greek and Roman Egypt: A Sourcebook*. Cambridge: Cambridge University Press.

Russmann, E. R. (2005), 'Art in transition. The rise of the Eighteenth Dynasty and the emergence of the Thutmoside style in sculpture and relief', in Roehrig, C. H. (ed.), *Hatshepsut from Queen to Pharaoh*. New York: The Metropolitan Museum of Art, pp. 23–48.

Sabbahy, L. K. (1997), 'The titulary of the harem of Nebhepetre Mentuhotep, Once again'. *Journal of the American Research Center in Egypt*, 34, 163–66.

Sauneron, S. (1962), *Les Fêtes Religieuses d'Esna aux Derniers Siècles du Paganisme*. Cairo: Institut Français d'Archéologie Orientale.

—— (1982), *Le Temple d'Esna VIII*. Cairo: Imprimerie de l'Institut français d'archéologie orientale.

Savage, S. H. (2000), 'The status of women in predynastic Egypt as revealed through mortuary analysis', in Rautman, A. E. (ed.), *Reading the Body: Representaions and Remains in the Archaeological Record*. Philadelphia: University of Pennsylvania State, pp. 77–92.

Sayed, R. el- (1982), *La Déesse Neith de Saïs*. Cairo: Institut Français d'Archéologie Orientale.

Scharff, A. (1929), *Die Altertümer der Vor– und Frühzeit Ägyptens. Vol. 1.* Berlin: Karl Curtius.

Schneider, T. (2007), 'Contextualising the Tale of the Herdsman', in Schneider, T. and Szpakowska, K. (eds), *Egyptian Stories: A British Egyptological Tribute to Alan B. Lloyd on the Occasion of his Retirement*. Münster: Ugarit-Verlag, pp. 309–18.

Schulman, A., R. (1979), 'Diplomatic marriage in the Egyptian New Kingdom'. *Journal of Near Eastern Studies*, 38, 177–93.

Schultz, R. and Seidal, M. (2005), *Egypt: The World of the Pharaohs*. Cologne: Konemann.

Scott, E. (1999), *The Archaeology of Infancy and Infant Death*. Oxford: Archaeopress.

Sethe, K. (1926), *Die Ächtung Feindlicher Fürsten, Völker und Dinge auf Altägyptischen Tongefäßscherben des Mittleren Reiches*. Berlin: Verlag der Akademie der Wissenschaften.

—— (1933), *Urkunden des Alten Reiches*. Leipzig: J. C. Hinrichs.

Shaw, I. (2000), *The Oxford History of Ancient Egypt*. Oxford: Oxford University Press.

Sheridan, J. A. (1998), 'Not at a loss for words: the economic power of literate women in late antique Egypt'. *Transactions of the American Philological Association*, 128, 189–203.

Sherratt, A. (1981), 'Plough and pastrolism: Aspects of the secondary products revolution', in Hodder, I., Isaac, G. and Hammond, N. (eds), *Patterns of the Past: Studies in Honour of David Clarke*. Cambridge: Cambridge University Press, pp. 261–305.

—— (1983), 'The secondary exploitation of animals in the Old World'. *World Archaeology*, 15.1, 90–104.

Simpson, W. K. (1972), *The Literature of Ancient Egypt: An Anthology of Stories, Instructions and Poetry*. New Haven: Yale University Press.

—— (1974), 'Polygamy in Egypt in the Middle Kingdom'. *Journal of Egyptian Archaeology*, 60, 100–105.

—— (1977), 'Amor dei: Mtr mrr rmt m tA wA (Sh. Sai. 147–148) and the Embrace', in Assmann, J., Feucht, E. and Grieshammer, R. (eds), *Fragen an die Altägyptische Literatur: Studien zum Gedenken an Eberhard Otto*. Wiesbaden: Harrassowitz, pp. 493–98.

Smith, H. S. (1992), 'The making of Egypt: A review of the influence of Susa and Sumer on Upper Egypt and Lower Nubia in the 4th millennium B.C.', in Friedman, R. and Adams, B. (eds), *The Followers of Horus. Studies Dedicated to Michael Allen Hoffman 1944–1990*. Oxford: Oxbow Books.

Spence, K. (1999), 'The North Palace at Amarna', *Egyptian Archaeology*, 15, 14–16.

—— (2007), 'Court and palace in ancient Egypt: The Amarna period and later Eighteenth Dynasty', in Spawthorpe, A. J. S. (ed.), *The Court and Court Society in Ancient Monarchies*. Cambridge: Cambridge University Press, pp. 267–328.

Steindorff, G. (1946), 'The magical knives of ancient Egypt'. *Journal of the Walters Art Gallery*, 9, 41–51, 106–107.

Strouhal, E. and Callender, G. (1992), 'A profile of Queen Mutnodjemet'. *Bulletin of the Australian Centre for Egyptology*, 3, 67–73.

Strouhal, E. and Forman, W. (1992), *Life in Ancient Egypt*. Cambridge: Cambridge University Press.

Sweeney, D. (1993), 'Women's correspondence from Deir el-Medineh', in Zaccone, G. M. and di Nero, T. R. (eds), *Sesto Congresso Internazionale di Egittologia: Atti, II*. Turin: Comitato Organizzativo del Congresso.

—— (2001), 'Walking alone forever, following you. Gender and mourners laments from ancient Egypt'. *NIN Journal of Gender Studies in Antiquity*, 2, 27–48.

—— (2004), 'Forever young? The representation of older and ageing women in ancient Egyptian art'. *Journal of the American Research Center in Egypt*, 41, 67–84.

—— (2006), 'Women growing older in Deir el-Medina', in Dorn, A. and Hofmann, T. (eds), *Living and Writing in el-Medine. Socio-historical embodiement of Deir el-Medine Texts*. Basel: Schwabe, pp. 135–53.

—— (2008), 'Gender and requests in New Kingdom literature', in Graves-Brown, C. A. (eds), *Sex and Gender in Ancient Egypt: 'Don Your Wig for a Joyful Hour'*. Swansea: Classical Press of Wales, pp. 191–214.

Szpakowska, K. (2003), *Behind Closed Eyes: Dreams and Nightmares in Ancient Egypt*. Swansea: Classical Press of Wales.

—— (2007), 'Flesh for fantasy. Reflections of women in two ancient Egyptian dream manuals', in Schneider, T. and Szpakowska, K. (eds), *Egyptian Stories. A British Egyptological Tribute to Alan B. Lloyd on the Occasion of his Retirement*. Münster: Ugarit-Verlag, pp. 393–404.

—— (2008), *Daily Life in Ancient Egypt: Recreating Lahun*. Oxford: Blackwell.

Taylor, J. H. (2001), *Death and the Afterlife in Ancient Egypt*. London: Published for the Trustees of The British Museum by the British Museum Press.

Teeter, E. (1999), 'Celibacy and adoption among god's wives of Amun and singers in the temple of Amun: A re-examination of the evidence', in Teeter, E. and Larson, J. A. (eds), *Gold of Praise. Studies on Ancient Egypt in Honour of Edward F. Wente*. Chicago: University of Chicago Press, pp. 405–14.

Teeter, E. and Johnson, J. H. (eds) (2009), *The Life of Meresamun. A Temple Singer in Ancient Egypt*. Chicago: The Oriental Institute of the University of Chicago.

Thomas, A. P. (1981), *Gurob: A New Kingdom Town*. Warminster, England: Aris & Phillips.

Tobin, V. (1986), 'Myth symbolism in the Amarna System'. *Journal of the Society for the Study of Egyptian Antiquities*, 16(1), 5–18.

Toivari–Viitala (2001), *Women at Deir el-Medina. A Study of the Status and Roles of the Female Inhabitants in the Workmen's Community During the Ramesside Period*. Leiden: Nederlands Instituut Voor Het Nabije Oosten.

Tosi, M. and Roccati, A. (1972), *Stele e altre epigrafi di Deir el Medina. N.50001–N. 50262*. Torino: Edizioni d'Arte Fratelli Pozzo.

Troy, L. (1984), 'Good and bad women. Maxim 18/284–288 of the Instructions of Ptahhotep'. *Göttinger Miszellen*, 80, 77–81.

—— (1986), *Patterns of Queenship in Ancient Egyptian Myth and History*. Uppsala: Acta Universitatis Upsaliensis.

—— (1997), 'Mut enthroned', in van Dijk, J. (ed.), *Essays on Ancient Egypt in Honour of Herman te Velde*. Groningen: Styx Publications, pp. 301–15.

—— (2002), 'The ancient Egyptian queenship as an icon of the state'. *NIN Journal of Gender Studies in Antiquity*, 3, 1–24.

Tyldesley, J. (1994), *Daughter of Isis. Women of Ancient Egypt*. London: Penguin.

Tylor, J. J., Griffith, F. L. and Clarke, S. (1895), *The Tomb of Paheri*. London: Egypt Exploration Fund.

Ucko, P. J. (1968), *Anthropomorphic Figurines of Predynastic Egypt and Neolithic Crete with Comparative Material from the Prehistoric Near East and Mainland Greece*. London: A. Szmidla.

Vandier d'Abbadie, J. (1938), 'Une fresque civile de Deir el Médineh'. *Revue d'Egyptologie*, 3, 27–35.

Vogelsang-Eastwood, G. (1993), *Pharaonic Egyptian Clothing*. Leiden and New York: Brill.

—— (2000), 'Textiles', in Nicholson, P. T. and Shaw, I. (eds), *Ancient Egyptian Materials and Technology*. Cambridge: Cambridge University Press, pp. 268–98.

—— (2001), 'Weaving, looms and textiles', in Redford, D. (ed.), *The Oxford Encyclopedia of Ancient Egypt*. 4 Oxford: Oxford University Press, pp. 488–92.

Walsem, R. v. (1997), *The Coffin of Djedmontuiufankh in the National Museum of Antiquities at Leiden*. Leiden: Nederlands Instituut Voor Het Nabije Oosten.

Ward, W. A. (1972), 'A unique beset figurine'. *Orientalia*, 41, 149–59.

—— (1983), 'Reflections on some Egyptian terms presumed to mean "harem, harem-women, concubine"'. *Berytus*, 31, 67–74.

—— (1984), 'The case of Mrs. Tchat and her sons at Beni Hasan' *Göttinger Miszellen*, 71, 51–59.

—— (1986), *Essays on Feminine Titles of the Middle Kingdom and Related Subjects*. Beirut: American University of Beirut.

—— (1989), 'Non-Royal Women and their occupations in the Middle Kingdom', in Lesko, B. S. (ed.), *Women's Earliest Records From Ancient Egypt and Western Asia. Proceedings of the Conference on Women in the Ancient Near East. Brown University, Providence, Rhode Island, November 5–7, 1987*. Atlanta: Scholars Press, pp. 33–43.

—— (1995), *The Egyptian Economy and Non-royal Women: Their Status in Public Life. Lecture, Brown University, 21 June, 1995*, Available at http://www.stoa.org. Accessed 2008.

Wegner, J. (2002), 'A decorated birth-brick from South Abydos'. *Egyptian Archaeology*, 3–4.

Wengrow, D. (2001), 'Rethinking "cattle cults" in Early Egypt: Towards a Prehistoric perspective on the Narmer Palette'. *Cambridge Archaeological Journal*, 11(1), 91–104.

—— (2006), *The Archaeology of Early Egypt. Social Transformations in North-East Africa, 10,000 to 2650 BC*. Cambridge: Cambridge University Press.

Wente, E. F. (1969), 'Hathor at the Jubilee', in Kadish, J. E. (ed.), *Studies in Honor of John A Wilson*. Chicago: University of Chicago Press, pp. 83–91.

—— (1982), 'Mysticism in Pharaonic Egypt?'. *Journal of Near Eastern Studies*, 41, 161–179.

—— (1984), 'Some graffiti from the reign of Hatshepsut'. *Journal of Near Eastern Studies*, 43(1), 47–54.

—— (1990), *Letters from Ancient Egypt*. Atlanta: Scholars Press.

Westendorf, W. (1967), 'Bemerkungen zur "Kammer der Wiedergeburt" im Tutanchamungrab'. *Zeitschrift für Ägyptische Sprache und Altertumskunde*, 94, 139–150.

—— (1977), 'Götter, androgyne', in Helk, W. (ed.), *Lexikon der Ägyptologie*. II Weisbaden: Harassowitz, pp. 634–35.

Whale, S. (1989), *The Family in the Eighteenth Dynasty of Egypt*. Sydney: The Australian Centre for Egyptology.

Wildung, D. (2001), 'Nofretes Neues Gesicht'. *Amun–Magazin für die Freunde der Ägyptischen Museen*, 3/11, 6–9.

Wilfong, T. G. (1999), 'Menstrual synchrony and the "place of women" in ancient Egypt', in Teeter, E. and Larson, J. A. (eds), *Gold of Praise. Studies on Ancient Egypt in Honour of Edward F. Wente*. Chicago: University of Chicago Press, pp. 419–34.

—— (2002), '"Friendship and physical desire": The discourse of female homoeroticism in fifth century CE Egypt', in Rabinowitz, N. S. and Auanger, L. (eds), *Among Women: From the Homosocial to the Homoerotic in the Ancient World*. Austin: University of Texas Press, pp. 304–29.

Wilkinson, A. (1971), *Ancient Egyptian Jewellery*. London: Methuen.

Wilkinson, T. A. H. (1999), *Early Dynastic Egypt*. London and New York: Routledge.

Willems, H. (1983), 'A description of Egyptian kinship terminology of the Middle Kingdom c.2000–1650 B.C.' *Bijdragen tot de Taal, Land–en Volkenkunde*, 139, 152–68.

Williams, B. (1988), *Decorated Pottery and the Art of Naqada III, A Documentary Essay*. Munich: Deutscher Kunstverlag.

Winlock, H. E. (1923), 'The Museum's excavations at Thebes'. *Bulletin of the Metropolitan Museum of Art, New York*, 20, 11–39.

—— (1942), *Excavations at Deir el Bahri, 1911–1931*. New York: Macmillan.

Wrobel, G. D. (2004), 'The benefits of an archaeology of gender for predynastic Egypt', in Pyburn, K. A. (ed.), *Ungendering Civilization*. New York and London: Routledge, pp. 156–78.

Xekalaki, G. (2007), 'The procession of royal daughters in Medinet Habu and their ritualistic role: origins and evolution', in Goyon, J. C. and Cardin, C. (eds), *The Proceedings of the Ninth International Congress of Egyptologists Grenoble, 6–12 September 2004*. Leuven: Peeters, pp. 1959–966.

Yamazaki, N. (2003), *Zaubersprüche für Mutter und Kind: Papyrus Berlin 3027*. Berlin: Achet Verlag.

Zandee, J. (1992), 'The birth-giving creator god in ancient Egypt', in Lloyd, A. B. (ed.), *Studies In Pharaonic Religion and Society*. London: Egypt Exploration Society, pp. 169–85.

Zeuner, F. (1963), *A History of Domesticated Animals*. London: Hutchinson.

Index